The Lost Art of Being Happy

The Lost Art of Being Happy

Spirituality for Sceptics

Tony Wilkinson

FINDHORN PRESS

First published by Findhorn Press 2007

ISBN: 978-1-84409-116-4

Edited by Jean Semrau
Cover design by Damian Keenan
Layout by Pam Bochel
Printed and bound by WS Bookwell, Finland

1 2 3 4 5 6 7 8 9 10 11 12 13 12 11 10 09 08 07

Published by
Findhorn Press
305A The Park,
Findhorn, Forres
Scotland IV36 3TE

Tel 01309 690582
Fax 01309 690036
email: info@findhornpress.com
www.findhornpress.com

In memory of my brother David,
1947–2005

Contents

Part One

HAPPINESS AND THE INNER LIFE

Chapter 1:
Something to think about

What do you most want out of your life?

It's a tricky question, I know, because most of us want a whole shopping list of things. We have ambitions or goals for every major area of our lives. You have an idea about what you want to achieve in your work, what you want for your family and in your personal relationships, a financial target, maybe goals for your hobbies, and so on. If you are at all religious, you might have a goal or goals to do with your religious beliefs, like salvation or enlightenment or serving God. But just think for a moment, even if it seems artificial, which of your many goals is the most important, the one you would choose if you had to choose only one. What would you choose, and why?

I have no idea what your answer is likely to be, of course. But the "why?" is easier to guess. The answer is almost certainly that you want to be happy or to live happily. Anything else you choose – health, wealth, power, pleasure – is likely to be something you want *because* you believe it will make you happier, now and/or in the future. For some people "future" might even mean in a future life, but it makes no difference. Happiness in some form and at some time is what we all want. It is the common denominator of all our efforts.

There is something fundamental, then, about living happily. But what does it really mean and how are we to do it? We can find direct attempts to answer this question hundreds of years before the current era, from the Indian and Chinese sages to the Greek philosophers. We find answers offered by every religion there has ever been and in every popular culture, even today in the commercial breaks in our television programmes. There are so many possible answers that we generally just stop thinking about it and get on as best we can. But every now and then something happens to remind us, even if we mostly live comfortably, that life is precarious and happiness even more so. Working out what is really important to us, what it takes for us to live happily, is not a party game or an academic exercise. It is at some stage an essential task for all of us.

There is however a way of thinking about this vital question which leads to a very satisfying and above all useful conclusion. This is not something I can claim to have invented, for I have taken fragments and sometimes whole chunks of it from different and sometimes ancient sources. But it is here presented in a form which I hope makes clear its relevance to today. Such a process of restatement is necessary for all ideas which last as this one has through many ages, for the idiom of one age obscures the message for another. The idea is this. There is an art to living happily and like every art it depends on learning, practising and if possible mastering certain skills. If we are not happy, it is because we lack these skills. But these are not skills of action or speech or anything external, they are skills of what I will call the inner life, the inner world of thought, emotion, belief, feeling, desire, perception, and so on. The inner life is not something esoteric or unusual, it is just your own conscious experience. But it is all-important. *The inner life and the practice of its skills are the keys to living happily.*

This is the "big idea" of the book and what follows amounts to working out the implications, which are astonishingly far-reaching. My first task is therefore to show how and why this idea is true. Then we will look at what these "happiness skills" might be and how you can acquire them. But you can see at once that if we could identify such skills it would make great sense to build them up in ourselves – in fact it would be absurd not to! We could thus become happier by training ourselves in these skills, training our inner lives. In fact we can go further, because it will become clear that our own happiness can provide a central value in our lives. That doesn't sound right, I know, it sounds rampantly selfish, but in fact altruism and concern for others survive intact. All will be explained!

To put anything forward as the key to living happily is obviously an ambitious claim. You might think science, probably psychology in some form, might answer such an important question and indeed you would find no shortage of eminent scientists prepared to argue that science potentially answers all the relevant questions. Unfortunately, "scientific" psychology spend several decades denying the importance if not the existence of the inner life, a mistake now happily being rectified but which leaves us today with only the beginnings of a science of the inner life. More fundamentally however this is not just a question about observable facts but about values and about how we might live our lives. And science is not about those kinds of question. The knowledge science will one day give us about our inner lives will indeed transform the way we think about ourselves, but it will still be the skill with which we use and apply that knowledge which will determine how we live. Science will inform the art of living, not replace it. As for values, we all crave a coherent view of the world to help us make sense of living, which is one reason why people faced with extreme circumstances are so often drawn to extreme ideologies. Some argue that there just is no sense we can make of our lives, but to me that view is neither satisfactory nor particularly scientific. This book attempts to construct a point of view which supports values and a principled way of living, organised around the simple idea of being happy. In so doing it implicitly offers a challenge. If happiness is indeed about the inner life, why is the inner life not our most pressing concern and if it were, what could we do about it?

Because religion has traditionally supplied direction and value to people's lives, particularly their inner lives, you may think if you are religious that you already have this area covered. If you are not you may think you are about to be sold a religion. Neither of these is true. (Well, the first might be, it depends on the religion, but in most cases it isn't.) We will explore a way towards a happier life which is not a question of finding or believing the right doctrines about anything supernatural, nor of relationships with a supernatural Being or beings. This way doesn't depend on faith at all; it is a matter of cultivating the inner life and its skills, steadily removing the obstacles to our own happiness that we put in our own way. But the process of building up inner skills still amounts to a type of spirituality. It has much in common with spiritual practice undertaken for religious reasons, hence the idea of spirituality for sceptics. Living happily, we will find, is sufficient motivation for spirituality in this sense and in fact spirituality is necessary for living happily. But this spirituality is not about spirits and is not a religion, although it does not preclude religion if you adhere to one for other reasons.

I believe the challenges of our modern lives and our society absolutely require an attempt to reconstruct the idea of spirituality along these lines. With a focus on developing the inner life we can tread a middle path between religion and materialism, between superstition and nihilism. This is an ancient path, as many will recognise, but it is just as important to see it clearly and stay on it today as it has ever been. Many people recoil from the selfishness and triviality of much of our "western" culture by turning back to see if religion, and if so which one, has the answer. Many more just wonder why consumerism, "success", or affluence don't seem as satisfying as expected. Secular thinking has not supplied that central core of meaning to our lives which religion once provided, while religion now is too often used as a badge or cover for political tribalism. The value of the inner life is far from being a new discovery, but we have tended to forget about it and thus we have forgotten how to live happily. But the path is still there. It is possible to cultivate happiness and fill yourself with a profound inner peace. You already have all you need to start the process and yet at the same time it will transform your life.

Chapter 2:
Introducing the inner life

The external life, the inner life, and Colin

You lead a double life. But don't be alarmed, I am not about to reveal your guilty secrets, if you have any. We all lead at least two lives, the external life and the inner life.

The external life includes all the recorded facts and figures about you, the details of your life in the world and among other people, your circumstances, your relationships, your possessions. But it also includes all the things you do in private, on your own, that nobody sees and perhaps even your biographer might not be interested in. It includes everything, in fact, that you do or say and it even includes your health and the state of your body at each moment. External, then, doesn't mean easily observable. There are those who lead duplicitous lives, presenting different faces to different people. Some other people like to keep a sharp line between their public and their private lives, however difficult that might be in the modern world. Some people's lives change so completely at some crucial point that it is as if they have embarked, without dying, on a new life. But these three examples – the clandestine life, the public/private division and the person with a "new life" – are all just different patterns in external lives.

The distinction we need to make goes beyond such patterns. Imagine that you were accompanied everywhere and at every moment from birth to death by an all-seeing recording device, a personal Big Brother that captured everything you did and said, monitored your biometric data every instant and noticed everything that happened around you. You might give a name to that extremely obtrusive device to make it seem less scary. I will call mine Colin.

Colin would provide a complete record of my external life. He (it?) would not, however, be able to record my other life, namely my inner life. My inner life includes the whole of my inner experience. It thus comprises all my thoughts and feelings, all my sensations, perceptions, feelings, beliefs, emotions, desires, judgements and imaginings, everything of which I am aware from moment to moment. My inner life is suspended from time to time when I sleep, but my dreams are also part of my inner life. I am directly aware of my inner life in a way I can never be of yours or anyone else's. I may understand what you are feeling or know what you are thinking but your thoughts and feelings are not part of my inner life, they are part of yours.

Colin could guess or assume that certain things might be happening in my inner life from my actions, words, or appearance, just as you and I decide all the time that other people are thinking or feeling certain things. Colin would also have the benefit of looking at changes in my physiological data, including my brain patterns. But he could not share or record my experiences directly. If I were mentally picturing an apple, for example, Colin might be able to guess from past experience and my brain waves what was happening. But he could not see the picture. If I were feeling sad, Colin might work it out from my demeanour and expression, from my voice or again from the patterns in my brain. But he could not feel the sadness or access it directly.

The value of the inner life

This distinction is of course a familiar one, between our consciousness and the rest of the world. But why does it matter in this context? After all, Colins for each of us are still, we may hope, a little way off. The answer to this question is very simple, almost commonplace, yet quite remarkable.

The distinction matters because what happens in your inner life determines whether or not you live happily. If your inner life is lived happily, you will live happily, it is as simple as that. Whatever external triumphs and disasters you meet, if your inner life is steady, calm and peaceful you will live happily. How you "take" things matters more than what happens to you. We see this all the time, don't we? Two people have accidents in similar circumstances – let's say they each break an arm. One is full of self-pity and anger; the other just accepts that "these things happen" and makes light of it. Two people are told they have life-threatening illnesses. One is bitter, looks for someone to blame, expects friends and family to put him first; the other looks forward optimistically to the treatment but is determined to live her life to the full, even if it turns out to be short. In these examples it is the inner reaction in terms of emotion, belief and desire which determines happiness: it is the inner life which matters, not external circumstances.

This simple but absolutely fundamental fact has been known, expressed by many philosophers, prophets and poets, forgotten and rediscovered again and again for thousands of years. It is true whether you are rich or poor, lucky or unlucky, successful or unsuccessful. We know that rich people, for example, can be miserable while beggars can be content. It does not by any means follow just from this that you should give away all you possess if you want to live happily. On the contrary, it is probably easier to be happy if you are materially comfortable. The point is that material comfort does not guarantee happiness. If you do not have peace of mind you will not be happy, no matter what else you have. It's not that external circumstances make no difference, a point we will explore later, but that the inner life dominates the outcome. That is why it matters so much to think about it.

Deep peace of mind, inner peace, will help you to transcend the sufferings and sadnesses of everyday life and live happily, come what may. Even the fear of death can be overcome and your own inevitable death can be accepted with equanimity if you progress far enough along this path. It is very bad-mannered even to try to talk to anyone about their own death in our society, but after all no one and nothing that lives can avoid dying. If we are to focus on living happily we must be able at least to describe how we might come to think about death without dread, otherwise the exercise is at best superficial.

You might, incidentally, prefer the word "mind" to "inner life", but as we discuss in a later chapter "mind" means very different things to different people and therefore raises special problems of its own. Just for now, I especially ask you to remember that the inner life includes a lot more than just reasoning or thinking or the intellect. It includes your emotional life, your wishes and desires and dislikes, and also your beliefs and prejudices. Without this wider perspective, it would be easy to jump to the conclusion that some kind of positive thinking was the answer, or that there was some crucial piece of knowledge which would make everything clear. The real answer is not complicated, but it's not quite that simple!

Chapter 3:
The inner life and happiness

George and Jenny

We need to look a little further at the crucial idea that it is not external circumstances which determine our happiness, but our inner reactions and our inner lives in general. The idea that the inner life is what *really* matters for living happily is, after all, completely at odds with the way most of us live most of our lives. But we will then add a new concept, the habit basis, which is an important step to help understand the relationship between the inner life and external circumstances and what we can do about our own inner lives.

Let's start with a little story as an example. Imagine two people – I will call them George and Jenny – who are enjoying a holiday. They need to choose a restaurant in which to have dinner. There are many to choose from and it isn't easy because they are in a region renowned for its food but also for offering poor value to tourists. Eventually and after much discussion they make a choice, but the meal is awful. George becomes morose and bad-tempered; in his eyes the evening has been spoiled, an opportunity lost and money wasted. Jenny, on the other hand, refuses to allow the bad experience to dent her holiday mood. The meal could have been better, sure, but such are the hazards of touring. They were fed, the mistake was hard to avoid, the evening is still warm and pleasant and the old town where they are sitting is full of charm.

Let's agree that George and Jenny here are exposed to exactly the same external circumstances. But their experiences are nonetheless very different. George tells himself one story, about the importance of getting a good dinner. Jenny tells herself another, about the importance of enjoying the holiday. George reacts with disappointment and increasing grumpiness, Jenny shrugs off the disappointment and focuses on the positive aspects of the evening. It is not possible to say that one of them is objectively right and the other wrong, nor even that they have different opinions about the essential facts, for both would agree that the meal was awful and the surroundings pleasant. But they end up poles apart in their emotional reactions, their moods, their recollections of the evening, and so on. Their inner lives have taken them in different directions. Jenny is happy and George is not.

Happiness works inside out

We can generalise this little cautionary tale. If your inner life at any moment is full of peace and contentment, you will be happy. If it is not, you will struggle to be happy however good things look from the outside – even if you get a good dinner! Thus your inner life is vital to your happiness. Happiness comes from the inside, from your reactions and responses to things and events, not from the things and events themselves.

But can we really generalise like this? Is it really true that the peace and contentment of the inner life are essential for living happily? You would not think so looking at everyday life in most Western countries. Consumer capitalism, probably the dominant, most successful idea in the world today, is based on the premise that happiness is to be pursued in the acquisition, possession or consumption of goods and services. Even when we think we have everything we need, which we rarely do anyway, along come new, improved versions and we have to start again. It is almost essential to the system that we remain in a state of permanent if mild discontent, or at least that our moments of contented equilibrium are relatively short-lived and capable of being upset by a new call to shop. If this sounds grudging, let me add at once that this is the best system for taking care of material needs that anyone has ever devised. The drive to consume ensures both that there are goods produced and people willing to work to produce them. The point is, though, that even as we have become better at dealing with the material circumstances of our lives, individually and collectively, we have come to neglect our inner lives.

To confirm that it is the inner life which really matters, consider as an example how owning something affects your happiness. What you own is less important for your happiness than your attitude to it, the beliefs and feelings and thoughts which surround it. Suppose you are rich: for the sake of argument let us say you have five million pounds. (Dollars or euros will do just as well!) This information alone tells us little about whether you are happy. You might be unhappy for reasons quite unconnected with your wealth, of course, such as your health or your children or your love life. But even in the financial sphere you might be happy or unhappy. Maybe you have just won a lottery, had a windfall, pulled off a financial coup or sold a business you successfully built up. Result: happiness. Maybe, though, your fortune is at risk and you are consumed by worry, maybe this is a recent inheritance from a loved one for whom you are grieving, or maybe you had fifty million last week and this five is all that a crashing market has left you! Result: unhappiness. Your beliefs, your feelings, your desires – all features of your inner life – are the key factors determining whether or not you are happy, not the external fact that you own or don't own a certain sum.

You might object that what makes the difference here is not the inner life but a host of other external circumstances which I have added to the story to surround the possession of the money. But important as the external circumstances are, they are not crucial and we can always adjust the details of the story to show this. At the very least, it is not the facts but what you believe to be the facts (for you could be mistaken) which will affect you. Even if your beliefs are correct your attitude will also make a difference. One person will shrug off setbacks another would find crushing, one person will worry while another will remain unruffled and so on. You could say this is just a matter of character and you would be right, but that is just another way of saying that it is a person's inner responses rather than their circumstances which matter.

What is true of five million pounds is just as true of five. It just needs more imagination to think of convincing stories in which a person's happiness hinges on smaller sums. In appropriate circumstances, unfortunate in themselves, the same argument works with a bowl or a handful of food as the external possession. For example, if you needed and expected more to feed your family you might be unhappy; if you expected to go hungry you might be very content.

Nevertheless, we haven't yet got the full story. External circumstances can obviously still be important. If someone is, for example, living in extreme poverty and hunger in the harshest conditions it would be absurd and unreasonable to expect them to be happy. Even though people are amazingly resilient and endure hardships we might expect them to find impossible, we can readily believe that there are some external conditions which only very exceptional people, and perhaps no one, could tolerate and retain any shred of inner peace or happiness.

If you or I were caught up in some catastrophe tomorrow we might remain serene, accepting and peaceful throughout, but it's just possible we might not! It's not a matter of choice, of choosing to be calm, choosing to retain our peace of mind. Whatever happens in the very near future, the way we react depends on the way we are, on our nature or character. We cannot call up the patience of a saint or a stoic ability to ignore hardships when we need them unless they are qualities or skills we already possess when the moment arises. Hence external circumstances will always affect our inner lives and therefore our happiness. So are we back to square one? What exactly is the relationship between living happily, the inner life and the external circumstances we face?

The habit basis

Confusion over the relationship between inner and external is probably the major reason why the importance of the inner life is underestimated. To understand it we need to distinguish:

1. The particular external circumstances you face at this moment, which in themselves might affect different people in different ways.
2. The inner skills, habits and dispositions which you have at this moment, which determine how particular external circumstances affect your inner life. We will call this set of skills and habits your "habit basis".
3. The resulting effect which the external circumstances actually have on your inner life at this moment given your current habit basis – how you actually think and feel, what you actually believe or want to do in these circumstances. The overall effect might be happiness, or it might not.

Thus when we say that happiness depends on your inner life we have to take into account that your inner life is affected both by external circumstances and by the underlying habit basis of your inner life at the time. Two causes, external circumstance and habit basis, combine to produce the effect. In some ways this is so obvious that your first reaction may be, "So what?" But it is hugely important. I may not be able to change the effect a particular event has on me: it finds me with the habit basis I happen to have at the time and I react from there. But if I can work on my habit basis so that, as time goes by, I am less and less affected by such events, I can free myself from the unhappiness they might otherwise cause me. Furthermore, if we think in general about the circumstances we are likely to meet in our lives which might shake our happiness or peace of mind, we may hope to identify the resources we are likely to need and then develop them so that we have them when we need them. These resources are the skills of the inner life.

Good things and bad things happen to everyone and therefore they will probably happen to you, regardless of your merits. Your external circumstances over time are likely to contain things and events which cause you pleasure but also things and events which cause you pain. You can control these external circumstances to a certain extent, of course; you can make choices and changes and impose your will on events to a degree. I am certainly not suggesting that you should give up trying to do so. But it is very unlikely that you can arrange everything to please you all the time. Even if you are the most fortunate person who ever lived, you will still get old, you may get sick, you have to live knowing that you will die and one day you will actually die. If living happily meant avoiding all unpleasant things we would have to say that living happily was impossible. If living happily is possible, the unpleasant things as well as the pleasant ones simply form the background against which it has to be achieved. But while we may not be able to choose our inner reaction to this or that at any particular moment, if we know the sort of reaction which would be most helpful to us we can work on ourselves to produce that reaction in the future. *We can change in a systematic and thoughtful way the inner effects unpleasant things and events have on us and thus we can cease to be at the mercy of circumstances.* Working on the inner life, changing the responses and the experiences of the inner life, means working on the habit basis so that different effects are produced. This process is a process of acquiring skills because a skill is nothing more than a useful habit we have or take the trouble to acquire.

Suppose a lighted match (bad external circumstance) falls on a pile of straw (your current state of inner resources, your habit basis). Will there be a fire (unhappiness in some form)? It depends of course on the straw. If the straw is dry and combustible there will be a fire. But if the straw is wet, there will be none. Practising the skills of the inner life is like wetting the straw, which makes very good sense if you know the lighted match is on its way. We all know that in our lives there will be a lighted match sooner or later.

Suppose you like to compete, maybe at tennis or golf or running. Whether you win today depends partly on what your opponent does. He or she is like the external circumstance which you cannot control. But the result also depends on your underlying skill and fitness, corresponding to the habit basis of your inner life. Your performance depends on the interaction between these two, just as your happiness in general depends on the interaction between external event and habit basis. You cannot change your level of skill and fitness instantaneously however much you want to, unless it's a computer game! But you can change your level over time by practice and training, so that the opponent you cannot handle today might be beatable next month or next year. Your level of skill and fitness is the foundation of your game and you can work on it. Your habit basis is the foundation of your happiness and you can work on that.

To keep the argument simple, we have concentrated on external circumstances and their effects, but the same applies if we consider an event of the inner life and its effects. Suppose, for example, you suddenly recall an unhappy memory. The further effects of that inner event – for a memory recalled is an inner event; nothing external need have happened – on your inner life also depend on your inner resources and dispositions. You might start to experience again the sadness you felt in the past, you might want to do something like seeking revenge, you might have beliefs about yourself which are reinforced or perhaps undermined by the memory, and so on. The reactions and responses of the inner life can be triggered by an external event or by an inner one, but in both cases it is the existing basis of dispositions, the habit basis, which determines what the response will be and whether the outcome will be happiness or not.

So right now, the basis of your inner life is just as it is, with whatever inner skills, habits and resources you have. It is, incidentally, no use berating or blaming yourself if you don't have the resources you currently need; it will just make you feel worse without achieving anything. There are some difficult circumstances you can meet with equanimity and other circumstances which upset you. A snapshot might therefore suggest that whether or not you are happy depends only on your external circumstances, but we have now seen that if you change your habit basis and thus the responses of your inner life then you might be able to cope happily in future with circumstances which today cause you unhappiness. Most of us have experienced this. We learn again and again to cope with and even master particular circumstances which on first acquaintance are quite daunting: think of the last time you started a new job. But now we can go much further. The basis of the inner life can be made skilful ("full of skill") to a point at which we can live happily and peacefully in most if not all circumstances.

Chapter 4:
Habit, change and the habit basis

The habit basis revisited

Now we need to look a bit further at the idea that everyone's inner life rests on a basis of habits or dispositions and that it is this basis we need to change if we want to live more happily. The vast and complex sum of all these dispositions to form experiences in any individual we have called their "*habit basis*" – with apologies for introducing a piece of jargon, but it is the only one we will need! No two habit bases are the same. No one's habit basis stays the same: as long as there is new experience the habit basis is constantly changed, even if it is only to cut well-worn grooves more deeply. Every time you learn something – and of course you can learn simply by seeing or doing something – your habit basis has changed, however marginally, and therefore in a sense you have changed. Even your most obdurate characteristics can be changed by circumstances or by deliberate effort.

As a collection of habits, dispositions and potentialities my habit basis is not something I am usually conscious of. This does not mean it is mysterious or hidden, but it certainly does not mean it is not "real". It is just something of which I am unaware for most of the time. Some of it I might be able to call into consciousness and review, like beliefs or memories; some of it will simply be latent, like the tendency to be afraid of snakes. The habit basis of the inner life underlies all our experience, but it is not itself part of that experience.

It is of course a shorthand to call all the patterns underlying and in part creating the inner life "habits", but this label is not meant to suggest anything about how such tendencies come about. It does not matter for this purpose whether a pattern is innate or acquired, whether it is, for example, an instinct from an earlier stage of evolution, a genetic trait or a product of personal upbringing, whether it is "natural" or affected. All that matters here is that there are patterns of experience or response and that it is possible to change these patterns.

Habits R Us

It is easy to accept in many instances how important habit is in our lives. We meet every day with many familiar circumstances and deal with them by a habitual response, both inwardly and in our outer actions. We react in defined ways to certain people, for example, because we know them and we know what to expect from them – this one is amusing and a friend, this one is a bore but we should be nice, this one we respect, this one is not to be trusted, and so on. These are already quite complex patterns. Even if we think only of the responses of the inner life and leave out our outward behaviour, the sorts of things mentioned involve many kinds of responses.

However, not everything in life is routine. We also meet with fresh circumstances, new people, new problems, new delights every day. Since they are new, how can it be said that we respond to them out of habit? But of course, we do. As we encounter a new person or a new experience, for example, we already have a set of responses ready. Let us say you are introduced to someone you have never met before: what do you do? Many of your responses are embedded in the language you use, for language itself is already based on habits or skills. Your inner responses, for example what you think and feel in these circumstances, are similarly the product of the same habitual language skills. How do you think without language? As for your feelings and wishes, a thought or an impression about this newcomer might call up emotions, perhaps instant like or dislike; or desires, for example to find out certain things about them or create a certain impression on them; or perhaps remind you of beliefs and prejudices, for example that people of this type (they are already assigned to a category, notice, which is another habit in operation) should be treated this way or that; and so on.

Repeating patterns and habits run through all that we experience. Just by themselves the patterns which are embedded in the language we use are all-pervasive and tend to dominate our patterns of thought and even belief. But we have emotional patterns and habits of wanting or desire as well, habits of memory and recall, likes and dislikes. Look at a few examples:

- Ms A finds that talking to her mother always makes her feel inadequate, like a little girl again.
- Mr B finds his temper fraying whenever he drives home through the rush hour.

- Mrs C doesn't feel right unless she has a cup of tea after lunch.
- Every time he looks at a suspension bridge, Mr D recalls his late brother.
- Ms E can't work without a tidy desk.
- Mr F can't stand Mr G.
- Mrs H feels fearful if she is alone at night.
- Mr J loves to watch the sunset.
- Mr K likes to salsa.
- Ms L feels self-conscious about her clothes whenever she is with Ms M.
- Mrs N believes in life after death but Mr P doesn't.
- Ms Q is afraid of spiders.

All of these are repeating patterns of inner experience, or habits in our sense. If you asked the person concerned about them, they might say, "That's what I'm like, that's just the way I am", but equally they might not be aware of the pattern, not having joined the dots, so to speak. These are by no means profound examples, but they begin to make the point that habits and repeating patterns are all-pervasive in our inner lives. It isn't just a question of certain major habits we have, like an addiction to smoking or caffeine, and it isn't just a question of other people being stuck in a rut. If you allow yourself to examine your own inner life as objectively as you can, you will quickly discover that everything you think, feel, desire, or believe – everything, in fact, which you experience – is in some way dependent on habit, or forms part of a repeating pattern in your experience or responses. Just begin to look for the patterns and you will find that you notice them more and more. The inner life is based on habit; it is quite literally a creature of habit. Our habits are us.

But we often do not realise that the habits of our own inner life are the source of our unhappiness. We may find ourselves, say, regularly fuming and unhappy at the end of a drive or cycle home through the city traffic. We might attribute this to the terrible driving and lack of consideration shown by (other) motorists. It never occurs to us that since we have no control over their driving habits the easiest solution might be to change our own attitude, relax about it and not let it get to us. This would of course amount to changing or breaking a strong inner habit of our own and it might not be a trivial undertaking, but it is likely to be easier than changing the driving habits of a whole city of strangers. Exactly the same reasoning can be applied to the tensions induced by public transport, shopping, dealing with colleagues, looking after children or any social interaction. One way or another, we place the problem or the solution "out there" in the external world and we fail to consider that our own inner life is partly the source of the difficulty and certainly one source of a solution.

We can in fact become quite attached to and even proud of the habits of our inner life, even when they are unhelpful and sometimes even when we recognise their unhelpfulness. "I just can't help it, that's the sort of person I am", we say ruefully but indulgently. This may make us reluctant to change even unhelpful habits because it means changing ourselves in ways which may seem scary or uncomfortable, just not "us". But such change is the only way forward if we are taking our own happiness seriously, because we know now that happiness depends on the inner life and therefore on these very habits. If we are not willing to make changes, we cannot expect to get different results, which means we cannot expect to start or keep moving in the direction of deeper inner peace.

Habit, skill and change

It is a crucial assumption that we ***can*** change the habits of the inner life in ways which are helpful to inner peace and happiness. We know, of course, that habits and patterns change all the time where external actions or behaviours are concerned and we know that we can train ourselves to do things by practice and repetition, as in sports, arts or at work. Often the objective in, for example, sports training is to "groove in" external behaviour so deeply that it becomes virtually automatic and the trainee can hardly do it wrong. Then under the intense pressure of competition the bat, club, boot or racquet swings in the desired arc (say) without conscious control and even in spite of interference from emotions like anger or anxiety. In some arts likewise the objective may be to avoid interference from extraneous thought and allow emotion-free expression in words or music. But for us the key question is whether such deliberate changes in pattern can be brought about in the inner life. Can we in fact train ourselves to respond differently inwardly, as we know we can do outwardly? Can we deliberately replace one pattern of emotional response with another, change our desires, change the tenor of the thoughts which spring into our minds, free ourselves from the grip of a crippling belief, and so on?

We can hardly doubt that the patterns of our inner lives do change over time. Your tastes and interests at age 20 or 30 are or were not the same as your tastes and interests at 10. Throughout your life the things you learn and the things you experience constantly change your opinions, your tastes, desires and beliefs. The only extra step we need to take is to recognize that we can bring about such change deliberately, or that we can choose the direction in which change takes place. But this is not so different from changing an outward habit, as when we learn a sport or work skill. It's just that we are not used to thinking of our inner experiences as being based on skill. But a skill is nothing more than a useful habit, usually one we have taken some trouble to acquire or improve. If I say that responding inwardly to an experience can be a matter of skill, it does not mean that you have to choose that response deliberately every time. On the contrary, habit takes the choice out of the particular occasion and the point of skill is that the habit which operates is one you have chosen and practised. Tiger Woods does not have to choose or think about the exact geometric trajectory of his club each time he strikes a ball; he has honed his skill to such perfection that his mind and body just do it right. And in the same way our habits will govern our inner responses, either helpfully or not, depending on the level of skill we have acquired, without our having to make deliberate decisions.

Suppose as an example (a thought experiment, if you like) that there is someone at work or at home who constantly irritates you by their unhelpful attitude. Instead of asking yourself, "Why do they have to take that line?", or "Why don't they get out of my way?", try asking, "What must it be like to be them? What must they think and feel to respond like that? How do I and my requests appear to them? What would it take to let them enjoy helping me?" Do this not once, but every time the problem occurs. Now reflect on two things. First, you have in fact created a new inner pattern or habit at will simply by remembering to ask these questions. Second, does your level of irritation stay the same? Probably not. These questions may not have useful, practical answers, but asking them reframes the situation so that the unhelpful person stops being seen as just a problem or an obstacle and becomes (just about!) a human being with problems and issues of their own. This may or may not help to resolve the external situation but it changes the way you view that person and therefore changes your inner take on the situation. If you do this consistently, you will find yourself becoming less irritated and more patient, little by little, in these circumstances. Thus you will have changed, however slightly, the patterns or habits of both your thoughts and your emotional responses. So, yes, we can change inner habits, and in much the same ways as we change external habits, basically by noticing what is happening, setting up a different pattern and establishing that new pattern by repetition until it weakens or replaces the old unhelpful pattern. And this process is properly described as building up skill in our inner lives because we are changing habits in directions we choose.

If you know what changes you want to bring about and you persist, you can thus create the inner life you want by changing your habits, or building your skills. It isn't always easy, but then creating external change isn't always easy either. It depends on the magnitude of the change you need to make. To become competent at an external skill – take for example cooking, painting or martial arts – might take several years of practice. To become expertly skilful might take decades of practice. You would only persist if you got some reward and satisfaction from the practice itself and if you were completely convinced of the value of the end goal. Aspects of the inner life might take the same degree of effort, but the interim benefit is to live more and more happily as practice proceeds. And as for the end goal, would it not be something to make yourself expert in the art of living happily?

Practice and skill

It would be a lot to ask that you should have acquired all the inner skills you might ever need to a sufficiently high degree just by chance and experience. Think of the skills of a sport for example, or of a craft or any art: some people are naturally "gifted" but few if any have all the skills they need without practice. So if we can work out which inner skills might help to deal with anything life throws at us, it would be a good plan to practice them and then we can be ready for anything. All the better if these skills also help with easier, everyday challenges.

In the sport analogy we used earlier, we said it was the fitness and skill of the inner life with which we should be concerned. Just as the desirable levels of physical fitness or skill are relative to the demands we make of our bodies, so we might suspect that the desirable levels of fitness and skill of the inner life may be relative to the demands made on them. But whereas we can be sure as occasional athletes that we will not be picked at random for the Olympics, say, and suddenly need phenomenal physical fitness and skill, we cannot be sure that in life external circumstances will not suddenly make exceptional demands on our inner life. In fact, we know that everyone has to meet major difficulties at some time. Trying to develop the resources you need when the trouble is already upon you will be difficult if not impossible, like trying to live up to an unexpected call from the Olympic selectors. Therefore it makes more sense to develop the skills and the fitness gradually, day by day. We may still find it difficult to deal with some situations, we may still be overwhelmed like a club level player suddenly faced with an international level opponent. But we will have a better chance if we devote time to training even when it doesn't seem to be needed, when there is no immediate challenge.

Happiness is a matter of degree, though, like fitness. You would not expect to go from gloom to bliss on the basis of a few moments' effort. But you can expect to get progressively happier, better able to cope with difficulties, calmer and more joyful. The quality of your life can be transformed, little by little, as you progress, not because of any change in your external circumstances but because your inner life is stronger. You can develop qualities both to deal with whatever difficulties come your way and to enjoy the good things all the more.

Competition and other people's habits

My happiness is about my inner life, your happiness is about your inner life. My happiness can be improved by eliminating or at least weakening unhelpful inner habits which stand in the way of my being happy and building up more useful ones. Your happiness depends on your doing the same in respect of *your* habits, not mine. It follows that we are not in competition for happiness. We may compete for external resources, at the worst for food, water, land or shelter, or perhaps less vitally (although it may not seem so to us) for anything from political or organisational power, jobs, promotion, the success of our children and the choice of partners to sale bargains and social approval. But we do not compete for happiness unless we ourselves choose to make these external things essential to our happiness – unless, that is, our inner habits demand these things in order to be satisfied. If we allow that to happen, we have already potentially sacrificed our peace of mind by our own choice, because we cannot guarantee that these external things will always be available. We cannot prevent their being vulnerable to consumption, removal, decay or attack, although we can spend our time warding off these dangers. If we commit ourselves to doing whatever is necessary to secure our external conditions, we do so implicitly at the cost of our peace of mind. If we accept, on the other hand, that happiness depends on the inner life, then there is no competition for happiness; there cannot be.

A related point is that if I act badly towards you, I am probably acting out of ignorance and it might help you to remember that. I am likely to be acting in order, as I see it, to enhance my own happiness in some way and I must presumably believe that this action of mine will contribute to that happiness. Perhaps I believe it will enhance my inner life. But more likely I think mistakenly that my happiness depends on externals, like making you "respect" or fear me, or on possessing your car or your mobile phone, your job or your wallet. In any case I am ignorant or misguided. I am trying to make myself happy, but I am heading in the wrong direction.

It does not follow by any means that you should allow me to have my way. That would depend on the (external) circumstances and you might well resist me vigorously. But the thought that you are dealing with ignorance can make a big difference to your inner response, avoiding loss of your peace of mind to negative emotion. You are dealing not with some malevolent demon but with a person like you striving to be happy, only ignorant or mistaken about how happiness is to be achieved. Even if I am physically attacking you, to take an extreme case, your peace of mind will be less disturbed if you can deal with the attack without hatred or anger. In such circumstances the attacker does enough harm without being allowed to take away your peace of mind as well. A mind clouded by hatred or fear or with an obsession for revenge is just as much injured as a broken arm. Again, it does not follow at all that you should be externally passive in the face of this attack. You might choose to do whatever you can to protect yourself and others. But your inner response to the incident would be more like your response to an accident or a natural disaster. If you were injured by a branch falling from a tree or by a landslide you might likewise experience fear and pain but you would not harbour a grudge against trees or rocks. You would do everything you could to escape or to mitigate the effects of the accident but it would not help to be outraged at the trees or the earth. Your external response might well be more effective, more focused, if you kept your cool with the elements: your inner response would certainly be less damaging. The same principles can be applied in responding to human aggression and injustice. This may seem like a very small comfort and no one would suggest it is easy to achieve, but it is an important and powerful idea if it can be absorbed, a radical change of perspective with radical effects.

There is a Taoist parable or teaching story which makes the point very well:

> A man is drifting in a boat on a river on a foggy day. Out of the mist there suddenly looms another boat which crashes into his, spilling him into the bottom of his boat. If the other boat

is empty, just being carried by the current, he might be shaken by the collision but he would quickly recover and regard the bump as an accident, just one of the hazards of being afloat. But if he sees that there is someone in the other boat he is likely to become angry, to blame the other person for carelessness or worse.

Yet why the difference? The physical damage and the shock is the same in both cases, but just because there is someone to blame (a target for blame) our boatman abandons his peace of mind, inflicting anger and/or other negative emotions on himself. We can understand it, it is what we all do, but if we could learn not to do it we would live more happily

Different strokes

My inner life habits are very unlikely to be exactly the same as yours. Since habits are formed by constant interplay between environment and individual, two initially similar individuals in broadly similar environments might react initially in only slightly different ways but over time the difference might be magnified until very different habits resulted. Think of the well-known butterfly effect described in chaos theory: it is said that the tiny effect of a butterfly's wingbeat might cause a chain of consequences as one movement in the air causes another until a hurricane results on the other side of the world. But most of us do not start out identical anyway and over the years your experiences and mine, your reactions and mine, will in all probability have been very different and so our inner habits will be very different.

Now, if you and I have different inner habits, it is highly likely that we have different unhelpful habits, that is to say different ways of stopping ourselves from being happy. What you need to work on will not be the same as what I need to work on. We can think of the result as being like different training regimes for different athletes: even if we both have the same objective, I may need to polish certain skills and improve some techniques and you may have more need to practice others. Moreover, what we both need will vary over time: we improve one skill and then realise that something else is letting us down or needs attention, so we work on that. And so it goes on.

As with a physical training regime, we might expect that there are basic or core skills which everyone needs to keep honed. There are few sports people, for example, who do not need strength, flexibility, endurance and co-ordination as well as the skills of their particular sport. And everyone needs to work again and again at the basics of their sport, however high their level of achievement. So with the skills of the inner life: there are some very common issues and problems which affect most of us to some extent. But it is also true that we may have particular problems from time to time. Each person's practice has a core but also has a changing component to deal with the issues of that person's own inner life. The same analogy also suggests that a guide or friend, like an athlete's coach, might sometimes be needed to help us if we are stuck as to what is holding us back. But mostly we need to develop the skill of watching and listening to our own inner responses and observing what it is we should work on.

Happiness as a central focus

It is in the nature of the habit basis that it changes all the time, but left to itself such change need have no overall direction. Your habit basis will change continually whether you are aware of it or not. It can be changed by your responses to external conditions or by any of your thoughts or emotions. If you see a cat catching a butterfly in the garden, your tendency will be increased to recall butterflies when you next see a cat, or cats when you next see a butterfly, and perhaps your emotional responses to cats and butterflies will marginally change. If you do or experience something new, you will introduce a new element into your inner life. But even if you just do, think or feel as you always have you will reinforce habits, you will cut the grooves of habit deeper and that is a change.

Once you accept that the inner life is what matters for living happily, it is natural to want to choose a direction for this change. Why not, indeed, change the habit basis in the direction of a happier, more peaceful inner life? You would thus choose to become happier, which doesn't seem like a choice you need to agonise over. However, although this doesn't mean you have to abandon your everyday life it is still a choice with far reaching consequences. The basis of the inner life touches your experience at every moment and can be affected at any moment by what goes on. Thus a decision to take charge of the direction in which it changes could amount to a decision to change your whole life, albeit from the inside. Happiness – understood as a condition of the inner life and a function of your habit basis – would become a central focus of your efforts.

"But hang on: can it be right that *my* happiness should be the central focus of my life? Isn't this just hedonism, or extreme selfishness? How can I possibly choose my own happiness over everything else and still be a nice person? What becomes of altruism and concern for others, loving my neighbour and selflessness, all the things I have always been told are the essence of being good?"

It is absolutely right that your happiness should be a central concern of your life, but this isn't at all selfish. Crucially, once we understand that happiness depends on the inner life and that the inner life depends on its habit basis, happiness ceases to be a selfish goal. More happiness for me does not mean less for you, because my happiness depends on my inner life and yours on your inner life. Moreover, I cannot directly change your habit basis in a helpful direction; you have to do it for yourself, although I can certainly help you. **We do not compete and we cannot do the work for each other.** And therefore it is not selfishness to make my happiness my central concern, it is just common sense, because my happiness cannot be achieved or brought about by anyone else.

It is a bit like those instructions in planes which say that you must put on your own oxygen mask before helping others, for the obvious reason that otherwise you might both pass out before either of you got any oxygen. If I really want to help you to be happy and happiness is a matter of a peaceful inner life, then the best plan would be for me to help you create a peaceful inner life for yourself. For me to seek my own inner peace will certainly not hinder your progress. In fact, it is unlikely that I could help you unless I had some idea of the skills involved and how to practice them, which means I must at least understand, if not be following, the same path myself or I would be useless to you.

Helping others, even a whole life dedicated to helping others, is not precluded by this concern with creating happiness for myself. Some people will naturally gravitate in this direction and it will suit them and bring them great satisfaction. We will see later that helping others is a helpful practice anyway in developing some of the necessary skills of the inner life. We will also see that the desire to help others naturally grows as these skills are developed. But helping others can only mean making their external circumstances better, or creating circumstances in which they can profitably work on their inner habits, or at most guiding them to create their own peaceful inner life. We cannot do the inner work for them, which means we cannot "make them happy". Making someone's external life better is often important and valuable work, of course, and it may involve putting their *external* comfort ahead of yours. But it does not involve putting their happiness ahead of yours, because their happiness is up to them and yours is up to you.

Direction and meaning

Once you accept that your happiness depends on your own inner life and that you can potentially change your inner responses to make yourself happier, there is an immediate bonus. The process of development towards peace of mind is a potential source of meaning in your life. This may also seem surprising, because we are used to thinking that meaning, in the sense in which it is applied to living rather than words, is a function of what we believe. We are used to thinking that we must find a creed, perhaps but not necessarily a set of doctrines about the supernatural, which can put everything in context for us. If we could understand why things happen as they do and what our place and role in the world should be (we think) this knowledge would give our lives meaning. So, many of us seek for or adhere to a faith to make sense of the world because only thus, we believe, can our lives have a sense of meaning and purpose.

But the idea that faith is the only alternative to meaninglessness is just not true. If we do have beliefs which provide us with a context and explanation for everything, they may indeed provide a sense of meaning to our lives; that much is true. But belief is not necessary. It is *direction* which gives meaning to living. People who have a clear direction, whether it is provided by faith, ambition or a political cause do not lack a sense of meaning. People struggling with a loss or a lack of belief or ambition or commitment on the other hand sometimes say they have "lost their way" or lost their direction. Belief can certainly provide direction, but developing the basis of the inner life to generate happiness also provides direction. And so it provides meaning.

Developing the skills of the inner life is in this sense a kind of spirituality. It transcends concern with the external and the material and it gives direction and therefore meaning. It provides a spiritual quality to living, as long as you can allow that it makes sense to speak of spirituality without spirits. Indeed, a desire for inner peace or peace of mind is often what moves people to turn to spirituality even in a religious context. But here we have a spirituality without any supernatural belief. It can stand by itself as a rational, humanistic, secular way of thinking. It is precisely what many people miss and are looking for in the modern world, a middle way between the difficulties of belief on one side and the emptiness of materialism on the other. In fact, because it is a spirituality without belief it can be used either as a substitute for belief or as a supplement to it: you can have no supernatural beliefs or you can accept the importance of training the inner life alongside your beliefs. You do not have to give up faith to follow this course, but you do not have to adopt a faith either. This an important theme and we will return to it later, after we have discussed more fully in later chapters what skills of the inner life will help to establish the inner peace we need.

Chapter 5:
A short zoology of the inner life

The inner life and the mind

We need now to start developing techniques to think about, examine, analyse and eventually change our inner lives in helpful ways. But first let me explain, in case you have been wondering, why I have used the term "inner life" all along instead of "mind". There are three main reasons.

First, if this was a book about "the mind" you might have expected a scientific work on psychology or psychotherapy or perhaps neuroscience. There are plenty of good books on these subjects already, better ones every day. Research has much that is interesting and important to say on these subjects, of course, which we should certainly take into account. But our inner lives are of immediate, personal concern to each of us. We may gain knowledge from brain science (say) of the mechanisms underlying the inner life, but we still have to live on the level of thoughts and feelings and desires. As an analogy, you know from your school science lessons that your table is made of atoms and even smaller energetic particles vibrating or whirling in space. But you still have to deal with it as a table. However deep your knowledge of the equations of particle movement at the subatomic level, it won't help you when you have to move the table across the room. You have to think about it and operate on it at a different level. Likewise, science will no doubt one day reveal all there is to know about our external lives, our brains and our bodies. Like Colin the spy machine science will even make some links between what is going on in the brain and what is going on in the inner life. But we will still live our inner lives in the world of experience and our experience is what we need to change if we want to live happily. We have to think about it and operate on it at a different level from the neuroscientific one. In any case, we have to choose now how to live our lives, and science cannot tell us that. It can help with background information, but living is not about information but rather about choosing, doing and experiencing. The quality of your life and mine depends on whether and to what extent we each cultivate our own inner life. There is some urgency about this, because our lives are ticking by.

Second, the term "mind" for many people means something narrower than we need. People distinguish between the mind and the heart, for example, or the mind and the emotions, leaving "mind" to refer to something like intellect or reasoning capacity. And then, quite rightly I think, they reject the view that happiness is just a question of exercising the mind in that sense, because happiness is clearly not just a matter of thought or intellect. This usage of the word "mind" to mean intellect or reason is perhaps mistaken anyway, but we have already seen that there is much more to the inner life than just thinking or reasoning. We need a term to refer to the whole of our inner experience because the whole of our experience is relevant, including emotion and desire and the rest. "Inner life" comes closer to what we need, or at least is less at risk of misinterpretation.

Third, if we talk about "mind" or "the mind" it can sound as if we are talking about a thing, or even a strange sort of substance (as in "mind and matter", for example). Philosophy in the last century showed us that this is not really so, that the way the words are used misleads us. There is experience and the way we talk about experience but it does not follow that there is a thing, a sort of metaphysical organism, to which the term "mind" refers. But words have a power of their own and if we talk about the mind it is hard not to slip into thinking of this "thing", sitting there (somewhere) performing activities like thinking and feeling and sensing and so on. Pretty soon we want to ask about "the nature of the mind" – or worse, "the true nature of the mind" – or about how the mind and the body are related. And then we are lost in a maze of speculation. "The inner life" carries less of this baggage. A life sounds more like a process, a series of events rather than a thing. If it has a "nature", we can describe it by describing what happens and why it happens and we feel less need to look behind these events for something hidden. So, "inner life" it is.

The busy inner life

I ask you to take the next step now by taking a quick look at your own inner life. Close your eyes and indulge for a few minutes in a little introspection. Turn your attention inwards so that you observe what is going on in your inner life rather than what is going on around you. Do this whenever it suits you, you need not take long over it, and then (please!) come back to the book.

You will quickly have observed how busy it is in there! There are thoughts, of course, but what are they like? Sometimes words (do you see them or hear them?), sometimes pictures, sometimes whole sentences or ideas. Some may surprise you, some you are comfortable with, others not. You can direct the stream of thought to some extent but if you do not it flows on anyway. It is very difficult to stop thinking. Then there are emotions and feelings: perhaps you feel a little anxious about this introspection, or impatient to move on, or cross to be asked to do something so trivial. Perhaps you cannot shake off the mood or the emotional tone induced by something else which has happened to you today. You will also find drives, desires and dislikes. Don't you want a cup of coffee yet? And why is this seat so uncomfortable?

The longer and more closely you look, the more variety and confusion you will find. All the things we have mentioned are in any case usually overlaid and half obscured by a barrage of incoming data from all your senses. Sights, sounds, smells and all the rest beg to be noticed and perhaps need interpretations and decisions, or perhaps they trigger further thoughts, emotions and desires. And so it goes on, all the time we are awake. This is the inner life and most of the time we just live it, take it as it comes. If we try to understand it and do something about it, it can seem very confusing.

Zoology and scaffolding

If we want to observe and discuss the jumble of events which seem to make up the inner life it would be helpful to have some system of classification. I suggest that four categories cover most of the ground:

> Thought
> Belief
> Emotions / feelings
> Will / desire.

I will sometimes refer to these categories as the dimensions of the inner life. Experience of course blends and mixes them constantly, or, to put it another way, experience is experience and these are categories we can apply later when thinking about experience. The dimensions of the inner life give us a tool to help us understand how the inner life and happiness are related and, far more importantly, what we can do about it.

This is not a scientific classification and I certainly do not claim that these four categories leave nothing out, nor that they divide the subject into neat, mutually-exclusive compartments. Surprisingly perhaps, it doesn't matter. Concepts are useful insofar as they do the job we need them to do and these will do well enough for now. For we really only need at this stage to do two things.

First, we need to give colour to the idea of the inner life and make the concept fuller and clearer. This is important because, while everyone has an inner life and thus roughly understands what we mean by the term, each person's inner life is private and particular to them. Thus we cannot point to or hold up an inner life and say, "Look, this is what I mean" – as we might do if we were referring to some external object. So our classification supports our definition. We are referring to items in these categories with which we are all familiar from our own experience and perhaps to other things like them. It is like the process of explaining to a child what animals are: they are lions and tigers and elephants, fish and birds, insects and reptiles, and so on. It is primitive zoology, but it works.

Second, we want above all to reach some conclusions about what to do. For this, we really need a serviceable framework of concepts we can use to make distinctions among the complicated swirling of the inner life. As with most complex problems, the first thing we have to do is break the problem down into manageable bits. But since this happens at a stage before a solution is found, the breaking process may not have much analytical significance in itself. So the classification does not need to be complete, exhaustive or fully articulated; in fact, it probably cannot be. Carpenter's tools are sometimes more useful than surgical instruments, depending on what you need to do. We need something with which we can get started, something to help us get to grips with the complexity in the first instance. If someone wants to add more categories, collapse existing ones or even use a completely different set, that is not a problem. Our argument needs some categories but does not depend on these particular ones being the only place to start. Again, we are in a position not unlike the early zoologists who started to build systems of classification partly just to get a grip on what was otherwise bewildering diversity and complexity.

Changing the metaphor, we might think of our four dimensions as a form of conceptual scaffolding. Scaffolding is important only insofar as it is sufficient to get us to our goal – building a wall or mending a roof, say. It must be strong enough to do the job but otherwise the appearance and qualities of the scaffolding are uninteresting. So with our conceptual scheme: it needs to be just robust enough, but it does not have to be anywhere near perfect. If necessary, we can amend or develop it as we go.

As far as completeness of coverage is concerned, many people would include "reason" and "imagination" as categories, but thought and belief, as we will use them, cover these areas. Memory is another strong candidate, but again we can say that we have thoughts and beliefs about our past and that will suffice. We might also include dreams, which are certainly a feature of the inner life, but if you really want completeness let us say they are a form of sleeping thought.

For many people the strangest omission from our list will be perception. Most people would name the senses and their effects on consciousness as one of the defining characteristics of the inner life. It is also true that many of the old "systems" of thought or philosophy of mind felt obliged to start with perception. But we will have relatively little to say about perception. If perception takes place without any thought or judgement, without our forming or altering beliefs about the world (however trivially), or forming or altering any desires or aversions or intentions, it is relatively uninteresting for our purposes. If it involves any of these other things, which in fact it usually does, it takes only a small adjustment to regard perception under one of the other categories.

The following sections in this chapter enlarge on each of our dimensions of the inner life to help understand some of the detail involved and, in particular, to introduce some of the ways in which elements of our inner lives affect our happiness. A good place to start is to look at the negative side, the patterns of the inner life which lead to unhappiness or prevent us from being happy, because if we can break down or remove those patterns we are already making progress. What is immediately clear just from introducing our dimensions is that the inner life is not simple. If we want to identify skills which will help us to be happier by displacing unhelpful habits, we probably need to look for a set of skills rather than a single magic solution.

Some of the patterns or habits we will mention are so subtle that we hardly notice them. Sometimes they are so much part of us that we cannot imagine not having them. "It's only natural to feel/think/want X!" we say to ourselves. And of course we may be right, whether because the habit in question is based on instinct, perhaps a leftover from our evolutionary past; because this habit is a part of our particular nature, the sort of person we are; or just because a lot of people we know are like that, so the herd instinct approves it. It may therefore be natural to be unhappy. It does not follow that you have no choice. You can decide: would you rather be natural or happy? We will continue on the assumption that you chose to be happy.

Thought

Thought is a significant part of what makes us human. In the category of thought we include language and thus verbalising, conceptualising, reasoning, abstraction, problem solving, judgement, mathematical activity and so on. But we also include memory (or at least recall), visualisation, imagination, fantasy and other non-verbal forms of mental activity which might be possible for creatures without language. We include both directed thought, the kind we do on purpose like trying to solve a problem or a puzzle, and undirected thought, the kind that just flits through when the mental gears are in neutral. We *exclude* belief, partly because it seems to involve something more than just the articulation of a thought, but more importantly for our purpose because it presents special problems and therefore is awarded a category of its own.

We don't have to be expert zoologists to understand what a tremendous advantage language and the ability to think have given us as a species. They are the main reason why an otherwise puny species of upright apes was able to adapt almost without limit to changing conditions and different environments. We were able to create food by farming and husbandry where none was offered, store and channel water where needed, harness fire and natural materials, outwit stronger predators and create social structures which grew in complexity to become cities. Our debt to language and thought is considerable!

However, all this power does not come without a price. A significant part of the price is that we cannot stop thinking, or at least we find it very difficult to stop. A particular subject may bother us, as when we yearn for something or someone, worry about something about to happen, obsess about something which already has happened, find a problem nagging at us, or can't switch off from the day's work. These things significantly disrupt our peace of mind and they are all made possible only because we think. On the whole, your cat or dog does not seem to indulge much in these activities. But for us it gets even worse: we think even when we have nothing to think about. We "chatter" internally. Our minds are hardly (if ever) still, as if, to use an ancient Indian metaphor, our unruly thoughts were a tribe of monkeys squabbling and chattering and playing in the branches of our consciousness. No doubt one day someone will provide a convincing scientific explanation of this phenomenon in terms of the activity of the brain and we will understand why our minds chatter. But this will still leave us to deal with the internal noise.

Thus, although language and thought are powerful, essential, even magnificent tools when we need them, they are so powerful that sometimes it seems we cannot stop using them. We cannot switch them off. To change the metaphor from Indian monkeys, it is like having a powerful motor on which the throttle is jammed open. We may be able to steer a bit, but we can't stop and it isn't always clear whether the motor serves us or the other way round.

If you take the time to observe how thoughts crowd into your mind, sometimes following a train of association, sometimes rising up seemingly at random and disappearing again, you cannot help being struck by how little control you seem to have. You can edit, certainly, which is what everyday concentration usually amounts to, pushing away whatever seems irrelevant and holding on to the useful. But you have little control over what arises in the first place. Is this not curious? This is your mind, your thoughts – and yet you are seemingly not in charge. People have theorised and experimented extensively about this, of course, but for now let us just note as a feature of the inner life that the arising of thoughts is only under our control to a very limited extent.

A very interesting thing to ask about the tumult of thought is what the inner life would be like without it. Of course it stops when we are unconscious, but is it possible to be conscious and, in a literal sense, thoughtless? Because we are not generally familiar with the still mind, it is not much prized or sought after. But even relative stillness, it turns out, is associated with a great sense of clarity and joy quite unlike any other experience.

Chattering is, however, not the only unhelpful feature of thought and perhaps it is a habit of which we only become aware once we have made some progress towards quieting the mind. Here are some other common ones:

- Dwelling on the past. Our past is often in our minds, whether alone or accompanied by guilt, regret for past mistakes, or nostalgia for past pleasures. It hardly matters, incidentally, whether the recall is accurate. Thinking about the past is not a problem in itself (otherwise all historians would be unhappy) but it can be the root of some common problems. Maybe past difficulties are relived so that we get a second dose of unhappiness from them. ("Those were terrible times, how we suffered." "I can never forgive what he did to me.") Or we implicitly compare the present unfavourably with the past. ("Those were the days, if only it were like that now.") Or we trigger any one of the many emotions incompatible with happiness. ("Even though it's years ago, I get so angry when I think about it.") Thus we prevent ourselves from being happy now because of the past.

• Fear and worry. Fear and worry are based on thinking about the future. Again, thinking about the future is not always or necessarily a problem in itself. We need to plan and sometimes to rehearse what we will do. But sometimes we think about some future event and imagine how bad it might be or what could go wrong, triggering fear and anxiety. ("I'm going to the dentist on Monday….") Of course, worry does not help at all when the feared future becomes the present, but we cannot let go of the idea that if we keep thinking about it we will think of a "solution". Thus we prevent ourselves from being happy now because of the future.

• Distraction. Thoughts often have a way of seizing our attention so that we do not notice the present. This might even be helpful – for example, if we can distract ourselves from the pain of a toothache. But distraction as a technique is one thing: distraction as a habit may cause us literally to miss chunks of our lives.

• Shadows and imaginings. We all have a store of imaginings, confused memories perhaps of childhood experiences or fears, dream images, ideas from stories and so on – what some schools of psychology would call the contents of the unconscious or subconscious mind. These can suddenly appear in consciousness, triggered by causes we may not notice or understand. They are of course illusions, in a sense, but they can have very real consequences in terms of our reactions to them: they may trigger further thoughts, emotions or desires which may disturb us greatly, or certainly prevent that moment from being happy.

• Stories. Our thoughts form stories and we form stories around our thoughts. We can call this speculation, deduction, interpolation, guesswork, projection or anything we like, but we do it all the time and often unconsciously, in the sense that we do not realise what we have done. As the holidaymakers we met earlier drive along, George, for example, might realise that this is not the best route and then decide that Jenny blames him for choosing it, on no better evidence than that she is silent. Jenny is in fact wondering whether she should have packed warmer clothes, but she notices that George seems rather tense and fears he is critical of her map reading. As they frame completely different stories, layer upon layer of potential misunderstanding can ensue. It isn't even necessary to believe the stories; it can be enough to entertain them for a second or two, whereupon they generate negative emotions which have their own consequences. Communication could of course dispel the stories quite quickly in some cases, but we may fear to communicate about the very story we need to tackle. It doesn't even take two to cause confusion; we are quite capable of wrapping ourselves in layers of story which generate fears and anxieties and discomfort. Later we will discuss the explicit use of story as a skill, one of the keys to freeing ourselves from much self-inflicted unhappiness. Let us note for now that this internal story-telling can be a major source of potential problems.

Belief

Belief is different from thought. For one thing, it involves assent or agreement. I may entertain the thought that there is an elephant in my garage, perhaps as part of a child's game, but this is not the same as the belief that there is one. Fiction would hardly be possible if there were not a difference. But there is more to the distinction than this. I have beliefs which I do not think about and many thoughts which never become beliefs. It is not clear that it makes sense to speak of "unconscious thoughts", but it makes some sense to talk of "unconscious beliefs" – propositions, for example, which I do not articulate and with which I might not even readily agree, but with which my behaviour and attitudes are wholly consistent. Many prejudices are like this, but also many beliefs about myself and my place in the world which may give rise to "irrational" fears or behaviour. Some of the most potent psychological treatments for behavioural or psychiatric disorders depend on uncovering and dealing with such beliefs.

While thoughts distract and may disturb, beliefs have their own special ways of disturbing peace of mind or contributing to unhappiness. They shape our perceptions of people and events, they dictate our own external actions, they give context and meaning to the way we live or alternatively deprive us of such meaning. Beliefs may seem to justify actions and behaviours because "that's how things are and I need to deal with them". More importantly for the inner life, they may create emotions and feelings or be used to justify desires and impulses.

In an obvious and direct sense we each live in a world which our beliefs shape. The external world at most constrains our beliefs and does not completely determine them. We project many features onto the world which go beyond the available evidence – we do it all the time and sometimes we are right, sometimes wrong. We can easily jump to wrong conclusions, particularly when we form beliefs on insufficient evidence, or we mistakenly focus on those aspects of a situation which feed some underlying fear. We saw this with George and Jenny. The boundary between thought and belief is certainly thin: a thought may be dismissed at first but if it survives it may become suspicion and, gradually, belief. As often as not, we realise we have made a mistake and everything is fine again. But not always: think of Othello. The list of difficulties with belief is long and probably more complicated than for any other dimension of the inner life. Here are some of the difficulties:

- Dogmatism, the belief that I know the absolute and complete truth about a subject. My mind is therefore closed to further discussion or argument. If the subject is relatively trivial, like the merits of a football team or the direction of the stock market, the worst I may suffer is exasperation at others' inability to grasp what I am certain is not only true but obvious. I may, of course, get a rude shock when I turn out to be wrong. More seriously, I may ruin my relationship with a relative or loved one because, for example, I cannot see their side of a story. More seriously still, someone might build a whole structure of beliefs and emotional support, the whole under-pinning of their system of meaning and making sense of the world, on the back of such dogmatism. Then when events challenge their beliefs they are left without support. Whenever our minds are closed on a subject there is a danger that circumstances will open them in a painful way. A common instance is when we elevate a lover, a teacher or a leader to pedestal status and refuse to look at the facts until they are forced upon us.
- Assimilative thinking, forming generalised beliefs on the basis of one or two unscientific examples. We come across one or two tall people with red hair who are rude to us and decide that all tall, red-haired people are rude. When we come across some tall red-heads who are not rude, instead of abandoning the belief we decide that these newcomers are somehow limited exceptions to our excellent general rule. This seemingly silly habit can generate serious prejudices and hatreds, all the way up to wars and genocide.
- Beliefs about the inner lives of others. As we saw above, whether we project our own bad habits, misread the signs or jump to conclusions, this is a constant source of potential difficulty.
- Beliefs about ourselves. We might believe that we are superior to others or inferior, more or less deserving, blessed or doomed by

fate. Some people suffer, for example, from a chronic lack of self-esteem. It is easy to accumulate evidence for such a belief from the everyday setbacks which the world offers everyone impartially; all it takes is selective attention to the detail. Others have an exaggerated sense of their ability at work or play: same selective attention, just a different selection. We might believe that we must be perfect at work or in our relationships or that striving to be so is a condition of others' liking and accepting us. We might believe that duty compels us to forego our pleasures for the sake of the well-being of others, or conversely that others should sacrifice their comfort for us. Unhelpful beliefs about ourselves are perhaps the largest category among unhelpful beliefs.

- Beliefs about our past and future. Our memories are incredibly selective and frankly unreliable much of the time. Even if they were perfect they could at best recall events from our own very particular point of view, missing out much detail including nearly everything about other people's motivation for actions and other information about their inner lives (and perhaps ours) which might change the whole significance of events. Yet we tend to have fixed beliefs about the past, our past, which dominate our present attitudes, emotions and desires. A common and therapeutically rich instance is the set of beliefs we have about our relationship to our parents when we were little. Likewise, we know relatively little about the future but we readily form opinions on the subject, optimistic or pessimistic according to our temperament. Particularly common constricting beliefs about the future are either that change from the status quo is undesirable or that it is impossible. Equally unhelpful can be the belief that progress is inevitable: both extremes are examples of dogmatism about the future.

- Beliefs about our rights and entitlements and the way things "should" be. Clearly we all have some of these, and life would be difficult without them. However, such beliefs easily accumulate and it is possible to spend a lot of time feeling that we have been wronged, casually or deliberately, by insensitive colleagues, family members, repairmen, officials, shop assistants or whomever. We can come to feel that the world is unjust whenever it is simply not to our liking.

- Suspicion, or the belief that we are under threat. In an advanced form this belief clearly amounts to a form of mental illness, although perhaps this is true of all problems of belief. But in less extreme forms it is tolerated and even encouraged by large sections of society. Politicians like to encourage us to feel threatened, whether by other nations or by enemies within, because their own power is thereby increased. Marketers of many types of products encourage our insecurities about others – what they might do, what they might think of us, and so on – in order to sell us the product which we hope will remove our anxiety. Sadly, some religious leaders encourage their followers to feel threatened by or at least uneasy about "unbelievers", who are often portrayed as refusing to believe out of sheer wickedness.

• World view. It is not, of course, a problem to have a world view – in fact, we all have one, more or less coherently. But each such view is full of consequences. It is a story from within which we live our lives, perceive the world, relate to others and interpret their actions. Features of any world view can produce inner consequences as well as external action. So we believe ourselves or others to be good or bad, are swept up by fear or hatred because of how we perceive the actions of others, desire some things and abhor others – all because of our world view. And this view may be not so much dogmatically held as simply invisible, because we cannot conceive of the world's being any other way. It is difficult to see your own point of view, literally the point from which you view everything, because you are standing on it.

All beliefs can be curiously invisible, in fact, because the whole essence of believing something is that you take it to be true, you regard it as a fact about the world. This means that beliefs can seem to be something we have no choice about – you can't argue with the facts, can you? – but it can also mean that we do not notice what we believe. We make lots of hidden assumptions. We could hardly function without so doing, but an assumption need not be true just because it is hidden. Crucially, it need not be helpful, either, so far as our peace of mind is concerned. Thus one of the most useful things we can do to counteract problems of belief is to make ourselves aware of our beliefs and the effects they are having on our inner lives.

Emotions / feelings

It is easy to understand how our emotional habits can be obstacles to our happiness. For example, it is extremely difficult if not impossible to be angry and happy at the same moment. Envy and jealousy are notorious destroyers of peace of mind. Fear, hatred, despair and disgust do not foster contentment. We do not need a full list of negative emotions to understand that such habits need attention if we are to become happier. These emotions are almost wholly negative in the sense that they are incompatible with peace of mind. It is, of course, possible that they may have positive aspects in other ways – for example, in evolutionary terms or because one negative emotion can overwhelm another, like anger conquering fear. But it is difficult to make a convincing case for these emotions being in any way compatible with happiness.

It is easy, too, to see that even more positive emotions can have their darker side. Love can be tainted with possessiveness or grow into obsession. The elation of achievement can grow into pride or arrogance. Even happiness, the externally-directed variety, can carry the seed of its own destruction if it depends on something changeable and perishable. (As, for example, when we are happy because we have a new car...until the first scratch.)

Thus the idea that emotional habits may need attention in order to increase our happiness seems easy to accept, even if there are still many difficulties about how to do it. But many people are nevertheless reluctant to hear that emotional habits may be a problem for happiness, perhaps because they fear that such a view may lead to a one-sided, rationalist approach to happiness. It can also be the case that our emotional patterns, more than patterns in other dimensions of the inner life, seem very much an essential part of "us", so that we fear we will lose something of ourselves if we alter them. We might regard it, for example, as rather to our credit that bullying makes us angry: that's the sort of people we are, we stick up for the underdog. But this is to confuse the inner with the external again. If you want to stick up for the underdog and combat bullying, good luck to you. If you allow the bully to determine the state of your inner life, however, you have joined the list of victims. You have a choice about whether you intervene, but you also have a choice about how you feel and whether your inner life is peaceful or disturbed. Or at least, you could have a choice if you could get to the point where habit did not cause anger to sweep you away. Getting to that point is what practice is for, the reason why you may need to increase the skills of your inner life.

It doesn't help that the word "feelings" is sometimes used as a synonym for "emotions" and sometimes to denote awareness of the body – even, confusingly, awareness of the physical effects of emotions. People sometimes say that their feelings guide them in life. We are often told to trust our feelings, and sometimes we use our feelings to help make a decision about something or someone as a complement to or even in contradiction of the overt evidence. Sometimes we call this intuition or instinct and it is an important feature of the inner life.

Such feelings or intuition may in fact come from our perception of changes in our own physical state or our perception of aspects of a situation of which we are not fully conscious. For example, it is well established that in our interactions with another person there may be many cues in their body language and facial expressions. We do not consciously read and explicitly draw conclusions from these, but we are nevertheless aware of them at some level and they influence our attitude to that person. In some cases, these "sub-conscious" perceptions may trigger a mild physical reaction in us and it is this reaction in our own body of which we become aware. For example: someone's body language is aggressive and, although we could not explain what is happening, we are aware that we feel uneasy in his presence. We may be experiencing a mild fear reaction, as if we were being threatened, although we are not consciously aware of it.

Intuition or feelings in this perceptive sense, then, are sometimes confused with emotions, partly because of the ambiguity of the word "feelings". So if it is suggested that we might weaken some unhelpful habits of feeling, it can seem as if we are denying the importance or authenticity of "feelings" in the perceptive sense. But this is surely a mistake. Emotions are not as such a form of perception. In fact, we may need to strengthen our awareness of what emotion we are experiencing in order to deal with emotional habits. We may need to become more conscious of the physical changes which occur during anger, say, or jealousy, in order, first, to realise how unhelpful such patterns of reaction are and, second, to catch or interrupt them sooner. Intuition or feelings in this sense are part of the solution, not part of the problem. Thus it is a mistake if a fear that feelings are being denied or betrayed lies behind a reluctance to tame the emotions.

Emotional patterns sometimes involve obvious physical aspects, so much so that we might be physically unable *not* to react in that way. Fear when faced with a charging lion would be one example, emotional swings induced by hormones or brain chemicals would be another. It might be premature, though, to conclude that training would be irrelevant in either case. A seasoned (and suitably armed) lion hunter, for example, would feel far less fear faced with the lion than I would. As for hormones, the connections between the body and the inner life are so complex and sensitive that I would not rule out the possibility that body chemicals could be influenced by training in various ways. However, to the extent that genuine examples can be found of emotional reactions which are inevitable and unchangeable, we can only accept them. It would not follow that no negative emotional habits can be changed, and we could still make ourselves happier by weakening the changeable ones. It would not follow, furthermore, that we do not have secondary emotional reactions which increase our unhappiness beyond that caused by any inevitable reaction. We could perhaps weaken these secondary habits if we tried, and thus lessen the overall effect of the inevitable one. We might just have to seek other means of dealing with the effects of unchangeable habits on our inner lives.

To be absolutely clear, I am not suggesting that negative emotions like anger are "bad" or that they should be suppressed or repressed. The argument is simply that they are unhelpful to the extent that they disturb our happiness, which they manifestly do in most cases. And the way forward in dealing with them is not to deny that they happen or to try to force them not to happen, but to work on gradually weakening the habit which produces them. They will probably still happen, but if we are successful their force and their frequency will lessen until they are only occasional visitors, they do not overwhelm our inner lives and they subside more quickly. In addition, we can set up other skills alongside them to lessen their impact on our peace of mind when they do occur. In this way we will retain more of our serenity. We can imagine in principle that these negative emotions might, if not disappear altogether, at least become dormant. Whether we get that far along the path depends on how long we persist with the attempt.

Will / desire

Wanting some things and not wanting others takes up a lot of our time. It is of course not just things, as such, that we want. There are states like wealth or motherhood or achievement. There are goods like love and power and fame, whose essence lies in the relationship we have to others. There are goals we set ourselves, like passing a driving test or getting a promotion. There are abstract goods like knowledge or understanding. There are transcendental goals like salvation or enlightenment. There are even wants and desires of the inner life itself, states of mind we find comfortable and pleasant and states we find uncomfortable and even painful. Our wants and desires can be big or small, we can have a hundred of them an hour and we may have one or two which drive us our whole lives and which may even be said to define us. Our aversions and dislikes have the same variety, ubiquity and power.

Broadly speaking, we might expect that we should be happier the more our desires are satisfied and the less we have to be averse to. It is not surprising then that many people regard happiness as a matter of getting what they want. When they get whatever it is, though, they often find that they are still not happy. Perhaps this is because they have confused the external with the state of their inner life; or else it is because each desire, once satisfied, is quickly replaced by another and so the treadmill keeps turning. It may seem obvious that satisfying our desires has a great deal to do with our happiness, but the relationship is not as straightforward as it might at first appear.

Peace of mind in respect of our desires is in some ways an equilibrium or balance, like the balancing of a pair of scales. To prevent desires from interfering with our happiness involves reaching an equilibrium between the intensity and number of our desires and their satisfaction, bringing the two sides into balance.

But there are always at least two ways of reaching any state of equilibrium: you can add to the lighter side of the scales or take away from the heavier. These two ways are not mutually exclusive, of course. In this case, one way forward is to take our desires as given and try to satisfy as many as we can, which is what most people strive to do – increase satisfaction to meet the demands. One problem with this is that circumstances may just not allow us to succeed; another is that demand tends to increase as it is fed, so that the more desires are satisfied, the more we want.

The other way of reaching equilibrium is to reduce your desires. A person with no unsatisfied desires is well on the way to being happy, but one way to have no unsatisfied desires is to have no desires in the first place. This is the traditional way of the ascetics, of course, and in its more extreme forms it is very unlikely to appeal to many of us. But reduction of desire explains one of the impulses to the ascetic life, a choice which many people find difficult to understand. A person may embrace such a life for many reasons but one of them is to become happier by gradually training oneself out of the habits of desire and aversion. We have seen already that not all habits of the inner life are about desire and aversion and thus even such an extreme life choice does not guarantee happiness unless there are other modes of training as well – which, to be fair, there usually are in such cases. But the basic idea is that unsatisfied desires and needs are incompatible with peace of mind, so that the fewer one has, the easier it might be to reach equilibrium and thus be happy.

There is a fundamental shift involved in thinking like this. Our desires drive most of us (indeed, "drives" is another name for them) and we rarely stop to consider whether the effort of striving to satisfy them is worthwhile. Some of our needs and desires must be satisfied or our lives will be very difficult indeed: we need to feed and keep ourselves warm, for example. After that, though, we seem to add needs and desires endlessly, so that endlessly we have to satisfy them. Whenever we pause for breath, we might notice that others are doing better than we are, and this spurs us on again. It doesn't really matter if "better" means here a bigger car or a more profound state of holiness: we judge our state of contentment against what others have achieved. If envy doesn't do the job, the advertising and marketing which surrounds us is there to manufacture additional desires. The boundary between "must have" and "nice to have" creeps relentlessly outwards and with its progress our dissatisfaction grows. You do not have to live naked in a cave to appreciate that enough is sometimes actually enough and that wanting things can create unhappiness for many reasons and indeed may itself *be* unhappiness. This is not at all to say that we should not enjoy what we have; in fact, to appreciate fully what we have is one of the ways we can retain our equilibrium. But it does suggest that if we could find ways of reducing our needs and desires we might increase our happiness rather than the reverse.

It would be a mistake, though, to conclude from our simple analogy with balance or equilibrium that we can thus deal with all unhelpful habits of will/desire. There are many common habits of desire and aversion which are simply harmful in themselves and incompatible with peace of mind. These include many of the habits which religious and ethical systems almost universally condemn as "sins". From our point of view they are unhelpful because they carry us away from any focus on improving our inner life and pin our attention on our external circumstances. These habits would include promiscuity, avarice, gluttony and sloth (excessive desire for rest). All of them could perhaps be seen as forms of greed directed at different ends. Greed in this sense amounts to desire overindulged or out of control, desire for something which is so excessive that it takes over as the central focus of our lives for however long it lasts. Instead of being focused on peace of mind and on living happily, we become obsessed with food, sex, money or whatever it is, which takes over as the main event regardless of the consequences. Peace of mind is forgotten. Thus these problem habits of desire could also be seen as failures of equilibrium. Hatred, incidentally, is the great "sin" of aversion, a profoundly unhelpful habit because it can destroy peace of mind in so many ways – outright anger, distaste, disgust, envy, the need to see the hated suffer, tolerance of injustice, and so on.

One of the most difficult habits of desire is the inability to accept that things change – in other words, a strong desire for the status quo.

Much effort and willpower may be expended trying to prevent change, only to meet with disappointment and unhappiness when change of some sort happens anyway. We all tend to do this to some extent, particularly in our relationships with other people, but it can happen in any context. We simply want the good times to last forever or we don't want to deal with the new. But it can be a fine balance: it can be equally harmful to want change so much that we miss the enjoyment to be had in the present, to focus on the destination so intently that we miss the journey.

Unhelpful habits of will/desire can sometimes arise from our view of how we want things to be: we suffer because things are not as we would like them or do not fit some mental "picture" or story we have adopted. It might be a major issue: we do not achieve the success or the fame or the wealth we crave or our family does not turn out the way we hoped. Or it could be minor: it might just be that we have run out of our favourite snack. We can even want to be different ourselves – better, stronger, thinner, wiser – and we become unhappy because we do not meet our own standards. Perfectionism, wanting ourselves or others or the world to be better and better, can be a terrible curse, leading to great unhappiness because, of course, the process has no end.

Success is another external goal often elevated to a central position in people's lives, which can cause great difficulties and unhappiness. Generally, we admire the "driven" person and we do not like to think that we are not driven enough, or not capable of driving ourselves. We admire the scientist whose desire to know carries them through all setbacks, the entrepreneur who overcomes all obstacles to become successful, the top athlete or the entertainer who produces great work. These are all people whose desire for their goal contributes in many cases to the welfare of others and often to their own. So we need to understand the relationship between the will to succeed and happiness.

The key is to remember the distinction between the inner life and external circumstances, in particular external action. The driven individual usually has an external goal which drives them: success in general is external. Having such a goal is fine, of course, but any relationship with increasing the driven person's happiness is accidental. Their happiness still depends on their inner life. In raising their external goal above all else they have implicitly adopted a different formula for living a happy life, but a formula which depends on external circumstances. For every person who succeeds in meeting their external goal there are many who do not and many ruin their health or even die in the attempt. Even among those who succeed, not all get the recognition, fame or reward they deserve or seek or believe will follow. Thus there are many external contingencies here, not all under the control of the individual concerned. But even if all the goals are reached, will the person be happy and fulfilled? Perhaps, and perhaps not. It depends on their inner life, as it did before they set out and at every step of the way. If their inner life is neglected and their habit basis is unhelpful, they will have no peace and happiness whatever their achievements.

As we saw earlier, there are a few external necessities without which happiness is almost impossible and the inner life can scarcely be developed – we need enough to eat, for example. Thus there are some external goals and drives which might take precedence over the development of the inner life. But not many, and not for many readers of this book. External goals might be adopted for many reasons – for example, because they are fun, because they seem worthwhile in themselves, because they will help others. We will all continue to frame and follow different external goals and there is nothing wrong in that. But if happiness is the central objective, every external goal is subsidiary. No external goal can be a substitute for trying to live happily by developing the inner life.

It is always useful to ask ourselves what inner habits are strengthened by pursuing an external goal. Are they are habits which will generally tend to take us in the direction of inner contentment and peace of mind, or at least not set us back? Only if this condition is satisfied will the achievement of the goal, still less trying and failing to achieve that goal, support happiness. Even dedicating yourself to helping others will not bring you happiness if it does not strengthen helpful habits of your inner life.

It is useful to remember, too, that all external goals are transitory. For example, wanting to be the best always ends in failure. Time always wins if no one else does. Every champion is defeated, retires, or dies and every politician leaves office. And, of course, however wealthy you are, you can't take it with you. It is perfectly possible to decide that happiness and living happily are not central and that you would rather adopt a different goal. It is also possible to adopt many external goals quite consistently with a central focus on happiness. But if you accept that living happily is a central objective, you cannot afford to ignore the inner life in the pursuit of external goals.

Chapter 6:
Basic skills

The art of living happily

With this chapter we come to a turning point, so let me first recap the story so far. I have suggested that the foundations of a happy life are generally misunderstood, although they have been pointed out frequently through centuries past. These foundations lie in what I have called the habit basis, the structures and dispositions underlying our inner life, rather than in external circumstances. Our habits of thought, belief, feeling and desire shape our inner landscape and how we react to external and inner events. In so doing they determine to a very large extent whether we are happy or not. Hence a reliable way to cultivate happiness is to pay attention to these habits of the inner life, to weaken the grip which our "unhelpful" (= not conducive to happiness and peace of mind) inner habits have over us and cultivate more helpful habits.

It is thus absolutely crucial that happiness is a matter of practice and training of the inner life and its habit basis. You can train yourself to be happier by training your inner life. You can practice being happy, meaning not that you go round with an artificial grin on your face but that you can practice the skills underlying happiness. This is not a matter of subscribing to a creed or set of beliefs – you may or may not subscribe to such a creed for other reasons – but is a matter of individual practice, of training yourself. We can cultivate inner skills to weaken and replace unhelpful habits just as we might cultivate physical skills to eliminate weaknesses in sporting or artistic technique. Only sustained practice will give us the inner skills to be happy in life and to face death fearlessly.

Another (ancient) way to put this is that we will seek to practice the art of happiness, the art of living happily. Skills, after all, are what all arts are based on, so to practice skills in a systematic fashion is to practice and prepare ourselves to practice an art. To regard living happily as an art is currently unfashionable, but it makes perfect sense and it is within the power and potential of all of us to choose this approach. An art is of course not the same as Art – I am not talking of an aesthetic approach to living, still less an arrangement of life for aesthetic effect. An art is a skill-based activity directed towards a desired result. Welding, cooking, gardening are arts in this sense as are, for example, martial arts or sports – and so are the fine arts like painting, poetry, or music. Living happily could be seen as the most important art we could seek to learn.

From theory to practice

But now we have to decide what exactly we are to practice, and how we are to go about it. What are the skills we need to acquire for what, if you accept the argument, is one of the most important tasks of our lives? Going back again to a sporting analogy, learning to play football or tennis is not a matter of learning a single skill called football or tennis, it is a matter of acquiring and practising a host of "sub-skills". When you have mastered, let us say, ball control, passing, reading the game, running off the ball, marking, tackling, shooting and many other skills, you may claim to have mastered football. When you have mastered the serve and the strokes and positional play and much else, you have mastered tennis. So if we are to live skilfully and happily we need to know what sub-skills to practice. What are the "sub-skills" of happiness?

It is relatively easy to identify inner skills which will do the job. Candidate skills are not hidden or esoteric and the knowledge of them is far from new – in fact, large parts of it have been known for thousands of years. We already know two important things about these skills. First, they are skills of the *inner* life, because that is where the work must be done. The other important point we have already covered is that, much as we all like simple solutions, a single skill is unlikely to be enough, because the inner life has so many dimensions in which problems may arise. We will suggest a system based around five skills. Each of them is in fact a group of skills, but grouping them in this way helps both in remembering them and in seeing what they are for and how they fit together. Each of the skills we have included would make a major difference to the life of anyone who practised it seriously, let alone mastered it. Together they provide a structure on which an organised system of practice can be based, to increase happiness significantly over time.

The five skills

Here then is an overview of the five skills of our suggested training system. As each skill is itself a complex of related skills, each might be regarded as a set or circle of skills – think of those Venn diagrams you might have seen in school, in this case with five circles intersecting and overlapping. The chapters following will discuss each skill circle in more detail.

Mindfulness

The first skill-set we will call ***mindfulness***. We could also call these ***attention skills.*** We need to be able to observe, sometimes with great patience, exactly what goes wrong: what happens in the inner life, what habits take us away from a point of happy equilibrium or disturb our peace of mind. For this we need ideally to make ourselves aware – as carefully and as objectively as possible and without jumping to conclusions or self-judgement – of each inner habit which contributes to our unhappiness. We might study and observe these habits, noticing for each of them, for example, how it operates, what triggers it, what course it runs and how it ends. The skill of mindfulness requires a kind of ***concentration*** or focused attention, but in a relaxed and fluid form, without strain. Mindfulness is a powerful tool for investigation and it also has curative properties of its own. For example, sometimes becoming aware of a bad habit is enough to weaken it.

The skill of mindfulness when practised intently leads to a state which is of particular use when the bad habit to be addressed operates in the dimension of thought. This is ***stillness,*** meaning stillness of mind rather than of body. In fact, I think it is closely related to ecstasy, in its original sense of standing outside oneself. It is a skill developed by many meditative practices, and also by physical activities requiring great concentration. (Is it a skill or a state? Getting there is certainly a skill.) States similar to meditative states have been reported, for example, by mountain climbers, athletes and racers. For some people aesthetic experiences have the same effect, and the state of inner stillness may also be achieved by various types of dance, from the whirling of Sufis to Roth's Five Rhythms. I think it may be the same as or closely related to the state of flow described by Mihaly Csikszentmihalyi, a leading member of the positive psychology movement. When thoughts and images are just allowed to come and go on our inner stage, with patience but without becoming absorbed in their content, they lessen in intensity and frequency and the mind settles or, as some people report it, "stops". This is where the practice of mindfulness becomes meditation or absorption. There can then be a feeling of inner spaciousness, wonder and joy, which make up the extraordinary positive side of this skill.

Benevolence

The second circle we consider are the ***benevolence skills,*** under which family we include ***compassion, kindness, love, forbearance, generosity*** and others. These may sound like very traditional virtues and of course they are. But they are also skills which we can inculcate through practice and it is essential for our purpose to think of them in this practical way. They have many uses but are particularly useful against negative emotional habits like anger, envy or hatred. These unhelpful emotional habits as we have seen are among the biggest obstacles most of us face to being happy, for a very simple reason: it is very hard indeed to be full of anger or hatred and to be happy at the same time.

Benevolence, though, does not necessarily start from feeling or emotion. It involves a concerted effort to change the way we see other people. It might start from as simple an exercise as trying to imagine how on earth the other person might think it reasonable to behave in their seemingly obnoxious manner – what would they have to believe or feel to do that? It might reach a point where one feels and acts with genuine kindness and compassion towards everyone, although perhaps only a few will ever get so far. But is this not an intriguing thought? It may not be surprising that compassion, a virtue at the heart of many religions, may become ingrained through the deliberate practice of "compassionate" thought and action. The surprise is that such practice may be motivated in the first instance simply by a pragmatic desire to be free of anger, hatred and other emotions incompatible with happiness. Thus the least selfish of virtues may be born not out of altruism but out of the simple desire to be happy.

Story

The third circle of skills has to do mainly with the ways in which we shape our beliefs and the ways they in turn shape our inner lives. I call them ***story skills.*** We can see all descriptive language as the telling of stories which operate on many different levels. Regardless of whether stories are true or false, what can matter more in the inner life is whether or not we believe them. Alternative stories about the same subject may appear incompatible, but still stand as complements to each other like the parallel stories about tables and atoms we saw earlier. Sometimes it is more a question of what is left out which defines a story. But every story defines and is defined by a point of view or perspective and selects from reality those bits we are interested in, or which we (or our habits) want to concentrate on. By changing stories we change our perspective or point of view and that can have dramatic effects on our inner lives.

We cannot get away from stories and still use language (still be thinking). If you can't escape from stories altogether, being able to switch between them may be the only way to free yourself from an unhelpful one. An important realisation is that all stories are partial and therefore all truth is partial. No story tells all there is to tell about any situation.

Before we even get to the job of describing the world or the bits of it that interest us, stories are already embedded in and implied by the language and concepts that we use, often so subtly that we do not notice them and their effects. For example, what is a chair, or what does "chair" mean? To answer this, you might use a dictionary-style definition: "a chair is a piece of furniture for one person at a time to sit on with their back supported". Not a bad answer, but it is already a complicated story, carefully distinguishing chairs from, say, sofas or stools or car seats because that is where we might expect confusions to arise. The answer has a point of view and assumes one on the questioner's part. If this assumption were wrong, you might have to launch into more description of what counts as a chair and what doesn't: when does a chair start and stop being a chair, what counts as sitting, how much back support is required to qualify, etc. Not all the possible questions have ready answers, especially if we leave chairs and consider more abstract or complex ideas, and so they lead to difficulty and puzzlement, even on occasion anguish. A particular concept we will look at in this regard is the idea of the self.

Playing with stories is so powerful that it is almost like playing with reality. Reality is not exactly ours to fashion as we like, but it is hard to separate reality from the stories we tell about it, simply because we cannot approach reality except through the medium of story. Hence story skills can be recognised not only in literature, mythology, politics and drama but also in science, medicine, and religious thought. They can even seem like magic.

Letting go

The fourth skill-set we will call the *letting go skills.* The skills of letting go are about the ability to release oneself from attachment, fixation or in the worst cases obsession with a thought, a memory, a belief, an emotion, a desire, a person or a thing. We often cause ourselves unhappiness by clinging to things, inner and outer, which are coming to an end, or have already ended, or perhaps never even existed but we wanted them to. We can be equally profligate with our aversions, which can be thought of as attachment to something's not being or not happening.

An important letting go skill is *forgiveness,* of ourselves as well as others – letting go of anger, guilt or shame about the past. Then *Non-attachment* is the skill of realising that everything changes and that only unhappiness will result from opposing change when it becomes inevitable. Non-attachment is being prepared to let go when the time comes. It is important that this attitude does not imply indifference or coldness. On the contrary, when we realise that change is both inevitable and an essential part of a person or thing, our love or enjoyment of them can be enhanced by the knowledge of their transient nature. The pleasure we take in a beautiful flower or a fine meal, for example, does not depend on a belief that the flower or the meal will last for ever. At its most developed, this is a skill which can greatly help us with the most difficult and least discussed problem of our lives – death.

There are many practices which help to develop these skills, the most extreme of which are forms of ascetic monasticism and isolation. But while asceticism is one path and a very good one for some people, the giving up of material goods is not really the point of letting go. What is given up is less important than the ability to recognise inner attachment and step away from it, reminding ourselves that this is a temporary pleasure and we might need to be able to do without it. This does not necessarily mean abandoning all comforts, still less abandoning external obligations or commitments. It does involve realising that we may have staked the continuation of our happiness on the continuation of something which is bound to end.

Enjoyment

Last to be discussed but not least in importance is the skill-set we will call *enjoyment skills.* To say that enjoyment is a core skill supporting happiness may sound like arguing round in a circle, but it is not. This set of skills is among other things a counter to the possible dryness of concentrating exclusively on removing the obstacles to happiness. There is a danger that we begin to think of happiness as something to be attained in the future, once the work is done, rather than something to be experienced now. Enjoyment is a matter of being joyful about – and most importantly in – the present moment, rather than postponing our enjoyment as we so often do because we want something else. It is the ability to see what is enjoyable or at least acceptable in any situation, however difficult. To encourage enjoyment or the sense of joy is a vital part of living skilfully, putting happiness at the core of our lives. Without it, the other practices can become barren, grim or even self-defeating, for a happy life is made up of happy moments and it would be a terrible mistake to postpone happiness while we train for it. We need to enjoy the training process, for the training process is our life.

Enjoyment skills include cultivating more of a sense of contentment about each moment of our lives, rather than striving so hard to improve our position that we are always discontented. For example, simply breathing in and out can be a pleasure if we are aware of it, but mostly we only notice when our breathing is difficult, as when we are ill. Also included are the skills of *acceptance* and *patience* when things do not go well. Acceptance does not mean passivity, but the ability to maintain equanimity in the face of hardship, recognising that it is here for now and until it can be removed.

Enjoyment also includes the habit of being grateful for the things we encounter. *Gratitude,* even a sense of *grace,* is a very important component of happiness. There does not necessarily have to be someone or something to whom we are grateful, although often there is. For many people it is natural, for example, to think and practice at all times in terms of gratitude to supernatural beings. But gratitude makes perfect sense as a state – and with practice a habit – of our own inner lives; it does not have to be a relationship to someone else. At the very least, the habit of gratitude helps us to remember what is right with any situation rather than becoming fixated with what is wrong: it encourages us to respond to both rather than focusing exclusively on what is wrong or not to our liking. And, last but not least, enjoyment of both life and practice needs *humour.*

Skilful = happy

These qualities or skills are in themselves so well known that the list may even seem banal at first glance, especially if you were expecting an amazing new discovery or revelation. Sorry, if you were! But the value of the list lies in the recognition that these are not just abstract qualities, however desirable. They are *skills* which pull together to form a vital art. The inclusion of each skill is rooted in the function that skill performs in taming the habits and dispositions which disturb inner peace and therefore prevent happiness.

Besides, knowing what's on the list is of no great consequence. It is *having* the skills and being able to apply them, having practised and internalised them, which makes a difference. And the difference which can be made is not at all banal, it is magnificent. It is the difference between living happily and just existing.

I do not claim for a moment that this is the only possible list of suitable inner skills – in fact, I know of other very good lists. This list is useful because it is based on the argument about happiness and not on any particular supernatural belief. *If you had mastered these five sets of skills, you would be able to deal inwardly with everything that life could throw at you.* You would have the wherewithal to live happily no matter what the circumstances because your inner life would be unshakeably serene in all circumstances. Mastery is a lot to expect, but even if your grasp of these skills were a little better than it is today, your life would be better and happier. So the more practice you can do, the more skilful you will be and the happier you will become. Even if you never reach the stage of mastery, your life will be happier than it might have been, perhaps as happy as you can make it.

Many of the skills, as we have noticed in passing, look like the virtues of faith and philosophical traditions. This is not a coincidence. To the extent that such traditions have always been concerned with the betterment of the inner life, they cover just this territory. Our focus and motivation for cultivating these skills is of course not quite the same as that of the faith traditions. But if we are at all concerned with living happily we need these skills of the inner life. If we do not have them (or a very similar list), our inner lives will be troubled and turbulent. Our own minds will not let us be happy. But I do not apologise for emphasising again that these are skills, useful habits which we can improve by practice. Thus the issue becomes a practical one, not a matter of eliminating sinfulness or defilement or lack of virtue or weakness, and certainly not a matter of being stuck with the negative consequences of unchangeable character. The issue becomes simply a matter of today's skill levels across a range of skills and how to improve them. And the reason for improving them is that our lives will be happier and will gradually fill with peace. Is this a spiritual goal? Yes, I think it is. Is it esoteric or supernatural? No, it is not.

Learning and living

No athlete's training regime consists simply of repeating the whole sporting performance again and again. There might be a fitness regime, special exercises to build up certain muscle groups, work on flexibility or stamina or balance or agility or whatever is most relevant or weakest. Then there will be practice and exercises to improve technique and eliminate technical weaknesses. There may be psychological coaching to handle the pressures of competition. And of course there will be plenty of performance, including competition with training partners and chosen opponents to sharpen and integrate the skills learned in training.

If we took the idea of training the inner life seriously, we might seek and adopt for ourselves a varied training regime aimed at strengthening the five skill sets. Not every such regime would look the same, for a training regime is a very personal thing and it must depend on your starting point. But each one would have the same objective: to improve and perfect the skills of the inner life so as to live happily and skilfully, free from the unhelpful habits which drag us down. As you read the next few chapters you might ask yourself: "What should I include in my inner training regime? What skills do I lack or most need to strengthen? And what shall I do about strengthening them?"

But while our skills can be nurtured and helped by exercises and practices performed in a separate space, life itself continually faces us with choices which will strengthen either a skill or an unhelpful habit, depending on which way we go. Unless you intend to seclude yourself (and even then you will have your own thoughts, emotions, desires, etc., to contend with) it is pointless and arguably simply impossible to separate your life into two components, practice and "real life". Thus the idea of practising to improve the skills of the inner life becomes something which pervades the whole of our lives. Life may not be a rehearsal, but it is always practice!

The ideal of mastering the inner skills

A skill is not the sort of thing you have either completely acquired or you completely lack. There are of course different degrees of skilfulness, a continuum from a shaky grasp of some of the basics up to complete mastery. In competitive fields, mastery means a stage at which few if any can beat you, but even masters in this sense usually know that they could be better. With the skills of the inner life, mastery might mean that one met every circumstance with the perfectly appropriate inner response, with continuous and uninterrupted equanimity and peace of mind, making automatically the choice which reinforced the skills still further. This may sound like an unachievable goal but there certainly have been people who have seemed to master completely the skills of the inner life, among them the great spiritual masters, male and female, of many traditions.

Whether complete mastery is achievable, though, doesn't make any practical difference because we can all continue to increase our level and degree of inner skills, and more skill will always be better (= more conducive to living happily) than less. You may not be a master chef, by way of analogy, but that need not stop you from preparing an enjoyable dinner and it need not stop you, if you choose, from being a far better cook next month or next year than you are today.

There is no point meanwhile in making yourself more unhappy about not yet being as happy as you would like to be! Happiness, we might say, is a direction we would like our lives to go in. There are road signs in certain places which say "The North" or "The South". You will never reach a sign which says "You have now arrived in The North" or wherever, but the sign is still useful because it is not the name of a place but of a direction. Profound happiness, perfection of the skills, mastery, even enlightenment – however you like to think of it, it is best thought of as a direction, not a destination. Ideals are fine, but not as idols.

Just do it!

Regardless of whether our particular list of skills is acceptable, it is something of a puzzle why training ourselves to lead happy lives is not a central issue in our individual and collective lives. The idea that the inner life is important for happiness is hardly new, after all – in fact, it is centuries old. So why isn't teaching our children the skills they need to be happy placed right at the top of the school curriculum? Do you remember the happiness lessons at school, the ones which discussed how to deal with adversity and difficulties, how to retain your sense of balance and inner peace whatever the circumstances, how to cope with loss and tragedy, how to see and enjoy the best in people, places and situations? No? It's odd, neither do I. Perhaps we were both off school that day.

There are at least three confusions which obscure the importance of practising happiness skills. The first is that people think happiness is about external conditions rather than the inner life. The second is that even if people do focus on the inner life, they believe that its development is a matter of religion. The third is that they believe that there is nothing systematic they can do to improve their inner life. None of these things is true, as by now I hope you are inclined to agree.

It is of course crucial that skills are practised, not just talked or thought about. You cannot get better at a sport or craft by reading a book unless you turn what the book says into action. The same applies to the inner skills. Again, there may be lots of different ways of approaching the acquisition of the skills of a complex art like happiness. A systematic approach of some kind is needed, a training system if you like, but there is seldom only one way of going about things. There is no point in arguing over the merits of rival lists, because all we need to do to make a big difference is to identify a reasonably sufficient set of skills and get on with the practice.

There are some preconditions for practice. First, you have to want to do it or at least understand the importance of it. Second, you have to be capable of sustaining the training. This is not a question of ability, class, education, intelligence or background but simply a question of focus and the determination to stick with it. The prize is happiness and an unshakeably peaceful mind but it is curiously easy to forget the magnitude of this prize and be distracted. Above all, the essential prerequisite may be responsibility, the willingness and vision to see that your happiness is your own responsibility. It doesn't matter in the end whether life has been cruel or kind to you, or whether other people have been cruel or kind to you. Of course it may be easier if external conditions are easier, but the good things of the external life can distract almost as much as the bad. You can take charge of your own life and destiny if you are willing to be responsible for your own happiness. Because happiness is a function of your inner life and your habit basis, this does not mean accumulating possessions or position by fair means or foul. It means being responsible for your inner life and for the direction in which your habit basis will change.

The important thing is not to leave the development of your habit basis to chance. We have only one real choice to make. We can choose not to practice, in which case our habits, good and bad, will still keep slowly changing but in random response to circumstances and without any deliberate direction. Or we can choose to practice and move our inner lives in the direction of greater happiness. Everyone who takes happiness seriously should have a framework for practice and some idea of how and in what direction their habit basis should evolve. If you lack such a plan or framework, your inner life may just drift and that means that your happiness will be at the mercy of circumstances. Whatever you decide about our particular group of five skills, everyone needs to practice and improve the skills of their inner life.

Jigsaw puzzles

Happiness, in the sense of profound peace of mind or inner peace, is the goal which holds any training programme together. If you bear this goal in mind, you can readily see how the different skills fit with one another and how they weaken habits or dispositions which will make it harder to attain peace of mind or sustain it once you have it. Everything fits together in the light of the central goal, like the pieces of a jigsaw puzzle which may make little sense on their own. We can work on difficulties of thought, belief, emotion and desire and just keep on improving and amending our habits until difficulties are gradually replaced by skills and we grow happier and more confident in our ability to be happy. Most of us have a lot of work to do but it doesn't matter – what else are you going to do?

It is useful that this goal of inner peace or happiness can give unity to a system of practice which might derive elements from many different traditions. A system of practice like this differs sharply from eclectic systems of belief. It is popular nowadays to browse the world's religions and faith traditions for doctrines which fit with our own preconceptions, tastes or experience. We might call this religious eclecticism or, less kindly, Pic'n'mix or DIY religion. It involves a rejection of "organised religion" and a decision to take responsibility for one's own beliefs. Brave though this might be in principle, what unfortunately but unsurprisingly results is that consistency is a bit of a problem. I read the other day, for example, an article by someone who declared themselves to be a Christian, but with the addition of a belief in re-incarnation. How on earth (or anywhere else) does that work? But the contradictions are brushed aside because, well, religion is meant to be hard to understand, isn't it? The outcome of this kind of jigsaw puzzle is often, excuse the pun, an unholy mess. If you believe contradictions you believe something which is not and cannot be true, however worthy your motives.

But this problem of consistency does not apply to an eclectic use of practices or techniques from different sources. Beliefs must be consistent or anything goes, but practices do not contradict each other. There might be practices which strengthened one skill at the expense of another and these we would naturally wish to avoid if we could find alternatives. But the test of a practice or a technique is not truth or consistency but effectiveness. If we know what effect we want to achieve, and we have good reason to think a certain practice will help, that is an acceptable reason to try it, whatever its source. In our case we know that happiness is the goal and that cultivating the skills of the inner life is the way forward. We thus have a simple test of effectiveness. In any case, if a particular practice does not work for us, the value of the whole enterprise is not called into question as it might be if some fundamental belief were challenged. If we make a mistake, we can try something else.

Happiness as our central goal binds together practices and skills, but happiness is made achievable by understanding it as a matter of cultivating inner peace through developing skills. Many people adopt meditation, mindfulness practices, good works, kindness to strangers, forgiveness, the observance of fasts and retreats – all these things are excellent for developing one or another skill of the inner life. But put them together according to your own needs and weaknesses, see that their goal and purpose is to develop these inner skills and that the end goal is to live in inner peace and happiness. Then you are on the path to something truly marvellous.

Part Two

THE SKILLS OF HAPPINESS

Chapter 7:
Mindfulness skills

Waves

Some years ago I was lucky enough to be on holiday on a beautiful island in Greece. But I was troubled at the time and despite the wonderful surroundings my mood, my thoughts and my emotions were unstable. Some days I was up, some days down. Each morning I would rise early, not out of choice but because the local poultry were already awake and noisy. I fell into the habit of taking a cup of coffee to the rocks at the sea's edge and sitting there watching the water. Some days the sea in the bay would be waveless, calm as a lake, the early light sparkling off it. The water was utterly transparent and the bottom of the bay could be seen clearly. Now and again shoals of tiny fish would arc out of the water and splash back. But on some days by contrast the water would be choppy, churned into white by wind and currents, nothing visible but the roughened surface. Once or twice the wind got up and the bay was full of racing waves which broke against the rocks in showers of spray.

Each day I sat with my coffee and watched the sea and my own thoughts, until one day it dawned on me that the two were very much the same. Sunny or stormy, calm or choppy, it was all just on the surface of things. You could imagine that a short way down in the water the happenings on the surface, which from my vantage on the rocks looked like the main event, were not even part of the story. Underneath, whatever changes were taking place had little to do with today's weather at the surface. The sea was not the waves or the calm, I was not my mood or the emotions or the thoughts flooding through me; both just looked that way from a certain perspective. Emotions and thoughts ruffled the surface of my inner life just as the wind and the waves ruffled the clarity of the water in the bay, but they were nothing fundamental. They passed through, and the next day or even the next minute they might be gone. With that realisation, suddenly the importance of these thoughts and emotions was put in perspective. My "troubles" were always, in fact, just ripples and waves on the surface of my inner life. But it took the calm and clarity of those early moments at the beginning of restful days to show me this. It was a spontaneous moment of insight made possible by stepping back, quite unintentionally in this case, from being swept along by the contents of the inner life and instead simply being aware of them. I had accidentally been mindful! But this was only a glimpse. Mindfulness is a great and deep skill, as we will now see.

Paying attention

If you want to train your inner life and change your habit basis for the better, you need at a minimum to discover what needs changing. But when you first try to observe your own inner life – observe the process of thinking, feeling and so on as it is actually occurring – you are likely to find it tricky.

For example, there is first the problem that what you observe is inevitably changed by observing it. You are observing the inner life with the inner life – you have nothing else to observe it with! – and thereby adding a new element. There is no way round this, although it turns out not to be such bad news. This "observation effect" can be used to advantage to interrupt unhelpful patterns, as we will see later. Second, there is generally so much going on that it is difficult to focus on what is happening and decide what to watch. It is like being faced with a hundred different monitor screens and simply being told to watch the important one – but which is it? Third, it is difficult to observe and not "join in", so that the attention is led away by a thought or a feeling. When that happens you are no longer observing but just thinking and feeling; your attention is involved in the content of the thought or the feeling rather than watching the process unfold. Fourth, it is difficult to hold the concentration required to watch because new thoughts and images, if not feelings and desires, keep popping up seemingly from nowhere.

The way round these difficulties is to cultivate mindfulness. Mindfulness is simply paying attention. But of course paying full and steady attention to anything is not at all simple. Deep, concentrated attention, especially when directed on the processes of the inner life, requires a level of skill which most of us do not have. We have to build up this skill, and the only way is by practice. So, yes, mindfulness is simply paying attention, but to master it is simply paying attention in rather the same way that Shakespeare was simply writing plays or winning Wimbledon is simply playing tennis!

Thinking, for example, is a particularly tricky process to observe because our thoughts ordinarily crowd in upon us so densely and quickly that there does not seem to be a gap between them. They tumble over each other like fighting puppies. And the content of our thoughts seizes the attention – that's what thinking is, after all – so that watching or paying attention to yourself thinking is difficult. Observing the inner life is not a simple matter.

Applying steady attention, otherwise known as concentrating, is in itself something we can all do, more or less, for relatively short periods. We tend to be better at it with external or physical tasks – for example, threading a needle or wiring a plug. But if we have to concentrate for long periods, our minds tend to stray from the task and we have to keep dragging our attention back. We think of other things: perhaps we worry about something or we daydream; an idea occurs to us about how we might tackle another problem; we feel hungry or lapse into sexual fantasy; we look forward to what we might do later; we think about the deadline for finishing what we are doing – then we realise our focus has strayed and we pull ourselves back to the task in hand. We can in fact carry on with many external tasks while we think about something else. Often our thoughts and feelings can be completely elsewhere while we perform a task on "auto-pilot", and not just routine tasks but quite complex activities like driving or operating machinery. Even when we do something which mainly involves thinking – like writing a business letter, composing a memo or calculating – we rarely concentrate completely and without being distracted for more than a few seconds. Everyday concentration is a matter of not allowing much to distract us, and not for long.

But there is no way we can observe the inner life like this. Each distraction will be a total distraction, every thought and feeling which captures our attention will bring at least a temporary end to the task. We can be thinking about our holidays or feeling upset about something which happened this morning and be aware of what it is we are doing, but the moment we fully engage with that thought or feeling, the awareness is gone. We then have no chance of spotting how our habits trot out some inner pattern which ends up with us feeling restless or unhappy. Sometimes we say that our thoughts or our feelings "carry us away" or even "sweep us away" and this language is spot on. They carry or sweep us away from being attentive. If we are going to try to observe our own inner lives at all closely, it is obvious that our concentration will be sorely tested and will need to be strengthened. Thus, improving our concentration, improving our ability to keep our attention steady and focused where we want it to be, will be an essential part of practice aimed at developing the habit basis.

We know that external skills of observation can be trained and sharpened by practice and by learning what to look for. The results can be surprising. A trained military observer, say, or a detective, an ornithologist, or an experienced hunter may notice external signs which would escape the attention of most of us. So Holmes was able to confound Watson in story after story! But inner observation or mindfulness can also be gradually improved by practice. The person practised in mindfulness may notice more and more about how their own inner life actually operates.

What's so great about just paying attention?

Mindfulness is generally underrated and undervalued in our lives because we simply don't realise how unaware we are. It already takes a certain degree of mindfulness to realise how important the skill is and how much we lack it. We generally allow ourselves to be run by our inner habits. We get angry, we worry, we fret about what we don't possess and others do, we think about the past and are full of minor and perhaps major regrets, we have all kinds of beliefs which limit what we do or drive us to do things. And all the time we may think we are in perfect control and know exactly what is going on, at least in our own minds. But it is simply not so. We react, or rather, our habits react for us. They are like inner reflexes. We think and feel and want and believe without making real choices – we get so that feeling comfortable with the habit feels like making a choice. But the effects do not leave us at peace; we cannot have peace of mind while we are full of anger or worry or regret or spinning thoughts. Mindfulness is the way out. Once we observe what is going on in our inner lives, we may create choices about whether we have peace of mind or not.

Mindfulness is like a sense, the sense which tells us about the inner life. We have many senses (sight, hearing, touch, taste, temperature, etc.) focused on telling us what is happening in the external world, and we often develop additional skills in using these senses to help us discriminate fine details in seeing or hearing or tasting. But the inner life has only one possible sense, mindfulness, and mostly we don't bother to develop it at all. We are without sensitivity or discrimination towards our own inner lives, which means we don't know what is going on and our habits have free rein.

Mindfulness is a skill particularly prized and encouraged by the Buddhist traditions, whose practitioners have done much to explore how to go about it and develop it and have thus greatly expanded the technology of mindfulness. This huge potential contribution to human happiness should be acknowledged with awe. If we understood their implications fully, these ancient discoveries would be prized alongside any of the most crucial technological discoveries of civilisation. But the idea of mindfulness need not be thought of as an exotic import from Eastern thought, because it is almost identical with some thoroughly Western ideals of self-knowledge and inward awareness. These range, for example, from the Greek oracle's "Know thyself" and perhaps Socrates' "The unexamined life is not worth living" through Marcus Aurelius and the Stoics. The idea of cultivating mindfulness occurs again and again in different guises in Christianity, Judaism and Islam, particularly in the mystical traditions which have always been strong within these religions.

This distinguished pedigree should not lead us to think, though, that mindfulness is something strange or complicated. It is a simple matter to understand and even to practice. The main difficulty lies in the dedication needed to train ourselves so that it becomes a constant and habitual activity. In this respect it has a lot in common with pursuing physical fitness or watching what you eat. You know you should do it, you know you will feel better in the long run if you take the trouble, but somehow, well, perhaps you will start again next week. Developing concentration and the habit of mindfulness does take some effort and time, preferably a little effort and time every day. There is a part of most of us that resists spending effort and time on such long-term projects. But if you accept the argument that happiness is a matter of the inner life and thus depends on the habit basis, developing this skill of mindfulness is absolutely essential to living a truly happy life.

We practice, as we shall see, by trying to hold the attention on one thing. It is an opposite to the short attention span, TV-type mind we all live with in the modern world and cultivate by our everyday activities. The flightiness we generally indulge cultivates a dissatisfaction with the moment, because we are always restlessly moving on to the next sensation and we get bored so easily. The idea of "resting content" is easily lost. So mindfulness is partly about slowing down, slowing the mind down so that we have a chance to appreciate our lives one moment at a time. That said, it can be practised in the whirl of activity, as when we concentrate on a physical skill to the extent that we become completely focused. Indeed, one way to reduce distractions is to occupy the body with so much activity that the mind has no choice but to stay still.

Mindfulness is not something separate from everyday life. It is used to weaken habits which affect happiness, but habits are weakened one instance at a time. Thus mindfulness helps all the time with everyday situations which might otherwise upset us. Suppose, for example, that the garage has just telephoned to say that your car, sent in for a minor service, needs a major and expensive repair. Now your day is ruined along with your budget, you feel, and the world is suddenly against you. Mindfulness means being aware that these reactions are taking place, retaining the ability in a small corner of your mind to observe your own irritability. You may not be able to prevent the negative reactions, but perhaps you can stand back a little from them, as if to say, "There I go again getting swept away by irritation at what cannot be helped while I own a car, allowing external chances to determine the quality of my life." After all, the garage's job is to repair cars (even if you suspect it is to relieve you of your money), but it is your job to shape your inner life and determine whether you live happily. Your reaction has allowed the garage to run your inner life. Mindfulness makes us aware of how we are reacting in any of the dimensions of the inner life, shows us what habits are operating and what we are doing to ourselves. Mindfulness helps us to say: fate has dealt me a blow but I still have a choice here, to be happy or not, to live this minute, this day, happily or not.

Clearly, mindfulness itself is a matter of degree. It is not a question of being totally unaware of anything or totally aware of everything in our inner life, like a light bulb switching off and on. We can be and generally are aware to a lesser or greater extent, more aware at some times than at others, more aware of certain features than of others. Some benefits of mindfulness will appear quickly, others will continue to unfold for years or even decades as practice continues. This ripening and deepening is indeed a mark of all our five skill sets. They are not quick fixes but elements of a training regime which becomes a way of living. I do not know of any upper limits to the effectiveness of such a programme and there may simply not be any. Think about it: it may just get better and better!

More benefits of mindfulness

Mindfulness, we have said, is a skill of surprising and extraordinary power. The greatest value of cultivating it is, of course, that it enables us gradually to become aware of the habits which govern our inner lives. The unconscious is brought into consciousness – meaning simply that we notice something which operates whether we notice it or not. The unconscious habits we all have are brought into awareness at the point at which they operate and their effects are made apparent.

A second benefit of mindfulness, however, is that many of the unhelpful habits of the inner life are weakened simply by our awareness of them. Suppose, for example, that George has a habit of becoming irritated whenever Jenny asks for help with her garden. Perhaps he feels that she is implicitly criticising him or perhaps he is reminded of some parental imposition which he resented at the time – we don't need to know why. Merely becoming aware of this tendency might cause George to be curious about it and to observe himself more closely the next time the situation occurs, perhaps in the hope of spotting the cause. This shift, even a partial shift, from irritation to observation, this slight dissociation from the emotional reaction, might in itself lessen the reaction and weaken the habit – and if the observation is successful, the habit might be understood and weakened even further.

I am not suggesting that habits can be made to disappear just by being noticed. In fact, there is generally no direct way of *immediately* breaking any inner habit, or if there is it is unusual. We can resolve to work on a particular habit whenever it appears, but there is no "act of will" we can perform which will banish a whole habit, a whole pattern of reaction, instantly. But we can interrupt the operation of a habit in a particular instance, if only we can become aware of it. We then give ourselves a choice as to how we react if we have not already reacted, or we can sometimes quell the reaction by catching it soon enough. If we do this in a sufficient number of instances, the habit will weaken, or a new one take its place. Attention and choice have to be applied to each instance in turn until the habit yields: the stronger the habit, the more instances may be needed. But in some cases, especially with habits of the emotions, awareness itself is a sufficient interruption of the habit in a particular instance. Perhaps the act of observation anchors the mind and stops the emotion from sweeping us away, or perhaps the awareness of the emotion is a sufficient dissociation to interrupt or weaken its operation.

Another benefit of mindfulness is that our conscious experience can be greatly enriched by merely practising the skill, and in this sense mindfulness could be considered an enjoyment skill. Developing mindfulness is the key to focusing on what is going on at the present moment and finding what pleasure there may be in that moment rather than mentally seeking to be elsewhere. Hence the frequently heard (but seldom explained and difficult to practice) exhortation to "live in the now". It is a curious thing that the present moment, really focused on, is immensely more rich and more full of life and joy than we usually suppose.

Thich Nhat Hanh, contemporary Zen master and one of the best sources of wisdom on the subject of mindfulness, uses the example of washing dishes. Usually we regard washing dishes as a chore to be completed as quickly as possible so that we can get finished, have clean dishes and go on to something more interesting and enjoyable. But an alternative is that we could wash the dishes mindfully, treating it as an important activity in itself, paying close attention to the sensations and sounds, noticing but not getting swept up by the thoughts and memories which flit into our heads and the feelings which arise, perhaps being amused by the frantic attempts of our inner life to distract us and "go" somewhere else. We could just concentrate on washing the dishes, treating this little segment of our lives as being just as important as any other, to be as fully lived and experienced as any other, not just thrown away as tedious. If we wash the dishes like this, just to experience washing the dishes, the activity takes on a different quality. It can, astonishingly, become almost a recreation, a source of pleasure, even joy. This is because we have fully lived and experienced these moments by focusing on them rather than giving way to the habits of dislike, of labelling this activity a chore or of wanting to be elsewhere.

It is of course an important aim of monastic training to live the whole of life in this focused manner – difficult to do unless one is prepared to simplify one's life greatly but a worthy aim and one which illustrates the power of mindfulness. We have less difficulty in absorbing ourselves in activities we expect to be pleasurable, but even in such cases increased mindfulness can greatly enhance the experience. Some people experience sex, for example, simply as the process which comes before orgasm. The orgasm becomes the objective, like having clean dishes, and the process is merely something leading up to it. Perhaps in such cases it would be helpful to adopt the advice on dish-washing – with a few suitable modifications.

Just as a caution, it is important to note that mindfulness is not and does not imply self-absorption. On the contrary, it involves an abandonment of the sense of self. Even when applied in examining the inner life, it looks objectively at what is actually going on, telling no stories about what should or might be going on, or what "I would like to" have going on. No stories, either, about why, or about who or what is responsible. We will look in a later chapter at the idea of self, which has a role as a social organising principle but can confuse us in the inner life. Depressed people for example are often very self-absorbed and focused on their own problems; indeed this narrow perspective may be one obstacle to their recovery. (I certainly do not suggest that they can change this perspective by some simple effort.) But this focus is a fixation, not mindfulness. In some ways it is an illness of the sense of self rather than a letting go of it.

Being mindful implies that we can react to what is really happening, rather than to what might be expected to be there. We don't travel on autopilot and that is why quite ordinary experiences, let alone intense ones, can take on a new freshness and intensity. Familiarity is a great duller of experience. Here is a story I heard so long ago I have forgotten where, but it makes the point well. It's a good story, anyway!

A boy was walking on the shore of a great sea when he saw someone in difficulties in the water. He plunged in without hesitation and rescued an old man. The boy dried the old man with his cloak, made a fire out of driftwood and gave him something to eat from his own meal. The old man was understandably impressed and grateful, and when he was sufficiently recovered he revealed, by way of thanks, a great secret that he had discovered through his researches, for it turned out he was an alchemist. There existed, he said, a stone which conferred eternal youth on anyone who possessed it. The old man had narrowed the search and discovered that this stone lay on that very beach, somewhere among all the other pebbles. That was why he had been there searching when he had been knocked over by a freak wave. You could identify this stone because it was hot to the touch. The boy was not much interested, because boys are not much interested in eternal youth. But many years later his life was touched by tragedy and he remembered the incident and resolved to find the stone. He went back to the beach and started to search. He would pick up a stone, feel it briefly to see if it was hot and then hurl it into the sea. He did this again and again, day after day, as his eagerness to find the stone grew. It became his life: weeks went by, seasons, years, then decades. And every day the now ageing man would walk the beach, picking up stone after stone, holding them for a second and then hurling them into the sea. The action became second nature, indeed became his nature, grooved in by years of repetition. Thus his life passed, until one day this old man picked up a certain stone and had time to register that it was hot, even though the day was cold. He held it for a second… and then hurled it into the sea.

Stillness, joy and compassion

Mindfulness has a few side effects, which are fortunately benign. Stillness is the first of these. For example, the "zone" entered by athletes at their best or the "groove" entered by musicians at theirs is probably a version of this stillness induced by concentration. The state of "no-mind" which is much prized in Japanese arts and has its origins in Zen is another example, as is "flow", which we have already mentioned. Stillness is a state in which the chattering of the mind diminishes or ceases but one remains fully awake and alert. It truly deserves the title of an altered state of consciousness, it is so different from our normal distracted state. It is the beginning of meditation proper, whether encountered in physical stillness or in activity, and it is reported to have many layers and degrees of refinement. It is a calm, restful and deeply refreshing state, which is where its immense value lies for anyone who wishes to cultivate happiness. Marcus Aurelius, Roman Emperor and Stoic philosopher, referred to a certain state of the inner life as like being able to take an inner holiday whenever you need one. It is tempting to think he meant exactly this ability to still the mind. It is easy to see how that might help one to be happy.

Stillness is again a question of degree. Between a mind tossing and whirling with thoughts and anxieties and a mind placid as a windless lake there are many intermediate stages. If you are lucky enough to approach the latter – and you will be if you persist in training yourself; it is a matter of practice not of talent – you will experience the sheer joy of absorption. This is what is properly called meditation, a word much misused to describe attempts to sit still. It can bring a joy so intense that many believe it to be a religious experience. Perhaps it is. It is produced, however, by your own effort. Something very similar seems to occur when the mind is concentrated in moments of great danger. The "noise" of the ordinarily chattering mind drops or fades away and one is left with a sense of total focus, "one-pointedness". The mind "settles", like muddy water clearing as the particles drop out of suspension, leaving clarity behind.

There is little point in trying to describe such a state, any more than there is a point in trying to describe the taste of chocolate. It has to be experienced to be fully understood, although many of us have at some time or another been so lost in an activity that no other thought intervenes, not even a sense of time passing. But here is a most important point: being able to reach this state from time to time is not the objective of developing mindfulness, at least not for us. Stillness is useful because it is in itself a state of great happiness, because it shows or reminds us what a peaceful mind is really like and because it may motivate us to keep practising. But it would be of little use, for example, to be able to achieve such stillness in a practice period only to become stressed, anxious or angry later in the day. That would be as if a person attended church or mosque or temple at every opportunity but lived a life of greed, hatred or cruelty the rest of the time – they would be missing the point completely. Our objective is to live happily in the whole of life by freeing ourselves from unhelpful habits of the inner life. Stillness is a moment of freedom from unhelpful habits, but unless we can remain there always we have not really freed ourselves.

Stillness develops or appears, gradually or suddenly, as you persist with practice. It will generally come through the practice of mindfulness anyway, but if you practised mindfulness solely to achieve it you might become discouraged and give up, thinking you were making no progress when stillness did not appear. It is therefore important to realise that, helpful though stillness is in being happy, it is not essential. If you regarded it as a mark of accomplishment or special spiritual progress, this would not be helpful at all. If you give stillness such a status you risk setting up some very unhelpful habits which will stand in your way: disappointment, disillusionment and self-disgust, for example, if you do not achieve it; pride and the desperate desire to hold on to it if you do. It is more helpful to practice mindfulness, in sitting and walking and in everyday life, and let it unfold for you whatever it unfolds.

Joy is another and closely related by-product of mindfulness. I use the word "happiness" to describe the state of inner peace in which it is possible to live our lives, but "joy" to describe a particularly intense feeling of well-being or euphoria which on occasion floods through body and mind. Joy occurs naturally in our lives, if we are fortunate, often after release from great strain or tension, as when danger passes or a difficult goal is achieved. But joy is also available in smaller doses – in hearing music, being awe-struck by something beautiful or realising that we are loved, for example. Joy in this sense is still a feeling, an emotion: it is not appropriate or possible in all circumstances and we may perhaps decide to leave it behind for the sake of a depth of inner peace. However, that is not an issue we face at this point!

Here we are concerned with joy as a by-product of the cultivation of mindfulness. It just happens: we practice mindfulness, we become calmer and stiller and we begin to feel joyful. It might happen early in the practice, in might take months, but it happens. At first it might just be flashes, like little stabs of pleasure. If we are patient it will grow and strengthen, we will feel it more often and for longer. It can indeed be a distraction, because we prefer to hold on to being joyful (indeed isn't that what we came for?) rather than going on with the practice of developing mindfulness. This would be a pity because in this case the joy is a product of the mindfulness and if we neglect the mindfulness we will lose the joy anyway. As with other feelings which arise, the best way is gently to detach ourselves from them, sufficiently at least to be able to watch them as they come and go, not to grab at them, not to regard their coming as an achievement or their going as a defeat. But as distractions go, joy is not a bad feeling to have to deal with and indeed it may strengthen our motivation to keep on with the practice.

The last side effect we will consider is compassion. This traditional, even archetypal, religious virtue forms a major part of the skill set of benevolence considered next, for compassion is a skill which can be cultivated in its own right and has a crucial role in weakening the most unhelpful emotional habits. But we are here concerned with compassion as a by-product of mindfulness. As we practice mindfulness we become more and more aware of our own inner life and how it works. We see how our habits cause this or that reaction in us, how we make ourselves unhappy by feeling this negative emotion towards one person or thinking that negative thought about another, seemingly without having made any conscious choice in the matter. We did not choose the reaction on this occasion and the reaction has made us unhappy, or less happy. It may begin to dawn on us that everyone has the same problem: everyone is in the grip of their habits just as we are and their inner lives are being buffeted by thoughts and feelings which diminish their happiness. There is no one who does not want to be happy, but there are plenty of people whose habits will not let them be happy. Or perhaps they are making conscious choices but are just mistaken in thinking that what they do (think, believe, desire, whatever) will help them to be happy. In either case they are speeding in the wrong direction, away from happiness when happiness is all they want, just like us.

This very thought process can be deliberately entertained to help us with our own issues, and in fact we will suggest doing just that. But it will also arise more or less spontaneously as a direct result of cultivating mindfulness. We become aware of our own inner obstacles and then it occurs to us that others have inner obstacles, just as we do. This is the beginning of compassion towards other people, our loved ones, our less loved ones and even people we do not know. The more we think like this, the more it becomes a habit. It is not a question of being nice because it is our duty or because we will be "better" people. It is just a by-product of practising mindfulness. But it is a great bonus because, as we shall see, this pattern of compassionate thought and feeling will help our own happiness immensely.

Gently does it

In applying mindfulness it is not helpful to judge or try to reject what is happening. We will often be tempted and will sometimes try these things, of course, but such attempts have nothing to do with the skill of mindfulness. In particular, we do not suppress particular contents of our inner lives just because we don't like the look of them – are ashamed or embarrassed or annoyed about them, for example. Most of the time we have no idea what energy or motive creates the contents of our consciousness, so to suppress such contents is unlikely to be successful anyway. It risks increasing their energy, or causing their re-emergence in an even more annoying form. Besides, by judging or reacting emotionally to inner life contents we are automatically strengthening habits of judgement and reaction which are probably unhelpful. If I get annoyed about distracting thoughts, for example, I am strengthening the habit of anger or being annoyed. This is clearly not a useful way to go.

This attitude of observing carefully and closely but letting things alone is itself very difficult, perhaps one of the most difficult things about developing the inner life. We are natural problem solvers, aren't we? If we see something not quite as we would like it or as we think it should be, our instinct is to correct it. But there are problems with this where the inner life is concerned. There is a danger that we jump to conclusions and replace one unhelpful habit with another. If we develop the skill of mindfulness and the other positive skills we discuss in later chapters, they will naturally tend to erode and displace unhelpful habits. As we have noted, many problem habits will erode just by being noticed, just by our becoming mindful of them. Attacking them, on the other hand, is a chancy business, not least because "our habits are us" so that in attacking our habits, even the unhelpful ones, we are attacking ourselves and we cannot be sure what damage we might do.

Thus we need patience in the process of change. It isn't that we do nothing, because we may need to work hard at developing positive habits or skills. We certainly need to continue observing with skill, attention and patience. But we cannot force the pace. Using our well-worn sporting analogy, concentrating on a technical difficulty in a sport by going over and over the problem might not always be the most helpful way forward and might even increase the difficulty. We need to be aware of the weakness, but then perhaps we need to practice in a different way to train up a new habit. Then we might hope that the new habit would displace the error and thus we might make progress without a direct attack on the problem.

So it is with our unhelpful inner habits. If you notice that whenever Joe or Agnes at work gives you the benefit of their views you begin to feel irritated, you might set yourself to observe how this comes about. Do you have a belief that they think themselves superior, do they remind you of someone who always irritated you in the past, do you find their delivery too slow, do you believe they have ulterior motives? Observe, find out what the mechanism is. Your first (and indeed your second) observation may be an excuse rather than an explanation, so look carefully. Perhaps you will see that you get irritated because of a particular unjustified thought or belief of your own, perhaps you need to find a way to develop patience and forbearance towards boring people, or perhaps the irritation subsides once you focus on it. There is no universal pattern. Mindfulness observes what is actually there.

First steps in mindfulness

To arrive at a useful skill of observing our own inner life, it makes sense at the outset, as with all learning, to simplify as much as possible. In this case, we need to practice in controlled conditions to strengthen concentration or steady observation, because our attention naturally flits about as thoughts and images crowd in on us. If we are to have any chance of steady observation, we need first to establish some measure of control, not over the contents of our minds but over the focus of our attention.

A powerful way forward is therefore to practice holding your attention on one thing. You just have to accept that your attention will stray and your thoughts will intervene and distract you. But when that inevitably happens, you bring your attention back to the object of concentration, not allowing the fact that you have been distracted to become the focus of your thoughts and thereby become a new distraction. If you berate yourself, get cross, decide that it is too hard or there must be a quicker way, or that you will go and get a cup of coffee, practice is effectively at an end. That's OK, of course, and as with most things it is a good idea to practice for only a short period to begin with – say 10 to 15 minutes. But if you want to get better at it, you have to put in the practice sometime. You would not stop practising controlling a football or hitting a tennis serve the first time you lost control of the ball or hit it into the net. We have to concentrate, even for a few seconds at a time, accept that our minds stray and try again when we catch ourselves, without fretting internally about the straying.

Your own mind may at first seem to conspire against you in this process. For instance, you may find yourself thinking, "Well, I'm getting good at this, I'm really concentrating, it's much better than yesterday..." – in which case you are not concentrating at all but rambling to yourself about your progress. The hardest thing at the start is to avoid getting discouraged by the sheer flightiness of the everyday, thinking mind. If you practice after watching TV or reading the newspaper, you will probably find that your mind is particularly jumpy, an indication of the rapid-fire habits of thought modern life cultivates unwittingly. No wonder we get tired!

What should you concentrate on for this purpose? Just because we are going to use the power of concentration to observe our own inner habits does not mean that we cannot start developing the skill of concentrated observation on an external object. But it is important that whatever you use as an object in the first instance should not be too interesting! If it is, it will spark off runs of thought in all directions and the chances of concentration will be even more remote. Thus an animal or another person might not be suitable, and even a devotional object (if you are devout) may be unsuitable at this stage, however much you would like to concentrate on it. On the other hand, an object like a stone may be too static to sustain your focus, and your mind will simply be dulled into sleep. One traditional method is to use a coloured disk – distinctive but not too interesting. Or you could simply focus on an internal count, counting down from 100, for example, and going back to the beginning when you find yourself distracted

Breathing

The concentration object "par excellence" is, however, your own breathing. It is something which can be used anywhere unobtrusively, is always available and is so ordinary as to be taken for granted much of the time; thus it is not too interesting and distracting in its own right. Yet it is always changing and its use as an object of concentration has a combination of advantages which almost nothing else possesses.

First, concentrating on the breath almost always has the effect, after even a short while, of calming, deepening and slowing the breath itself. This change is at worst harmless and more likely is beneficial to your health and sense of calm. You are, after all, doing this with the aim of increasing your happiness, so extra calm is a bonus. Concentrating on the breath is even recommended in some cases purely for its health benefits – for example, to help lower blood pressure or reduce stress.

Second, because the breath is always with us, it is easier to transfer the skill of watching it quietly to watching our inner life in other more difficult situations – in "real life". If we acquire any skill, particularly an internal one, it is important to be able to summon it when we need it and to do this it is useful to have an "anchor", to use a term from NLP, to call it up. An anchor in this sense is simply an external trigger which has been established by association to call up a certain state of mind or inner resource, a sort of conditioned reflex. The breath can itself be an anchor in this sense, but sometimes people use other anchors as well, like posture and gestures.

If we chose an external object as an anchor to evoke mindfulness, there might be an awkward gap between the initial practice and its application. If we were concentrating on a candle flame or a disc, for example, it would be more difficult to recall the same sense of mindfulness when, for example, we were shopping or driving or doing the laundry. Thus, if you start practising concentration with an external object, you will need at some stage to set up a more "portable" anchor. Breathing is something we can return to anywhere, at any time, and this gives it a practical advantage if we attach the habit of watchfulness to it. If you find yourself in turmoil for whatever reason, you can concentrate on your breathing for a few moments. Not only will this have a physically calming effect, but it will also remind you of the skill you have acquired during practice and give you the chance to bring that skill to bear on your present situation.

Third, the breath is fairly unique among physical functions in that we can assume conscious control of it if we wish, or we can concentrate on it without assuming control, or it continues anyway if we concentrate on something else. Thus we can develop concentration by watching the breath but then transfer that concentration seamlessly to aspects of the inner life. As thoughts and emotions arise, we can notice them and go back to the breath. If we are in danger of being swept away by emotion or feeling, we can go back to the breath to stabilise ourselves. If we realise we have been distracted by thought, we can go back to the breath to regain concentration. And if we need something to help us through pain or anxiety, the breath is always there.

Practising with the breath

There are hundreds of books of instruction which describe practice with the breath very well. The only difficulty is that many of the best of them tend to regard this as a religious exercise or the start of a religious practice of meditation. There is nothing wrong with that, but some people may be put off by the context of the instruction. Some very basic instructions are therefore repeated here.

In essence, you observe the in-breath, then you observe the out-breath. It's that simple. You might begin by taking a few deeper breaths to settle yourself, but after that do not try to force or change the breath in any way – if it is shallow and rapid, note that; if it is deep and slow, note that, too. If it changes while you are watching it, note that. Notice the gap between breaths, if there is one, or that there isn't. Notice whether the breath fills the chest first or whether it seems to fill the belly, or perhaps the back. Notice how the in-breath starts in the nostrils, where perhaps it feels cold, and how the exhaled air perhaps feels warmer. And so on. But just observe. Difficult as it is, try not to describe to yourself what you observe, as in a sports commentary. Just try to be as fully aware of what is happening as you can. Do not judge, do not decide what the ideal should be, do not try to change the breath or the breathing pattern, do not do breathing exercises. Just observe. Then you will realise that you have lost concentration and are thinking about something else and not observing! Try to go back without internal comment or recrimination to observing again.

If you have not tried this before, you may be surprised at how hard it is, given how easy it seems when described. The first few times it is an achievement to get through one whole cycle of breath – one in-breath and one out-breath – without losing it. It is good to practice for at least a few minutes at a time, losing concentration and going back to it, and remember that everyone gets better over time. Practice can last as long as you have time available, but more than half an hour without a break is probably counter-productive at first because the practice becomes futile as the mind starts to rebel and wander, or the practice develops into something else, or you fall asleep. It is more a question of patience than willpower. It is not really possible, certainly not helpful, to strain or force yourself into concentrating, although everyone tries that at some stage. The practice can be done any place where you will not be interrupted. Even a few minutes on the bus or the train are worth using, but obviously practice is easier in a quiet place with as few external distractions as possible, at least at the beginning. There will be enough internal distractions!

You can sit, stand or even walk while you watch the breath. After all, the inner habits you will come to observe can occur in any posture and at any time, so it does not do to be too picky about the style of your practice, except to make it easier to concentrate while your concentration is still fragile. If you walk, you can match the pace of the walk to the breath to help concentration. It doesn't have to be one step per breath, which is walking too slowly for most people; it can be three or four steps per breath, depending on how slowly you breathe. The rhythm of the walking helps to maintain concentration, but of course there are usually other distractions, such as bumping into things and people. So you need a quiet place to do this and one traditional way of doing it (but by no means the only way) is by pacing up and down a fixed path in an enclosed area so that you do not need to think about the route or about avoiding collisions

Lying down is another option, especially useful if you are ill or infirm. The problem is that the danger of falling asleep is high! Some people even use this kind of exercise to calm their thoughts and help them sleep, and it can be very effective. But there are very effective mindfulness techniques which can be learned in a prone position, such as the body-scan technique (similar to yoga nidra) taught by Dr. Jon Kabat-Zinn for the relief of stress.

If you sit to practice, the most important thing to get right is posture. This is not for any esoteric reason, but simply because you will quickly tire and will put strain on the back or neck if your posture needs to be constantly maintained in an unnatural position by your back or neck muscles. It is not necessary, for example, to sit in the lotus position or kneel on the floor astride a cushion, although these positions are very stable and very good if they come naturally to you or you can get used to them. Sitting cross-legged "nursery school style" without raising the buttocks on something or supporting the back is a poor position for posture and difficult to maintain. We are most used to sitting on chairs; sitting on a chair is just as good as sitting on the floor, although a low chair in which your hips are lower than your knees will not allow you to get a good posture. Orthopaedic stools or chairs which rock forward slightly are very good for helping keep the back relaxed and straight. In whatever case, the back must be straight, as if standing though without stiffness or undue tension. Slumped positions are not only bad for your back, they are more likely to send you to sleep. Tense positions will induce cramp or soreness within a few minutes. The mind needs to be relaxed but alert and the back should mirror this. Some people find it helpful to imagine that there is a cord drawing their spine upwards through the crown of the head, which is a good trick as long as you do not allow your cord to be too tight! The shoulders should be relaxed. As for the head, you should have the sense that it is perfectly balanced on the spine without any muscle effort needed to keep it there. Putting a gentle smile (but not a fixed grin!) on your face also helps. It relaxes the face muscles, may improve airflow in breathing and will also make you feel happier.

If you are calm and comfortable as you start to practice, you will probably find that the biggest internal problems are the thoughts that drift into consciousness and distract you from watching the breath. Sometimes when you start it seems that the thoughts appear even more profusely than they normally do, but this happens partly because you are more aware of them. So treat this as a good sign that you are already beginning to notice more of what goes on in your inner life. There are, however, two ways of dealing with these arising thoughts which, while perfectly natural, will slow your progress down. The first and most obvious is that you engage with them and are carried away by them: you start actively to "think" the thought, to follow the trail, as it were. For example, the memory suddenly pops into your head of a conversation you had yesterday and you start to rerun and rearrange it, saying the things you meant to say or now wish you had said. When you "come to" it can be surprising how far you have come from simply observing the breath, and how long you have been distracted. It doesn't help that our minds are used to "multi-tracking": we are quite capable of doing several things at once without paying full attention to any of them. But in this practice try just to observe that the thoughts are arising: try to detach yourself from the content of them and stay with or go back to the breath.

It is also quite natural to go to the other extreme and try to block out or push away the incoming thoughts. This can be especially relevant if the content of the thought is unwelcome or even shocking, which does sometimes happen. It is as if there were a part of the mind which actively wants to distract us and will try any trick in the book to do so. It shows how little control we have of this aspect of our own minds, which doesn't of course mean that anybody else controls them but that they are out of conscious control. But the issue here is that it doesn't work to try to block out arising thoughts, whatever their nature. "I mustn't think about elephants" is just as much a distracting thought (and incidentally a thought about elephants) as "Elephants", so trying to deal with arising thought by pushing it away actually strengthens its hold on our consciousness and certainly distracts you from watching the breath. The mind, especially whatever bit of the mind it is which throws things up into consciousness, apparently does not deal easily with negatives.

The only thing to do when distracting thoughts arise is to take the attention back to the breath. Do it again and again, as many times as it takes. Leave the arising thoughts alone, if you can. Just let them pop up and fade away again. Not that this is easy: it's a bit like not scratching an itch. Don't engage with the thought, don't follow the trail, but don't suppress it either. Just ignore it and it will (eventually) go away. Just concentrate on watching the breath, letting the thoughts flit in and out as they will. They are not your concern for the moment.

If it proves too difficult to leave your thoughts alone even for a few seconds, do not despair and above all do not decide either that you are useless or that the practice is a waste of time. Keep trying to observe the breath, if only for a few seconds at a time. If you were sitting, perhaps try another way, like walking. You are beginning to learn about how your mind works, how your inner life operates. Since that is your objective, to gain the ability to observe the inner life and the habits which lead you away from happiness, you are making progress; you are on the right path. You have already noticed that your mind is crowded with thoughts whether you want it to be or not and that this is a habit which is totally beyond your conscious control. Your first instinct may well be to stop it or control it, but that will not be possible. All you can do is to train yourself – and it is a long, patient process – to allow it to happen without getting caught up in it, neither to be carried away nor to suppress it.

There are, however, many other techniques which can be used to help keep your focus on the breath so that concentration is less broken by inner distractions. One is to use some simple phrase and recite it inwardly to coincide with the in-breath, reciting another to coincide with the out-breath. "I am breathing in, I am breathing out" will do, but any phrase will do as long as it does not distract attention away from the breath. Such phrases seem to give the "inner voice" something to do and thus occupy part of the mental space which might otherwise be filled with distractions. They also reinforce the attention by making it necessary to match the phrase with the breath: this helps concentration in the same way as a musician, say, has to concentrate when playing with others to match their timing. In the Vietnamese Zen tradition of Thich Nhat Hanh mentioned earlier, for example, "gathas" are used as a basic part of monastic training. These are simple phrases or verses used to maintain attention on what one is doing, in watching the breath but also in all other aspects of life. Watching the breath is not an end in itself but a practice which develops the skill needed to observe what is going on at all times in life, and the gatha system aims directly at increasing such awareness. Thich Nhat Hanh himself has provided in his writings many such gathas to help with mindfulness.

Other techniques involve examining different parts of the breath, focusing on the start of the in-breath, for example, or the gaps between in and out breaths, or the length of the breath, or the physical sensations of the body while breathing. Or one can count the breaths, counting up to ten cycles of in and out and then starting again. Most people lose the count and the idea is then just to start again with the count at "one". (Some claim that counting down is better than counting up.) Care needs to be taken with this technique not to put the count on "auto-pilot" and think about something else, congratulating oneself meanwhile that one has not lost the count. This is missing the point, which is not to get from one to ten repeatedly, but to stay focused on the exercise. Another method is to "send the breath" to different parts of the body, imagining breathing into each limb or organ in turn, or each chakra, if you wish. If the mind is just too active so that it seems the breath cannot compete for interest, try holding the breath out for a second or two, and you will find that your mind rapidly becomes much more interested in the next breath. You could imagine the breath as light or sound, if it helps to keep the attention steady. The practice does not have to be solemn: it might help at the beginning to treat it as a game which you play against your thoughts, in which you have to focus on your breath and they try to distract you. Another method is to watch the thoughts themselves, noticing how and when they appear and disappear relative to the breath, trying perhaps to watch the space around the thoughts rather than the content of them. And finally (but not exhaustively), a practice recommended by Jack Kornfield is to name the distractions – "thinking", "fantasising", "wishing", "wondering what time it is", "feeling uncomfortable", and so on – as a way of acknowledging them as distractions before returning to the breath without recriminations.

There are thus dozens of methods, each perhaps suitable for a different character and temperament. It is good to experiment with different methods for a little while and try new techniques from time to time. But we should not be distracted into thinking that we must find the method that is perfect for us before we can proceed. All such methods are just devices to help keep the concentration focused. If you persist, you will eventually be able to observe without strain, in a relaxed and easeful way which allows the inner distractions to come and go without breaking the focus. I do not think it ever gets trivially easy and there will be times when it seems very hard indeed, even when you have been practising for years. You have to motivate yourself sometimes by reminding yourself that this skill you are practising really is one of the keys to a happy life and that mindfulness therefore is one of the most worthwhile goals you can set or achieve. If you can make even a little progress towards this goal, perhaps just that you notice the loss of concentration a little sooner than you did, you will have taken a major step towards taking control of your inner life and shaping it in the direction of greater happiness.

Next steps or alternatives to breath-watching

As your concentration improves, or even as an exercise in concentration in itself, you can begin to observe your own inner life in everyday situations. You can observe what you do, how you think and feel when eating, working, playing, travelling. Mindfulness in eating is a good place to practice, and you may be surprised at how little attention you normally pay to eating your food even if you think you "enjoy" eating. Some people even find that paying close attention to the actual process of eating (slowing it down and taking more time, concentrating on flavours and textures and the look of the food, finishing each mouthful before even loading up the next) helps to prevent overeating and control weight, but this is a secondary benefit. As to mindfulness at work, even if you are very busy you might take two minutes in every hour to calm yourself, watch your breath and observe what your inner life is doing. You will find such an exercise helps you to work more efficiently, because your concentration is increased and your energy less dissipated in irritation or worry. (If you need to reassure yourself that you are not "wasting time", reflect that your overall efficiency has to increase only by about 3% to make up the "lost" minutes. If you really feel you are too busy to take two minutes every hour, you are probably so stressed that you need to take two minutes every half-hour!) Or just focus on your breath and ask yourself regularly, "What am I doing?" – meaning what is going on in your inner life. The habit or skill of mindfulness can be strengthened in such ways until it becomes the strongest of habits, capable of operating in any situation. It is a matter of progression.

In the end, of course, mindfulness is not just about observing the inner life. It is about being fully aware of what goes on around us as well as being aware of how we are responding inwardly – if indeed we are responding at all and not just dreaming. It is about being fully awake, taking full advantage of this wonderful capacity we have, this conscious life. The habits of the inner life can get in the way of being fully awake. We pick and choose, we judge, we jump to conclusions, we want this but not that, we get carried away by sadness or anger or whatever, we are reminded of something else, we worry about what may happen next, and so on. If we can develop the skill of mindfulness, perhaps first by something simple like watching the breath as we sit still or walk slowly, we can use it to notice the habits of our inner life and transform them. As we progress, we can observe the external world anew through our newly calm and mirror-like mind. Well, calmer and more mirror-like, at least. When we start there is always the desire to taste the fruits of the completed project immediately, so we sit for a bit then look out of the window to see if the world looks different. It is easy to kid yourself. Probably there are people who naturally find themselves with no or few unhelpful habits of the inner life, just as there are people with a natural aptitude for cooking or sports or mathematics. There is no point being envious or even competitive about it: remind yourself that happiness is not a competition anyway. The one certain thing is that you will get better, happier, more skilful with practice.

Mindfulness of the body

If you are suffering from great confusion of thought or feeling, or are particularly anxious or "wound up", mindfulness might be practised and focused on the body and the physical sensations from the body rather than on your disturbed thoughts and feelings. It might, for example, be better to attempt a physical activity like walking, jogging, or, if you like them, yoga or tai chi, where you can calm the mind by concentrating on the physical sensations of movement and posture. But whatever activity you choose needs to be done with concentration on the breath and the sensations of, say, walking, not just walking the body absently while the mind goes its own way. The point is to find an activity in the doing of which you can concentrate calmly on the physical sensations of the body, thus practising mindfulness of your body until the mind is calm enough to bear observation.

It would be wrong, though, to think of mindfulness of the body as a form of practice to be used only in cases of emotional turmoil. Mindfulness of the breath, after all, is no more than mindfulness of a certain aspect or activity of the body. Mindfulness of the body more generally can be used both as a way of developing attention and concentration and as an important source of information about the inner life and the habit basis. We have already seen that walking "meditation" is one of the traditional forms of practice, and we have seen that everyday activities like washing up can be the made the subject of mindfulness practice. The addition of alert, aware observation of what is going on can help to make chores interesting and less of a chore, while enjoyable experiences can be enhanced. All activities can be imbued with this quality of mindful intensity; it is a question of how and with what intention they are approached. Alertness, awareness, careful attention to the information from inner and outer senses, to arising thoughts and feelings and desires, but all without being swept along or taken up by the inner stream – this is mindfulness.

Visions and visitations

The deeper we get into the practice of mindfulness, the more likely it is that things will come into consciousness which seem out of the ordinary. Exactly why this happens is not clear but it is too commonly reported by those who practice and write about mindfulness practice to be ignored. It may be that if we achieve intense concentration it induces a kind of trance where we have access to parts of the brain which do not normally contribute to consciousness, rather like waking dreams. Or perhaps the quieting of mental activity which is usually in the foreground of the mental stage may allow things to come to attention which we usually do not notice or even work hard at not noticing. We may have suffered emotional damage in the past which we have "papered over" and which surfaces as we relax our minds. Whatever the mechanism, you may find thoughts, images and feelings coming into consciousness which are startling in their realism and intensity.

It is important to add that of course you may not have any such experience. If you do not, it does not mean that you have not progressed or that something is wrong with you or with the way you are practising. If we were undertaking a practice of meditation in order to experience "higher states of consciousness", we might be disappointed if nothing happened. But we are not: we are practising mindfulness in order to observe, slowly and patiently (which is the only way it can be done), the habits of our inner life and how they promote or inhibit our happiness. It is so important to keep this objective clear and it follows that any surprising "manifestations" in your consciousness may be potential distractions from what you are about. If you get too caught up in them, they will deflect you from your purpose. In that sense, if you have no surprises you are lucky.

These "by-product" experiences might be things of great beauty, states of peacefulness, visions of light, feelings of well-being and so on. Indeed, they may be highly enjoyable and fill you with happiness. If you have them, enjoy them; it may be very important and rewarding for you to realise that you are capable of this intensity of bliss. But when they are over it is vital to ask yourself two questions. First, am I able as a result of this experience to live my ordinary life with full peace of mind and happiness? Second, do I have any inner life habits remaining which in everyday circumstances, or even in times of stress, still inhibit my happiness? If the honest answer to the first question was "yes" and to the second "no", then you would indeed have achieved some sort of breakthrough. But the likelihood is, sadly, that while the pleasant experience is a precious and sustaining memory, everyday life still presents the same challenges and induces many of the same inner ups and downs as it always did. In that case, there is still work to be done.

Many people who have uplifting experiences, visions or feelings when they concentrate hard on their inner lives regard such experiences as definitive spiritual or supernatural insights. Perhaps they are right, although it is well to remember that such a conclusion is always an interpretation of experience and there may be other explanations. There are dangers, too, in such an interpretation. People may either believe they have reached the end of the road and have achieved all that practice can achieve or, more commonly, they reframe the purpose of practice to be the attainment or re-attainment of the experience they had. Very often then they suffer confusion and disappointment because they cannot repeat the experience. Now, this is not to say that there are not unusual states of consciousness which can be reached through the practice of meditation or deep concentration on the inner life. We simply come back to our focus on happiness and the habit basis of the inner life. Is it not a sufficiently ambitious objective to live in happiness and peace of mind no matter what the circumstances? Mindfulness is worth practising because it is a major part of what we need to do to reach this objective. If extraordinary experiences lead to happiness and the elimination of unhelpful habits they are useful, but if they lead to yearning for more such experiences, disappointment or even a rejection or tarnishing of everyday life, they are an obstacle. These experiences are features of your inner life, whatever other interpretation can be given them. Observe them, watch them arrive and depart, enjoy them and let them go.

Occasionally people are not so fortunate and experience disturbing or frightening visions or feelings. It is important in this case to keep hold of the fact that these are only objects of your inner life; they are quite definitely illusions, even if based on memories or past experiences. Their appearance may tell you something about yourself which you already know, or they may reveal a habit or tendency which was hidden from you. If you can, stay calm and observe them and they will eventually fade. They are visitors to your inner life and although what they have to tell you may be important, it may not be clear what the real message is. Whatever it is, it is never the whole story. You are more than this, you are not identical with this. But their persistence may outlast your patience or fortitude. Do not criticise yourself if this happens. Do not hesitate to seek help from someone else with experience, a health professional if need be. There is no need to be heroic about facing such difficulties which may be unique and frightening to you but which others may have encountered before. If you are disturbed, stop the practice and work on something else or, better, seek help until the experience is clear to you and you can face it.

Chapter 9:
Benevolence skills

Benevolence

Under the umbrella of benevolence I include some of the most useful, most widely acknowledged and yet in some ways controversial inner life skills, including compassion, kindness, love, forbearance, generosity, friendliness and others. These skills have a vital practical importance even if we do not consider any moral, religious or supernatural justification for practising them. Yes, you've guessed, they help to make us happy!

These skills weaken some of the most difficult and damaging habits of the inner life, namely the negative emotional habits which stand in the way of our happiness more than anything else. For example, it is virtually impossible to be gripped by anger or hatred or any of several other negative emotional responses and be happy and peaceful at the same time. The benevolence skills help us to address this problem.

Try this exercise if you are not convinced that happiness and anger are incompatible – it's not pleasant, but it makes the point. Think of an occasion on which you got really angry about something. It doesn't have to be something grand or important which caused your anger; it might be something quite trivial which just proved to be the last straw on that particular occasion. Stop for a moment and try to recall that anger as fully as possible. Picture the scene in your mind as vividly as you can: the colours and sounds, the other people, what was said and done. Move inside: exactly how did you feel and what did you think? Perhaps your thoughts were full of the harm done and maybe you cast around about how to do something about it, put it right or get even. Of course you probably had a few "if only's" – if only you had seen it coming, if only they had thought before speaking or doing what they did, if only you could defy them somehow, if only you could think of the right words, if only you had the power to change things, and so on. Then there are the feelings, that churning in the guts, the adrenaline rush that made you feel slightly out of control, maybe flushing or a lump in the chest or throat, tears of rage perhaps, tensions in the body, maybe even trembling. Try to recall. I know it's not pleasant, but try to feel it and remember it. What did you do, what did you feel, what did you say or want to say? Did you become violent? Did you have even the shade of a violent fantasy, perhaps? What did you want to do?

Enough. I am sorry but I wanted to make the point as vividly as possible. It doesn't feel good, does it? (Stuck with it? Take deep breaths, walk about a bit and imagine with equal detail an occasion on which you felt really calm and happy. Take your time and let the anger subside, and remember this was only a kind of fantasy, something you deliberately recalled on request.) Even if your anger was entirely justified on the occasion you recalled, in the sense that someone behaved outrageously or unacceptably, it doesn't feel good to be in that state. Actually, it sometimes feels worse the more your anger is justified, because the anger is stronger and, on top of everything else, you feel a sense of grievance that someone is putting you through this. You have no inner peace in that state. This doesn't mean that you should suppress your anger, it doesn't mean that you "should" anything. It just demonstrates that anger and inner peace don't go together, which means it's very hard to be angry and happy at the same time.

The benevolence skills are usually thought of as virtues, perhaps more than the other skills, which is a pity because thinking of them as virtues tends to give us mistaken ideas about them. We might think that they are innate qualities which we either possess or do not, depending on whether we are "good" people or not. Or perhaps we think that we "ought" to have them and it is a moral failure rather than a lack of skill if we don't. In the guise of virtues, benevolence skills are certainly acknowledged and prized by every ethical tradition. There is scarcely a religious tradition in the world which does not include some of these skills in their ethical recommendations, usually right at the heart of what it is to practice that faith. Whether called love, compassion, loving-kindness, understanding, kindness to strangers, generosity, charity or even just respect for one's neighbour or for fellow human beings, these skills are vital to most religious messages. The corrosive effects of anger and hatred are also strongly emphasised in the teachings of great religious figures of all traditions. But whether or not you believe qualities of benevolence have a supernatural significance beyond their incredible practical use, we will here simply treat them as skills which we can practice and indeed have to practice if we want to become happy. It is important that they can be built up by practice, rather than being innate, earned or supernaturally instilled.

If benevolence skills are at all controversial it is because they sometimes seem at odds with cherished modern maxims of self-assertiveness and self-expression. They may even seem like invitations to others to be aggressive, or as an acceptance of victim status, being a doormat. Although many traditions recognise the value of not meeting aggression with aggression (as, for example, in "turning the other cheek"), it is widely held today that verbal or physical expressions of righteous anger are not only good for us (getting things "off your chest") but may even be natural and inevitable. Psychological opinion has, it is true, turned against what psychologist Martin Seligman aptly calls the "hydraulic" theory, the idea that emotions must be let out somehow or pressure will build and they will explode in more harmful ways. But the idea still lingers in everyday belief. It is a staple of (admittedly often badly made) fiction that we should resist or avenge wrongs done against us or others, and to fight back against evildoers is widely regarded as a sign of maturity and strength. Benevolence in all its forms is seen by contrast as rather limp and wishy-washy. There are some important confusions in these views which need to be understood in order to avoid damaging consequences for the inner life. They stem mainly from the usual confusion between inner life and external action, as we shall see.

Anger, hatred and related beasts

The skills of benevolence, I have claimed, are worth pursuing because they weaken the negative habits of anger and hatred. They are also effective against related habits like envy, jealousy, suspiciousness, impatience, prejudice and many more. But anger and hatred would be enough; if we could sufficiently weaken these habits, we would make ourselves so much happier. There is plenty of evidence from physiological studies that people who are less prone to anger and hatred are, as might indeed be expected, less stressed and less likely to suffer from stress-related problems like high blood pressure and cardiovascular diseases. But from our perspective of focusing on the inner life as the key determinant of happiness it is enough to note that anger and hatred preclude happiness. You cannot be full of anger and at the same time be serene and peaceful. You cannot be experiencing the thoughts and emotions of hatred and at the same time be experiencing inner peace.

It is certainly possible to feel states of excitement, even exaltation, induced by anger or hatred – as in the adrenaline "high" people sometimes feel in confrontations. Although you might not be happy precisely while you are angry, perhaps your anger spurs you to seek redress for whatever made you angry and your happiness is thereby restored. Or again, you might rejoice at your enemies' defeat or discomfort, for example, which seems like an example of happiness and hatred combined. Or perhaps you are so fired with "righteous" anger or hatred of someone or something you feel is evil that you rejoice in your violent intentions or actions against them. So it may be that in some cases it is correct to say that an angry or hate-filled person finds pleasure in their emotion – perhaps they could even be said to be happy in some sense. But an angry person (to take anger as the example) is certainly not at peace. We say they "burn" with anger, their inner life is troubled and turbulent. There is an unsatisfied need or desire in them – for redress or revenge or justice. They may be distracted from other things; they certainly cannot rest in the moment, enjoying what comes. Can you burn with anger and fully enjoy a good meal or a beautiful sunset? Probably not. As you may have seen for yourself just a moment ago, thoughts are troubled and fixated on the grievance, beliefs are apt to run away along the lines of suspicion, the whole world view is coloured by the emotion of the moment. All this is without considering what actions might result from the anger and what consequences may ensue. In trying to slake our anger we may provoke another wrong, making us more angry and requiring an escalation of action, and so on. Anger is poison to the inner life. Strong anger tears the inner life apart and any consequent action is more a reaction to suffering than a free choice. People can readily accept that anger is unhelpful in the case of murderous rage or, say, uncontrolled temper towards family members, but all anger has the same quality and tends in the same direction. Anger is anger.

It doesn't matter anyway if you can think of an exotic example in which an angry or hate-filled person could be said to be happy. It is enough that it is rare to find anger and inner peace together. Hence anger and hatred and their cousins among the negative emotions are simply unhelpful if you accept the view that a peaceful inner life is the best way to live happily. If you can lessen the habits of anger and hatred, you will be happier – end of story. Anger is sometimes a natural reaction, sometimes a habit that has taken us over, but whether it is natural or acquired it is generally unhelpful if you want to be happy. Therefore it makes sense to weaken the habit or instinct as much as you can, and that is why the benevolence skills are worth cultivating.

It is very important that these remarks about anger and hatred are not in themselves moral judgements. I am not arguing that it is wrong or bad to be angry, although in many systems of ethics it is. But I am not trying to outline a system of ethics, just a framework of training the inner life so that we can live happily. Terrible things happen in the world and sometimes to you or me directly. Sometimes anger is the natural reaction. The point is that anger does not serve us if we have decided to live as happily as we can. The less anger we have, the more peaceful and therefore the happier we will be.

Compassion

I will concentrate first on compassion to illustrate the value of the benevolence skills. Compassion is a quality on which whole religions have rightly been founded, but it need not be complicated. We can understand it as the skill of putting ourselves in the place of another person so that we can see the world, if only fleetingly, from their point of view. If we can bring off this change of perspective, we will change the way we think about that person, change what we believe about them, change how we feel about them or their actions and change our will or desire in respect of them. We will treat them inwardly with the same indulgence with which we treat ourselves and our own actions. This might in fact be one interpretation of the famous but difficult injunction to "love your neighbour as yourself".

The important point here is that each of us generally treats "me" as a special case when we assess actions and behaviour. This may be because we have more information about ourselves (the data of our inner life, for example) or just because we are biased: generally, the special treatment we give ourselves is favourable! There are exceptions, of course, but on the whole we tend to feel that we ourselves act and think from wholesome or understandable motives in pursuit of legitimate needs and interests. We feel that we understand our own actions, even when they turn out to be mistaken or misguided, and to a large extent this is because we feel we understand our own inner lives. We are at least partially aware of our own motives and drives and we have access to the reasons and beliefs behind what we do, whereas we have to infer those of others. This sense that we understand may of course be an illusion and often is demonstrably so. But however unreasonable or objectionable our habitual behaviour may be, we have more sympathy with ourselves and our actions than we would have with the actions of others.

Notice that this may be true even of some people who would generally be regarded as downright evil. They do not start out to do whatever it is *because* it is evil or unreasonable. They generally have some justification for it in their own minds, a belief or a feeling which makes what they do seem acceptable or even necessary to them. To take a worst case, for example, those who have ordered or taken part in genocide through the centuries have often convinced themselves that it is their victims who are evil, guilty, dangerous or even subhuman. Or they have acted out of fear of the victims or of someone else. This does nothing to make such actions acceptable or tolerable, of course, but at least we can concede that there might be some basis for them, however twisted or crazed, in the minds of the perpetrators. We will undoubtedly want to rebut that basis with all possible strength, but it makes the actions approachable as human actions so that we do not fall into the same trap as the perpetrators and regard them in their turn as inhuman. Evil for evil's sake is perhaps quite rare and often ascribable to disease when it does occur. If this is too much for you to accept of real life evil, think of fictional villains. In fiction nothing is less convincing than a villain whose evil plan is motivated solely by wanting to be bad. Wanting power, wealth or revenge, yes, but not just wanting to be bad.

But to return to our own case, by whatever tests the world judges our actions, and regardless of whether its judgement is fair or well founded, our inner court admits different evidence and always hears mitigating pleas. We judge ourselves differently. Thus it is no trivial thing to imagine ourselves in the position of another person. To do so is not to condone their action or even fully to understand it, but it is to judge it differently, with the indulgence we would grant ourselves. It is not even necessary for this purpose that our imagining be accurate. If you try, for example, to think of some historical figure and try to put yourself in their shoes and understand their actions, you will almost certainly be wrong because you cannot have all the facts. But that is not the point. This is not history but an attempt to give someone else the benefit of the doubt we would like to claim for ourselves.

If we allow special pleading for ourselves, we also allow it to a more limited extent for our loved ones and friends. That indeed is one of the marks of whether someone is your friend, whether you will defend them against gossip, for example, or stand by them when they are accused of behaviour you feel is out of character. We feel we understand our friends and loved ones better than we understand mere acquaintances or strangers. Hence we could liken compassion, putting ourselves in another's position, to friendliness. If loving or understanding our neighbours as ourselves is too hard to start with, we could try understanding them as if they were friends.

Compassion defuses anger and hatred, and that is its great value. If I can view another with compassion, it is difficult to hate them and it is difficult to remain angry with them. I can see their harmful action as the result of ignorance or mistake or a misdirected attempt to be happy. They are like me with the same underlying motivation, wanting to be happy. Maybe I feel they should know better and frankly maybe they should. But the fact is they don't. What I choose to do about it is up to me and it certainly does not follow that I must stand by and smile indulgently. But if I choose to act, I can act without rancour in this frame of mind. My own inner life does not have to deal with anger and I can remain at peace while I deal externally with the situation – or decide not to.

Kindness

If "compassion" sounds like too big a word, how about "kindness"? The two are very close cousins. The change is useful, however, because kindness carries a different set of resonances for most of us. Kindness is an everyday and perfectly familiar thing, whereas "compassion" sounds perhaps a bit solemn and pious. One way of interpreting kindness is this: to be kind to someone is simply to promote their happiness and well-being, however casually or intermittently.

We are all kind some of the time. We all fail to be kind some of the time and sometimes we even notice what we have done and regret it. Kindness need not be a matter of action or speech; we can just think kindly or unkindly about someone – often we have to choose because, for example, we feel we have to decide how to interpret something they did or said. In such a case, our decision is often a matter of pre-judgement (prejudice by another name) because we ascribe positive motives and intentions to someone we like or feel good about at that moment and negative ones to someone we dislike or are suspicious about. The practice of kindness here might be to find the positive interpretation if the facts at all permit it.

But perhaps there is no possible positive interpretation. Imagine, if it's not too lurid, that I am being robbed in the street at knife point. This may be an unrealistic example because in the fear and confusion of the moment only a very seasoned practitioner would have the habit of kindness so deeply ingrained that they would think and feel kindly. But the example can still show us how kindness works. Now, it makes no sense even to try to think that this robber has a benign motivation, it's obvious he means me nothing but harm. But why, for what cause? If from an "evil nature", how did he get like that? If from chronic poverty, what was the cause of that and why is he different from law-abiding poor people? If from the need to feed a drug habit, what then? This vicious act has not appeared from nowhere, it has roots and causes, it is part of some process affecting a human being and twisting their inner life away from happiness. We come back to a basic stance of compassion or kindness: whatever this robber is doing, he acts because in his mistaken and possibly damaged mind he thinks it will make him happier. He has the same ultimate motivation as I have.

This attitude of compassion or kindness does not by itself dictate my action. I may decide to hand over my valuables or I may decide to fight back if I think I have a chance (there was a knife, remember!). But anger or hatred, for example, will only make an upsetting event even worse and prolong its effects on my happiness. It will not even help me to think clearly, to act successfully or to recover after the event. A habit of kindness will help me to keep my own mind more composed.

In this admittedly extreme example, fear would be a natural reaction. But fear also does nothing to help, which shows us two things. First, there are perfectly natural instinctive reactions (habits built in by nature, we might call them) which may not always be useful to us – in fact, if we could weaken them by training we might benefit in certain circumstances. Much military training, for example, is aimed at raising the threshold at which fear is experienced or increasing the capacity to operate successfully when experiencing fear. Most of us have fearful responses in more ordinary situations, from fear of insects to stage fright to exam nerves, and it may help to understand that these are habits which could be weakened by the right training techniques, if we can find and practise them.

Second, an unhelpful response is just that – unhelpful. This applies across the whole spectrum of happiness training. An unhelpful response is not something unnatural – what could be more natural than fear when attacked by a robber? It is not something to be ashamed of, it is not a sign of moral turpitude, it is not something for which to despise yourself. Do not say: "I felt fear, so I am a coward." It is simply where you are now, it is one of your responses. If it doesn't work for you, work on it. Or, if the situation in which it arises can be avoided, leave it alone. But do not set up freedom from fear, or freedom from unhelpful responses generally, as an ideal you have to live up to, because that is a sure way to allow your happiness to be compromised. Freedom of the inner life – freedom from unhelpful responses – is a direction to travel, not an ideal you have to match.

Kindness, compassion and indulgence

If compassion amounts to treating and regarding others as we treat and regard ourselves, it would still not imply that we treat them kindly unless we are kind to ourselves. Thus being kind to ourselves is an important step on the path to overcoming anger and the other negative emotions.

What could be meant by kindness to myself? It is certainly not the same thing as self-indulgence. We have suggested that kindness in general can be interpreted as seeking to promote the best interests and happiness of someone, so in this case it involves promoting my own happiness. Since we know happiness is a function of the inner life, kindness to myself becomes a question of promoting my happiness by developing my inner life and habit basis. So far as external circumstances are concerned, kindness to myself might include arranging them if possible to promote this aim of inner life development and to avoid overwhelming inner challenges.

It is useful to remember this distinction between kindness and indulgence, for it might influence not only our attitude to ourselves but our attitude to others. It is the grain of truth in the often-quoted tag about being cruel to be kind. Being cruel is never being kind, but refusing to indulge desires is often kind, either because we know they are harmful or because the habits thus formed will not be helpful. All parents have experienced this. The kindest thing we can do for ourselves is to promote our own happiness through developing our habit basis in the right direction and the kindest thing we can do for others is to help them develop theirs. But since we cannot do the work for others, the best we can usually do is to make their external conditions as conducive as possible to this end.

Being loved

Many people believe that what will make them happy is to be loved. The psychology of receiving love is very complicated and accounts for a good proportion of fictional literature, never mind psychological writing. Wanting to be loved is by no means an affliction of the weak. Even very successful people, such as for example politicians and film stars, are sometimes still driven by the longing to be loved. And this drive is often why people adopt a religion, because it is certainly comforting to believe that there is a Being who loves everyone, and therefore loves me even if no one else seems to.

But here is a harsh truth: it is a mistake to think that being loved can ever be the basis of inner peace, and therefore it is simply not the root of happiness. Being loved is a wonderful thing, make no mistake. Like good health, wealth or success it is one of the great gifts which life can bestow, and on the whole it is bestowed more liberally than any of the others. But it is neither a necessary nor a sufficient condition for happiness. Although it is offered in many quarters as an ideal around which we could organise our lives, being loved is not the way to ensure happiness. Romantic fiction is just that, fiction. Being loved is not a benevolence skill – in fact, it is not a skill of the inner life at all. Appreciating love given to us is another matter; it is part of the skill of gratitude, one of the enjoyment skills.

To seek to be loved is in fact a strategy for happiness based on external circumstances, which are fickle and changing. We look outside ourselves for somebody – another person, a supernatural being, even a pet – to love us. We want them to behave, in other words, in such a way as to produce in us the feeling or the belief that we are loved. Once this need or desire has hold of us, our happiness depends on the other's behaving as required, because only that will give us the feeling we need. If the other does not oblige, we are in trouble. Sadly, someone may even love us but their expression of that love does not fit the pattern we have settled on, or their love just doesn't count for us. Parental love often falls into this crevasse, but then parental love may often feel conditional to the recipient even when it isn't.

Believing that we are loved by inscrutable supernatural beings is exempt from this requirement that the other behave in certain ways, of course, which is another reason why such belief, if you have it, is very useful. But if you do not believe on other grounds, it would not be rational or sensible to believe just *because* belief fulfills this need, any more than it would be sensible for me to believe that I am loved by an invisible giant rabbit. Belief must have some other grounds or it is clearly a delusion. We will see in a later chapter that the skills of letting go can be helpful against overwhelming needs, as the desire to be loved can become. For now, we can perhaps see that we could regard the desire to be loved as the desire for someone else to give us what we want, for someone else to "make us happy". But we know, don't we, that nobody can make us happy, because happiness depends on our own inner life. If we could let go of the desire that someone else give us what we want, we might find that we are happier.

You might, as an alternative, reflect that if you love yourself you will indeed be loved. If that feels like cheating, or just not what you meant by being loved, it is worth asking why. Do you not love yourself? If not, why not, and why do you expect someone else to do what you refuse to do? A lack of self-love is a serious matter and it will certainly stand in the way of your happiness. It is important to examine its roots, with or without professional help. Perhaps you need to forgive yourself for something, which may require that you work first on the skill of forgiveness, which we discuss in a later chapter. Perhaps you have a particular sense or idea of what a person needs to be like in order for you to love them, in which case perhaps you could agree to show yourself kindness and compassion instead. Perhaps you have become trapped in some story about yourself, that you "must" (who says?) live up to some ideal you cannot reach. Or perhaps you have accepted a story from someone else about your own worth and that story needs examination. The point here is that this lack of self-love is a damaging habit. If you can change it, you will be happier, but you need first to accept that you have this habit and look at it fearlessly.

If you do love yourself, meaning that although you know you have faults you are on the whole comfortable with yourself, what does that feel like? The feeling must include both the feeling of loving and the feeling of being loved. Perhaps you can learn to distinguish them. Another exercise would be to imagine what it would be like to be loved as you wish. What do you imagine it would be like, and why do you crave it? What difference would it make to your inner life? What would you do differently if it were true? Can't you do that anyway? Why not behave as you imagine a person would behave if they were loved or felt loved and see where that takes you?

Partnership

Even if seeking love is not a viable basis for happiness, love between partners is important in most lives and I don't want to ignore it. It tends to be downplayed by many religious traditions because it can distract us from "duty" and perhaps lead us to value physical pleasures more than some traditions think is good for us. It is not without danger even in our terms because it can involve staking our happiness on something external, namely the beloved. As such it can notoriously disturb our inner peace and happiness. Our love may be unrequited, or the beloved may find someone or something else they prefer, or eventually they may die. On the other hand, as external circumstances go, a close relationship can obviously be deeply rewarding, a rich source of pleasure and learning. Sure, there is a risk that in the excitement or indeed the routine of a relationship we forget to take care of our inner lives. But if we avoid this pitfall and do not abandon our inner lives, we can use our relationship to foster and develop our inner skills and then we are lucky indeed.

Where better to learn kindness than in the minor frictions of a relationship? Where better to learn what it feels like to love than in loving someone? Where better to practice mindfulness than in taking care of the well-being of someone we love and observing the ebbs and flows of our inner life while we do it? Relationship may, it is true, magnify the weaknesses of our inner life. If we are even a little jealous or unkind by nature, then we may be jealous or unkind in our relationship, but it is hardly fair to blame the relationship. Far better, surely, to seek to change our habits and be grateful that the relationship has brought them into focus. Romantic love clearly involves much more than just the benevolence skills – for example, admiration, sexual attraction and the willingness to give the other a major part in our life story. But the proportions are not fixed and we can learn and grow more skilful by observing how they shift and change.

Love is all you need?

Many people hold out love for others as an ideal, perhaps the ideal to which we should aspire. We should love our neighbours, we should even love our enemies and thus we will be good people. I think this is a wonderful ideal, but seldom is it explained how we are to go about it.

It helps if we interpret love as compassion or kindness or even friendliness. Then loving others becomes a matter of taking *their* inner lives seriously, by putting ourselves in their shoes or putting them in the privileged position we ourselves occupy in our own judgements. We can generally only come to this position gradually, thinking and feeling our way in, applying over and over the key question: "What must go on in their inner life for them to do that?" From this practice grows habit, from habit grows instinctive understanding. We do not have to condone or like their actions, but we can understand the actors as being like us. They may be ignorant, muddled, or mired in unhelpful habits but at bottom they are just trying to be happy.

Is this too remote an understanding of love? What becomes of the warm feeling? But you cannot create the feeling directly. You can create the inner habits of responding with kindness, friendliness or compassion. You can practice them in your daily life, in your work, your relationships and your family, until if you persist they become second nature to you. Then the feeling will happen, the feeling of being kind and compassionate, the feeling of loving other people without wanting anything in return. You will get glimpses of it along the way. Everyone does, even if only a few get to the point where, we can only suppose, they feel it nearly all the time. But it doesn't matter if you don't perfect the skill: a bit is better than none and the joy of it is enough to confirm that you are on the right path. This is not religion, remember; you are engaged in arranging your own inner life to make you happier. And as with happiness itself, it might be helpful to think of love as a direction rather than a destination.

Kindness and compassion and the need to cultivate them are also an answer to a particular danger of focusing on the inner life, which is that we can become self-obsessed, even a little solipsistic. It is possible to focus so intently on rearranging the habits of my inner life that I actually have no time for the difficulties of others. I might even regard anyone else's difficulties as solely their own concern. Changing their habit basis may be something for which only they can take ultimate responsibility, but this attitude takes the idea that we are each responsible for developing our own inner life too far. Kindness and compassion require sympathy and engagement with others and a realisation that they are struggling with difficulties similar to my own. I want to be happy, they want to be happy and we are both making lots of mistakes along the way. To help them is quite literally to help myself because of the effect on my habit basis. What about refusing to help, what does that do to my habit basis? To refuse help out of meanness, or hatred, or indifference, or even because of a judgement that they do not deserve it, will do nothing to promote my own inner peace – in fact, it will tend strongly in the opposite direction. Shutting out others cultivates unhelpful habits. Helping others, or at least being kind and understanding about their difficulties, cultivates an attitude in me which helps me as well. In this way a sense of community with others becomes an important pillar of my inner life. Actually, when we are struggling with our own unhelpful habits it can be very helpful to remember that there are lots of other people engaged in similar struggles. None of us is uniquely awful! Vital as it is to be clear about our own needs and take responsibility for our own development, if we ignore or condemn the needs or faults of other people we can defeat our own progress.

Is love all we need, in the end? Are the benevolence skills enough to bring us complete happiness, or as much of it as we can manage? Since these skills are antidotes to some of the most disruptive forces which stop us from being happy, namely the negative emotions of anger and hatred and their cousins, benevolence can take us a long way. Perhaps if we perfected these skills as some of the greatest spiritual figures have done, we would need nothing else. But we do not start from perfection. Sublime compassion, like sublime mindfulness, may encompass all the skills and all the virtues and bring complete happiness. It does not follow that the practice of only one skill set will be a good strategy. If you were practising tennis, you would not confine yourself to practising only your serve, notwithstanding the knowledge that a brilliant serve would win you many games. Living happily is likely to be more complex than tennis and, besides, your life game may be lacking in more than one stroke! It would be a missed opportunity, therefore, to concentrate on developing the benevolence skills without the other skills, important though benevolence skills are. Love may be all you need, but the practice of love is probably not all the practice you need.

Chapter 10:
Benevolence practice

Cultivating compassion and kindness

All too often we hear news of an atrocity of some kind. We switch on the television or open a newspaper and learn about multiple murders, crimes against children, war crimes, massacres of innocents, indiscriminate bombing, terrible things happening daily. Occasionally the media will set about a "background story", trying to understand why someone might do such a thing, to trace the process by which a once-innocent child becomes the sort of person who can undertake such horror. Such pieces are not intended to excuse or justify the action. They are ways of helping people to grasp some understanding of an action which seems inhuman and incomprehensible.

There is a lesson here about how we might practice the skill of compassion, even in the more usual, everyday instances in which people offend us. The way to practice is through the imagination. A useful key, as we have seen, is the question: "What must that person's inner life be like for them to do or say that?" From such a viewpoint we can imagine what thoughts, beliefs, emotions and desires might support such behaviour. So the cruel or thoughtless action or the harsh word becomes something we can just about imagine having done or said ourselves. We might have justified it to ourselves by the circumstances as they appeared from that particular point of view. Nothing in this process implies that the person was "right" to do or say what they did or said. The action might be horrible or the words unequivocally damaging and cruel. We are not attempting to excuse or exonerate, just to imagine how it is possible that one person might want to do this to another. We do not even need to arrive at the correct understanding, the exact, forensically-correct sequence of causes, and in any case this will usually be impossible for us to reach. If you think that there are some actions which do not deserve such attempts at compassion, you do not have to be a Christian to remember the words of the dying Christ about his torturers: "Forgive them, for they know not what they do."

Very often it will happen that we can ascribe the harmful actions of another to a mistaken belief. The most generic such belief is that the action will contribute in some way to their own happiness, which we can readily sympathise with in principle even if we can see it is a mistake. For example, if I believe absolutely that I will be happier the more money I possess, then stealing from you or cheating you out of your money may seem like a good idea. This is a sadly common belief! In this particular case, you would probably still find it difficult to generate compassion for me as you fend me off, even if you broadly understand that I act out of mistaken belief. But the basic idea is sound.

It is in fact a central tenet of many religions that ignorance – meaning in particular the mistaken belief that certain actions are in one's own deepest interest when in fact they are not – is the wellspring of many unhelpful or evil actions. Of course, to recognise this ignorance in others does not justify feeling smug or superior that one is free from error oneself. Nor does recognising ignorance imply that we have to leave the erroneous belief unchallenged, still less the injurious action. The importance of recognising that a harmful action usually comes from mistaken belief lies in the fact that it helps us to imagine how the action might have come about, putting ourselves in the other's shoes or seeing the event from their point of view, and thus to react to the action without hatred or anger.

I do not mean to suggest that every wrongdoer has a conscious belief that this action on this occasion will make them happy. The action is of course likely to be part of a pattern, tied in with a pattern of beliefs and desires and feelings. We are dealing, in fact, with the habit basis of the wrongdoer, which in the worst cases may be pathologically damaged. But there are causes which have shaped that habit basis, either things done to the person or mistaken choices they have made themselves: fiery emotions, mistaken beliefs and desires all have roots and causes. We can always find a point from which the action can be understood in terms of an imagined inner life of the perpetrator. Ignorance or confusion of some sort will always play a major part, as it does in our own lapses. It is sometimes enough simply to know that there is always such a point. However much we despise what has been done, however strenuously we might support the prevention of such activity in the future, we can know that people might do this, under certain inner and external conditions. Whether we are considering an atrocity or a petty annoyance, it is a human action, driven by the same striving to live happily which drives us, but operating under mistake, ignorance, delusion, misperception or some other habit of the inner life which dominates that person.

Thus we try to replace the anger and hatred we might feel – if not with understanding, at least with the belief that this unpleasant action or harsh remark can be understood. Of course there might be malice in it, but malice is not the end of the story, ignorance and delusion are. This attempt to understand is perhaps like some methods of acting, where the actor seeks to give a convincing performance by trying to understand and generate in himself or herself the thoughts and emotions of his/her character which lie behind the outward action. The simulated action is thus driven by a simulated inner life and this, the actor hopes, will make it appear more authentic and believable to the audience. The actor's standard question to the director is said to be, "What's my character's motivation?" – not so different from asking, "What's my character's inner life doing?" Or in our context, "What's my neighbour's inner life doing?"

Notice that although cultivating compassion involves imagining the inner life of the person at whom you are in danger of directing your anger or hatred, the exercise does not confine itself to inner or psychological factors. It may make sense to start with questions about the inner life of the other person but there are also external circumstances to consider. The attempt to cultivate compassion might consider any or all circumstances, inner and external, frankly real or imaginary. The point is the effect on you, not the factual accuracy or the provability of the analysis of the other person. If you intend to reform the other person, the case is different, of course. In that case your analysis had better be accurate or your efforts are likely to be useless or even harmful. Compassion is moreover not incompatible with prevention or even punishment. It does not entail a "soft" attitude to prevention, deterrence and the protection of others. But these become practical matters, questions essentially about what will work.

Our own beliefs, whatever they may be, can be helpful in generating or reinforcing the habit of compassion. For example, those who believe that a spark of the divine is to be found in every human being may practice compassion for others out of reverence for that spark. It is helpful for Buddhists who believe in repeated reincarnations over millions of years to consider that over the generations every living thing has at some point been your kind parent and is thus deserving of your thanks and care. Or we might see everyone as a child of God. Those without a belief in the supernatural may find it easier to use psychological models to help the process. Thus a Freudian might understand malicious behaviour in terms of repressed sexuality or trauma, a behaviourist might see learned patterns of stimulus and response. Methods based on belief will necessarily vary widely according to the beliefs in question. It is not even essential that one fully subscribe to the belief: one of the uses of story and myth can be to arouse the relevant attitude and sympathy in us, even when we perfectly well understand that the myth is not literally true.

Faking it

But is this skill of weakening our anger or hatred towards others really compassion? Is it really the same thing as the virtue which is advocated by so many religions and creeds throughout time and throughout the world (and sometimes even practised!)? Surely this is just a mind game, whereas true compassion should "well up" from the soul or the heart? The answer is that we have to create a habit of response and we can only do that by directing the inner life along the path we want to follow. We have to fake it until we can make it. Spontaneity will come later, as we practice.

Frankly, it may be difficult to know when working (or playing) with the practice of compassion leaves off and genuine, spontaneous compassion takes over. But we can nevertheless see that there can be a sense of progression here. A person might start by using a compassion practice to deal with anger. Take road rage as an example – the low level, everyday kind, not the murderous madness we occasionally read about. Maybe we go from something like "That b*****d cut in front of me, why doesn't he learn to **** drive?!!" to something more like "That person doesn't understand the rules of the road" or "He must be having a bad day to drive like that" or even "He's young, I hope he learns before he kills himself". In so doing we reduce our own anger, reduce the effect the provocation has on us, avoid ten spoilt minutes of fuming and fretting. And if we do this regularly we will find it becomes less and less necessary to reframe the situation. The provocation itself loses its power over us, loses its power to disturb our equanimity. We do not need to deal with the anger because it does not arise, or at least not so strongly. We find the habit of getting angry in this type of situation begins to dissolve, maybe slowly, but it does lessen its grip. Maybe we also start to realise that other drivers are in the grip of the same tendency to anger which once ruined our drive through the rush hour. What is the harm in waving them through now and again instead of battling for the last metre of space on the road? At negligible cost we can avoid stirring up anxiety in ourselves and make someone else's journey marginally more tolerable. Or we may reason that the fewer angry or fraught drivers there are on the road, the safer the road will be for ourselves and everyone. So we start to drive more considerately ourselves and after a while this may itself become a habit. And so on.

It may be a long way from better driving to universal love, but the practice and the progression is the same. A practice which starts out as a way of dealing with, say, an irritating work colleague can in the course of its success lead to habits which take us onward and result in changes of attitude (habit) of which we were not even aware at the outset. The beneficial habits we develop to solve one problem may suddenly illuminate a different area which is holding us back, perhaps without our realising. More importantly, the deliberate practice of thought, feeling and action "as if" we were compassionate leads to the genuine habits of compassionate thought, feeling and action – in other words, to being compassionate. If it helps, you could think of the initial rather deliberate practice of compassionate thought as the practice of "pre-compassion". The names do not matter, the practice does.

Speaking kindly

The practice of kindness of speech or word obviously takes us into the realm of the external where our thoughts and feelings directly impact the lives of others. But our own words also affect our own inner lives. If we want to cultivate a kind and quiet mind, then harsh words spoken are no more consistent or helpful than harsh words entertained silently. We cannot, for example, encourage the inner habits which will weaken anger and hatred in our own inner lives if we retain the external habit of angry or hateful words. It just won't happen. What you say and what you think interact in complex ways, for your habits of speech affect – indeed become –your habits of mind. Thus kindness in our words is an essential part of kindness in our minds.

Thinking kindly requires vigilance and effort because the habits of judgement we have learned from experience are deeply set. We are not trying to see everyone else as "good", because many people manifestly are not. We are trying to see other people's faults as having causes which at some level are beyond their control if only because certain responses have become habitual. Their faults are often the product of a lack of knowledge, experience, judgement or wisdom, just like our faults. These people may not be good but they are usually not evil, only ignorant, even if sometimes profoundly so. And even those for whom evil is the only correct description were once innocent, until their habit bases became corrupted by their mistaken choices, their physiology or their experiences.

A good start is to practice being careful with criticism or harsh words, quick to praise and encourage. The practical benefits are great. There are few people who do not react better to praise than to blame and many successful management techniques are based on this idea. But praise must be sincere and believable. I have a close friend who has a habit of praising something in the appearance of nearly every woman she meets. This is something which requires great skill, although most of us could do it more than we do. (Women, in my experience, do it much better than men.) My friend carries it off because it is done sincerely and she has an eye for detail. What she praises is only what she finds praiseworthy; she does not dissemble but always finds something worth a compliment. The effect is wonderful to watch: people light up, their spirits visibly lift. And as a by-product, they are always glad to see my friend.

It is so easy to hurt with words, even accidentally, for we do not always appreciate the effect our words have, particularly the resonance they have in other people's inner lives. A word of anger, for example, can be for us just a release of our feelings and then forgotten, but it can sometimes be devastating far beyond our intentions for our target. If everyone had achieved perfect equanimity it might not matter what we said because their inner lives would be sufficiently robust, but since we know that most people have not achieved equanimity, even a casual remark can be vicious in its effects. So the practice of kindness dictates that we be very careful in what we say and how we say it, that we exercise restraint, think before we speak. Similarly, since we cannot be sure how and in what context things might be repeated or used, kindness suggests that we should be careful what we say about others even when they are not present.

Kind action

Kindness in our actions, like kindness of speech, models and shapes our attitudes to other people and therefore has a direct effect on the habits of our inner lives even though the action itself is something external. So from the point of view of training the inner life, kind actions are helpful to us because of the attitudes and feelings and thoughts which go with the actions. To act insincerely – giving with the expectation of reward, for example, or helping reluctantly or disdainfully – is of no use for this purpose at all, even though the recipient of our kindness might not notice the difference.

The most obvious form of kindness in action is **generosity**, a powerful practice and a virtue recognised in every system of ethics.

What we give may be something material, or it may be our time, our effort, our expertise or just our willingness to listen. The important thing is that we help someone with their need. We may not necessarily put their needs ahead of ours: we might on occasion, but to do it always is simply not possible given the vast needs of the world. The attitude we might seek to cultivate is that we put others on a par with ourselves in however small a respect. By being generous we try to treat others as we treat ourselves. Even this is hard enough. Many skills come together here. We can simultaneously practice the skill of letting go or non-attachment, helping us not to stake our happiness on acquisition or possession, about which more later. We also practice gratitude, one of the key skills under the headline of enjoyment, which helps us to acknowledge our own good fortune.

Of course kindness is not just a matter of giving. Kindness can be practised in how you treat other people, in your demeanour and your willingness to take their concerns seriously. It is never a matter of what they might think of you, or what a third party might think, or even whether anyone might notice what you do. Helping someone else always helps you because it strengthens your habit basis in skilful reactions of thought, feeling and desire which block negative habits.

Kindness includes *forbearance* with others, for example when they are slow or repetitive or just dull. You can be rude, you can fume inwardly and fix a smile, or you can cultivate for a few moments the kindness of giving your attention. Why should you do this? First, you are not wasting your time, you are practising a skill of the inner life which will make you happier – not only because you will be better able to cope with such circumstances in the future, but also because by the practice you have helped your own habits in the direction of kindness and compassion. Second, you are finding a way to enjoy this moment of your life despite the unpromising circumstances, and the more you enjoy each moment the more you will have a happy life. Third, you give something to the other person which makes their external circumstances a tiny bit more pleasant. You cannot tell what all the consequences will be, but as well as the positive effect on your habits you have the immediate satisfaction of having helped another person when you could have hurt them.

When we looked at practising mindfulness of breathing, we noted that thoughts and feelings can arise which engage our attention and distract us from the practice. Sometimes it helps to compare external irritations with this internal distraction. If people around you are irritating or difficult to bear, is that any different from the distractions and irritations your own mind throws up when you try to be still and mindful? Both offer potential obstacles to your purpose of practising the skills of happiness. If your own mind can distract you so easily, why expect more of the external world and other people? In neither case will it help to get angry or try to suppress the distraction. If you bear with it, it will change anyway. Thus the practices of mindfulness and forbearance can inform and illuminate each other.

Loving yourself and loving others

Mahayana Buddhism is one of many traditions which have great wisdom on the subject of kindness and compassion. It contains a valuable practice called "metta meditation", which can be borrowed entire to help with the skills of kindness and compassion in our secular context. It goes like this.

First, still yourself as much as possible, as we discussed in the mindfulness chapters. Then reflect on the idea of kindness and try to generate a feeling of goodwill and the desire to promote the well-being of someone. It is important that the person at whom you direct these feelings and this desire in the first instance is yourself. This both strengthens the desire and the will to keep developing your habit basis and gets you more used to the idea that kindness to yourself is the foundation of some essential skills. Only when this practice has become established does the practice move on to direct the attention to others. Usually, in order, kindness and goodwill are directed at yourself, people you love and like, people whom you dislike or think of as your enemies and finally people to whom you are indifferent or whom you do not know. It is possible to attempt all four in a single sitting, but you may find it better to concentrate on one "target" per session and perhaps even stay with that target or class of targets for several weeks. It depends on how deep you wish to take the practice.

This may sound artificial but it is in fact a very powerful and valuable long-term practice. It is very important, however, that the first stage (yourself) should not be skimped in your natural desire to become a "better" person. Loving your neighbour as yourself, to change the tradition but not the message, is, as we have seen, of little help unless you love and are kind to yourself.

Chapter 11:
Story skills

Stories and language

Let's suppose we are making a film, let's say a nature documentary about elephants. We want it to be truthful and coherent, we want it to capture and hold viewers' interest but also to inform them, show them something about the world they did not know but which we feel is perhaps important for them to know. Do we just set up the camera pointing at where we hope the elephants will appear? Do we just follow the elephants around, filming them at whatever they do? We might do these things, of course, but what we would get is not a documentary; it would be at most part of the raw material for a documentary. We must shape the film to tell the story we want to tell, highlight some aspects of what the creatures do and ignore others, focus the viewers' attention visually and probably with a commentary, edit out repetitions, and much else besides. Our aim is to communicate something to the viewer and that involves selecting some bits of nature and missing out, well, most of it. And even when we have left only the bits we want, we have to go further and focus attention by words or pictures on just those aspects that are relevant to our purpose.

It would be the same if the film were a drama. We don't just film the actors acting and hope the viewers get the idea. We have to select some bits and not others, focus attention on the actions which carry the story forward, visually emphasise the clues, say, or perhaps temporarily mislead viewers in order to heighten the drama.

In each case we are telling a story, though stories of very different kinds. Every story is shaped, selected; some things are emphasised and much is left out. But story does not just happen in dramas and documentaries, in books or films or soap operas. It is the essence of language itself. We can do many different things with language, such as giving commands, expressing emotions and desires, asking questions. But what we do with it more than anything else is to describe, to ourselves and to others, just about anything and everything. This process of description is no more than the telling of stories – some meant to be true, some not – about ourselves, other people and worlds real and imaginary. All beliefs are stories in this sense, all the propositions of science, mathematics, religion, history, all the descriptive thoughts you could possibly think. And thus our inner lives depend to a massive extent on stories of one kind and another. Because of the importance of language we could say that stories dominate the inner life, so it is not surprising that some of them cause problems for the peace of the inner life and that we need skills to deal with such issues.

Stories are so ubiquitous, so much a part of the fabric of who we are, what the world is like and how our inner lives work, that it is often very hard even to notice them and how they operate. It would be very hard indeed to get away from them altogether even if we wanted to: the only way would be to stop thinking. But this is not a solution compatible with doing anything at all, because the thinking and the stories must begin again as soon as activity starts. A better way of living in the world and avoiding problems caused by stories is to learn to recognise how deep and complex the reach of story is and to develop skills to avoid getting caught out by or stuck in stories. As usual with our essential skills, to do this at an expert level is difficult. But we can all get better with practice.

The story skills are thus about learning to run the story rather than letting it run you. The skills involve the development of a great deal of flexibility of thought and belief, the ability to change perspective and understand other points of view. They involve a certain amount of good-humoured scepticism about your own ability to be right, and learning how to live with that uncertainty. They involve the recognition that all truth is only a part of the story and thus different points of view may give access to different aspects of the truth, as well as possibly their share of error. This does not mean abandoning the idea of truth so that anything goes. On the contrary, it involves being very particular about the truth, being as clear as we can about what we can establish and what we have to assume.

In this chapter we look at some of the aspects and consequences of story as the medium of our thoughts and a dominant influence on our inner lives. Simply to recognise this influence is already to take a different perspective and to have learned an important story skill. It is a massive subject and we can do little more than scratch the surface, but it is still important to get as far as we can. In the next chapter we will look at some simple techniques for shifting from one story to another, or to change perspective, often the only way to escape the unhelpful effects of a story on our inner lives. And in the chapter after that we will look at a pair of very powerful stories as illustrations of both the problems and the opportunities which stories offer the inner life.

Stories and the world

Our public and private worlds are entirely made of stories. I don't mean that there is nothing out there (or in here) to describe, nothing underlying the stories, but rather that we cannot think about or discuss anything without going through stories. The simplest description ("the cat sat on the mat") is already a story and as such it selects something about reality which we want to describe and misses out the vast bulk we are not interested in at the moment. We tell stories, even to ourselves, every time we articulate an experience. And thus, for us, the world as we experience it owes as much to our stories as to what actually exists.

As an example, suppose that you became interested in a new hobby, perhaps collecting something, fishing or growing vegetables. You would undoubtedly seek out information about your new interest from other enthusiasts, or from books or the internet. You would probably pick up some new terminology, learn what to look for – how to tell a valuable item from a fake, how to know where and when best to fish, how to tell a healthy plant from a diseased one, and so on. As a result your appreciation of your subject would change, you would actually notice different things, look with different eyes, come to different decisions. The "real world", the world of carpets or fish, antiques or vegetables, would not have changed in the slightest, but because of your new knowledge and skill it would seem utterly different to you. You would be telling and be able to tell different stories about it, because you would have more language tools at your disposal and you would focus your attention on different aspects of the world. Thus your experience of the world would have changed. And although you would of course realise that the change was in you, it would be just as if the real world had changed. Stories create the world, or at least our experience of the world, which for us is effectively the same thing.

These stories we tell are often externalised and shared with others, but they dominate our inner lives to an extent we hardly appreciate. If all our beliefs are stories, so too are all our thoughts and imaginings. Any desire or emotion we recognise or articulate becomes the subject of a story (or sometimes many stories). Calling something a story tells you nothing about whether the story is true or false. It's not that your deeply-held beliefs are somehow real and the flaky ones are "just stories": every belief you have and everything you could possibly believe is a story. Some are true, some are not.

A story need not have words; pictures or images will do just as well – think of a silent movie or even a still picture. There are languages of symbol and image which can be read by those who understand what each image signifies – think of the symbolism used in different eras of painting, for example, or the many theories about how to interpret the images and stories of dreams. The drawings of M.C. Escher play tricks with perspective so that, for example, your eye follows a flight of stairs down until you realise that you have reached the top again. (You have to see them!) They are a good example of how we construct visual stories without noticing, until in this case we are made to notice because the story is deliberately subverted. In the inner life pictures are of great importance because, for most of us, vision is of great importance and usually the dominant sense. But pictures carry resonances and stir emotions just as words do so the stories we frame in pictures, whether externally or inwardly, can have great power over our inner lives.

Models can be stories: a famous example is the chemical structure of the genetic material DNA, the double helix, for which the building of a model not only told the story better than words could have done but provided the confirmation of how the various pieces of the puzzle fitted together. Ceremonies and rituals can be stories. They are often explicitly arranged as such with some element of drama, but even less formal ceremonies are stories. They carry symbolism and meaning, they can help to release emotions or make their expression acceptable, and most importantly they mark or create change. Hence the importance of rituals in all societies and also for individuals. Ceremony and ritual have effects on the inner life particularly through the change they create in emotion and belief. Hence it is useful to remember that ceremony can be a powerful technique for creating or facilitating change in the inner life. Of course public ceremony can become debased and meaningless, but it is not always so. And private rituals can be just as powerful and helpful if they have resonance for the change we need.

The big story onion

There are layers of story in our inner lives, like the layers of an onion. On the outside of this story onion are the very explicit and external uses of story. Some of these we know are false or, rather, their truth is not the point, such as in novels and films and also in the stories we might tell to our friends socially. These might be explicit fictions, like jokes, or they might be stories whose truth is not established, like gossip, or they might be partially true but embellished, like anecdotes of our own exploits. But in these outer layers we also have stories which everyone takes to be true, or which are meant to be true even if they are not, like the stories we deal in at work or in business, in public life such as in law, politics or finance. Most of what we learn in schools and colleges is story at this level; it might be science or history or mathematics, it might be established fact or unproven theory. But it can deeply affect the way we experience the world, and therefore it can deeply affect our inner lives.

Going a little deeper but still in the outer, external layers we have the stories we present daily about ourselves, our public personalities or masks, who we are or want people to think we are, what roles we play. It is not that these roles are necessarily false or insincere – they may or may not be – but that they are edited, they are at most a slice of who we are. One person might be a thrusting, ruthless executive at work but a caring mother at home, another might be a housekeeper and also a talented and productive artist, another might be a struggling salesman but a pillar of local community work. Most of us present different stories about ourselves in different contexts, and each story is clearly only a part of the truth.

Somewhere around this level, too, are the beliefs and attitudes we have towards other people, the stories we tell or accept about friends, people we meet, other groups, other countries and religions. Our prejudices are here, our instinctive responses and our store of stereotypes, for good or ill. We can hold some of these beliefs quite strongly, but often on very untested or flimsy evidence – for example, just hearsay or half-digested news reports. These stories are often rather general. We may or may not be prepared to countenance exceptions but we start off from the position that if someone is a Moslem or a Christian, say, or English or Spanish, they will have certain attitudes and behaviours. Our attitude to them is already partly formed by this story attached to a word or a label.

Deeper still we have the stories we usually tell only ourselves, the stories which make up our self image – for example, about what we are good at and what our limitations are. We can, of course, articulate and share these thoughts but often we hardly even articulate them fully to ourselves. One of the interesting things about this layer is that the stories are often made true by us, they are self-fulfilling. We fix on a story that we are not good at something, let's say singing, and so we never or hardly ever try it. Perhaps we try it occasionally but of course our lack of practice and our nervousness about it mean that we don't do very well, which of course supports exactly what we have always suspected, that we are no good at it. Parents and teachers often unwittingly load us up with these kinds of stories, which go in deep while we are young and impressionable and are hard to shake.

There are stories at or about this level concerning our place in the world, what kind of person we are, what tribes and groups we belong to. Our "fundamental beliefs" about the world might be stories at this level, too – our religious beliefs and deeply held convictions, for example – although often such beliefs are as much part of our public image as our self image. We can have a story we adopt about what our life is about, what we want to achieve, what is most important to us, and we can direct our lives to living out this script. Stories at this level can be very powerful indeed and if we come to adopt a new story at this level it can seem like a life-changing and deep experience – this is (part of) what happens in religious conversion or political awakening, for example. Conversely, if we are forced unwillingly to accept that a story we have cherished at this deep level is false, it can be shattering.

Deeper still into the onion we have stories of which we are not usually aware. How can this be? Well, there are for example personal stories we cannot easily recall but which still have an influence on us. These might be early traumas in some psychoanalytic sense or they might be experiences from any time of life too painful for us to think about. They might be the roots of mental disturbance or simply the causes of strong likes and dislikes we otherwise struggle to explain – a fear of spiders, for example. There might be strong emotions, anger or shame for example, which accompany these thoughts and memories and so we protect ourselves from them.

Some of the habits and patterns which make up the habit basis and drive the inner live may also be examples of unconscious stories. You see a stranger in the street and immediately you find yourself reacting to his appearance and the way he carries himself. Without your even trying to create one, a whole story fills your mind: he is dangerous or innocuous or attractive, you feel apprehension, interest, admiration – and yet you have only a glance to go on. It is as if the story was already there and you have slotted this stranger into it, you have fitted him into a pattern. In fact, many concepts are like this; we decide that a certain label applies in a particular case and a whole host of associations, patterns and consequences that already exist for us become attached along with the label. This brings us to the difficult and important topic of the stories which are embedded in language itself.

We easily forget that language is a toolset, with lots of tools we use for specific purposes. In order for it to work, we have to have certain implicit but shared conventions, and these conventions make or rest on assumptions about the world. It is often very hard to tell what is convention and what is an assumption or agreement about the world, so language itself already incorporates certain stories. For example, people used words for colours long before anyone understood anything about light of different wavelengths, how the eye sees colour or what creates the effects of one colour rather than another. Grasses and leaves are both green, sufficiently alike to be described by the same word even though they may be very different shades which in other contexts like printing or interior decorating we might be careful to distinguish. So what exactly is green, what exactly is it that light green grass and dark green leaves (say) share?

Don't you feel that language is already gently pushing us here to say that there is some attribute, "green-ness" perhaps, which both possess? Because attributes are what adjectives like "green" describe or ascribe, are they not? And if we don't think about it much (and why should we?) we might accept that something like this is so. Then we might get drawn further in and ask what such an attribute is and we might even decide that there is some universal standard green to which both grass and leaves can be compared or which both somehow emulate to different degrees. But in fact what we are talking about is just how a word is used. When a child learns the word she is told that this grass is called green and that leaf is also called green, that this splash of paint is green but that one is not, and even that we can argue in the case of certain shades as to whether they are in fact green or blue. She will somehow piece together how to use the word and after a bit of trial and error use it like everyone else. But in the course of so doing she may make or accept all kinds of assumptions, hardly noticed even by herself, which make sense of the rather haphazard process on which such usage rests. It may never matter, but in learning language several thousand such words and patterns of use will be learned. For each of them, what happens is that a habit or a group of habits has been acquired and some of these habits may have consequences for the peace of the inner life. This is unlikely to be true of "green", of course, but in other cases the way we use language can affect what we believe, what we think and even what we see. Think about all the different cultural, social and personal beliefs, viewpoints and prejudices which over many centuries and even today might surround the word "black".

Sometimes we have to investigate the assumptions and habits behind the way we look at the world, even those inherent in the way we use language, in order to perceive what is disturbing us, confusing us or making us unhappy. This is the basis of some psychotherapies and philosophical methods but it is something of significance in all our lives and most of us do not develop the skill. It is sometimes as if telling the story clearly can release us from its power, but sometimes it's just that once we articulate the story we can see clearly that it must be false.

We will see this process in action a little later. Let us now suppose that with the peeling away of the unconscious layers of the story onion and even the layers on which language rests, we reach its centre. What do we find? The reality behind all the stories, perhaps? Or perhaps nothing at all, the layers being all there are? However it is described, it must be right that we cannot talk about it or tell a story about it, because if there were another story to be told we would not yet have arrived at the centre of the onion. When all the stories by which we know and create the world are exhausted, we are left with silence or, as some people describe it, emptiness. Sometimes this can seem like a worrying idea, but all it means is that when all the stories are taken away there is no story left to be told. If the words emptiness and silence bother you or sound sinister, peace is just as accurate. (And inaccurate!)

Problems with story, or, the diseases of the onion

We have seen that story pervades our inner lives at every level, even the unconscious levels which drive the inner life. This is not in itself a problem or a difficulty, it is just the way our inner lives, and in particular the vast part of them which is tied up with using language and therefore story, work. But unfortunately, problems can arise with story at any layer of the "story onion" and they can have serious effects on the peace of the inner life. With the outer layers we are more familiar and practised at spotting problems – mistakes, falsehoods, gaps and vagueness, for example – but even in such cases we can very easily get it wrong, or get muddled. The further in we get the more difficult it can be to realise what the problem is.

Evidence and support

There are always questions of truth, evidence and support with stories. Most of the beliefs we have at any given time rest on flimsy, insufficient evidence. They have to, because we have thousands of beliefs and we can't go round checking every tiny detail of every one of them, especially since vast numbers of them are trivial or irrelevant to us anyway. As I walk down the street I see a hairy quadruped in the distance – a dog, of course, and I think no more of it, but it could have been another animal, or a robot dog, a hologram or a mirage, or maybe I was hallucinating. It isn't worth the effort to check because the dog explanation was by far the most probable and anyway this belief has no consequences for me. (Until of course the day when the world is taken over by dog-like aliens from another galaxy whose advance scouts have been here for some time....) We all form hundreds of beliefs (stories) every hour about other people, events, ourselves, our environment, and so on. These beliefs sometimes have major consequences for our inner and our external lives and it isn't always obvious which ones matter and which don't. But they are very often guesses, at best. Sometimes we could check them better than we do, but often we simply do not have the ability or the time or the resources to check. The point is not that we should become compulsive checkers of our beliefs, nor that we should devote our time to a Cartesian search for irrefutable truth, but that we might be wise to recognise that most beliefs are rather provisional things, working hypotheses at best.

Our beliefs are generally "invisible" to us. We don't notice that we are believing things. There are only a few areas, like politics and religion, where we say, "This is what I believe". Most of the time believing something means taking it for a fact, and having taken it we don't even think to question it unless something untoward makes us think again. We seldom have enough data but we have to get on with things. It is thus a good practice to remember that whatever we take for granted has been adopted as a story which may be quite wrong.

Vagueness and misunderstanding

A second area of difficulty concerns vagueness or lack of specificity in stories. With shared stories, misunderstandings often arise because important details are left out or left to be assumed by the listener: "Oh, I thought you meant something else!" we say when the mistake comes to light. We can also do this to ourselves, we can internalise a misunderstanding or misunderstand our own internal stories and lead ourselves into tangles of confusion or unhappiness.

One of the reasons this happens is that nothing defines exactly how a word should be used for every circumstance in which it might come to be used. Meanings are not created or defined by dictionaries, they are created of course by usage which the dictionaries then summarise. "Concepts", or the meanings of words, are consequently not fixed or determined in every circumstance. Often this incompleteness of concepts does not matter, but we can get into real tangles when we come across an area where a concept is not complete and we try to use it as if it applied clearly. This happens a lot in those areas where we try to push concepts to their limits and tease out all their implications, as sometimes happens in mathematics or physics or, more relevantly for our lives, in ethical conundrums. For example: suppose your brain was transplanted (never mind how!) into my body. Would the resultant individual be you, or me, or a new person? It feels like there should be an answer, indeed with some such questions it might even feel as if finding the answer were very important. But there isn't an answer, because the question has never arisen in earnest and so the concept of personal identity has never been stretched to give an answer. If it became relevant, we might just fall into a convenient usage, or we might have a great national debate about it because it was felt to be an important moral, legal, political or even religious issue. The story would have to be decided upon. But imagine the potential for confusion until a decision was accepted.

Consequences and other dimensions

A third area of difficulty is that stories have consequences, both in terms of other stories and in terms of other dimensions of the inner life, like our emotions and desires. Our beliefs do not exist in some rarefied, separate realm of rationality. They are mixed up in our inner lives with all the other dimensions and habits, they cause and are caused by our thoughts, they trigger and are influenced by emotions and desires, they notoriously determine our attitudes and our external behaviour. Even within the dimension of belief there are complications. We can believe things with certainty or with reservations, we may even decide that we do not believe something but still it influences us – for example, when we fear or worry that it might be true after all. We have beliefs that we protect and will not allow to be questioned, as happens often with religious beliefs and also with many beliefs about ourselves and our loved ones. These are much more like strong habits or addictions than rational decisions about propositions. And of course we all know that at any given time many of our beliefs are false; we just don't know which ones! But a false belief will affect our inner lives as if true because we will think and feel as if it were true. And the truth of a belief may matter less to the inner life than the likelihood of its being proved wrong. If I believed I could walk through walls and tried it regularly (or at all) the world would offer me painful evidence against my belief. If I believed I could walk through walls but that it was wrong or unwise of me to use this power, the belief might persist indefinitely.

The whole truth?

The last area of difficulty we will consider is that every story, every belief, however solid and convincing, is at most only an aspect or a part of the truth. The language we have at our disposal focuses our attention on the world and goes a long way towards determining which bits of it we notice. We saw this with the example of the new hobby. We are capable of noticing things we do not have words for, of course, but we are much more likely to notice something once it is drawn to our attention by language, by learning a concept and how to apply it. Language edits the world for us, like the editor of a newspaper or TV news programme who can shape how we perceive our world by showing us some bits but not others. But in the case of language the editing happens at such a deep level that the line between shaping our perceptions and actually shaping our world is sometimes difficult to draw.

Because of the necessary editing carried out by language, it is almost impossible to arrive at anything we might call the complete truth about anything. This is easy to accept in complex external situations like, say, reports about a war. Details get missed out, everyone takes a side so objectivity is impossible, things happen fast and evidence we might normally use to check things gets destroyed. In simpler situations, however, we can often get all that we are interested in and usually we call that the complete truth. You find that your coffee pot is broken, you ask how it happened, you are told a story and you accept that you have found out how the coffee pot came to be broken. The story may be true or false but it is told in a narrow context in which much is assumed and much else is considered fixed or irrelevant and the story does not seek to disturb this infrastructure.

Such stories are complete within a certain narrow context, but that is all. It is our interest or attention which has selected the context here;

there is nothing about the situation itself which makes the story complete. We could, for example, trace every atom of the coffee pot back through its complicated history right back to the beginning of the Universe. We could do the same for the protagonists involved in its manufacture, sale, use and breakage, adding layers of environmental, psychological and biological explanation about them and their role. We could speculatively project the consequences of the break forward in time. It would be pointless in this particular case, sure, but it could all be true and part of the extended story of the breaking of the coffee pot. The limits of the story are arbitrary. The tale need in principle have no beginning and no end.

The complete truth is thus impossible, even though enough truth is often readily available. We are always selective when we describe and talk about the world. We only notice and take into account the bits we deem relevant for our purposes, like documentary makers. This is not a defect of language, it is one of the reasons why language works as well as it does. If it were not so, we would be overwhelmed with detail and unable to get anywhere with our thoughts and beliefs. But it surely means that we miss, in our chosen stories, far more than we capture of the potential richness available. Our world is created, as far as our inner lives are concerned, by the stories we accept about it, which means also by the language and the concepts we use, and it is also limited by those stories and those concepts.

Language and our existing beliefs also interact to determine our point of view or perspective, the "place" from which we view the world. To continue the visual metaphor, where you stand will determine to a great extent what you see, and how you interpret it. The boss may regard a frequently late employee as unreliable by nature; the woman herself, on the other hand, struggles to do justice to both work and a sickly child. In this example, it may be relatively easy to share information and modify points of view. But in extreme cases, often tragic, we find that people with different backgrounds and experience look at the same situations and come to such different conclusions that they simply cannot understand each other. Each may think the other is guilty of bad faith in what they say and do – notoriously, one man's struggle for freedom is another man's insurrection, one man's attempt to maintain order is another man's state aggression.

Changing perspective or point of view changes what you see, in language and thought just as much as when we are spectators at some event. This means that a change of perspective can lead us to see that our original perspective gave rise to wrong or at least partial or oversimplified beliefs, because now we can see that important things were missed out. It can also mean that two radically different versions can both be true at the same time because the perspectives are so different, like the everyday view of a table and the scientific view that tells us the seemingly solid table is made up of particles rapidly moving in space.

It is always possible in theory to appreciate things or events from a different point of view, but we ourselves may find it hard to achieve such a shift at the time. It is always possible to tell a different story, but we get locked into patterns of interpretation so that we jump quickly to conclusions. These patterns can be so much part of the furniture of the inner life that we don't notice them and think we are looking at the world in a direct way, free of interpretation or expectation. We rarely are. That doesn't mean we are always wrong, still less that we can believe any old thing and it will be true. But it does mean that we might not notice when we are wrong, or partial, or when another interpretation might also fit the "facts", because our background habits of belief, our ways of looking at the world, are filtering or biasing the data. If we realise this, we can look deeper for a different story, another aspect of the story or perhaps a different interpretation of what we think we know.

We often protect our perspective jealously. For example, if I dislike some criticism you make of me, I can label it as prejudice. Whether it is or not doesn't matter here: your opinion may indeed be prejudiced, or mistaken in some other way but carefully considered, or it may even express a partial truth. But to say that it stems from prejudice means that I feel entirely justified in setting it aside without consideration. "Prejudice" is pejorative, prejudice is wrong and so if there is any fault it is now yours. I don't have to respond to the criticism or change my behaviour or my views because you are a bad person and your opinion counts for nothing. This condemnation by labelling is a staple piece of rhetoric in what passes for political debate but it may be done quite sincerely. If so, then my perspective is so fixed that communication is currently impossible; my inner life is closed and buffered against what might just be a grain of truth worth considering.

Sometimes when a person is told they have cancer, the enormity of what they have been told quite naturally blots out everything else. This becomes their point of view, they become "person with cancer" or "cancer victim"; fear, anger and a host of other emotions sweep them away. No one can deny that such a diagnosis is a huge challenge, perhaps one of the greatest challenges anyone could face. But what if the cancer story did not dominate all the other stories of that person's life? After all, everything that person was before the diagnosis does not go away. Other stories are still true, other processes are still continuing. (We will have more to say on processes later.) Dealing with the cancer of course becomes a priority, but there is still a life to be lived, a life perhaps all the more precious for the new sense of its finiteness. Living happily still remains a priority and the most important question to ask might be, how do I retain my peace of mind under these conditions? The story or stories we tell ourselves and allow ourselves to believe will determine the quality of the life we can lead even in these extreme circumstances, but that means that we have to retain the freedom to see life from other perspectives.

Relativity and relativism

We all know that any of our beliefs might be wrong simply because we have made a mistake. So it is useful to be able to stay aware of the alternatives and not to close our minds at the first opportunity. But now we can add that even when we are right, we have still adopted a story and other stories might also be applicable. There are always other ways of looking at the picture. Dogmatism, the idea that we know the only and complete truth about anything, is always false. There is a parallel with relativity in physics: no observer has a privileged or absolute perspective in space-time. We may move relative to each other but it makes no sense on a cosmic scale to contest whether you move and I stand still or the other way round. Similarly, there is no absolute, unbiased, complete point of view from which we or anyone else can view the world.

We have to be careful with this, however. What you see may depend on where you stand, but it does not follow that you can see anything you like if only you stand in the right place. There is indeed a mistaken line of thinking here in which the idea of truth becomes slippery. If everything is so relative to perspective and mindset, goes this line, then perhaps everything is true from some perspective and false from some other. Some people actually argue that this is so. (Or not, presumably.) Nevertheless, some things are true and some false whatever the perspective or mindset. The belief that I can walk through walls is false, even thought it may never be tested. You may say it is "true for me" but that is just a polite way of saying that I believe it although it is false. It isn't actually true for me because I can't walk through (the usual kinds of western) walls. Many points from which to "look at things" may be possible, but that does not mean we can arbitrarily choose what is true from any given perspective, nor that there will always be a point of view from which our pet belief is true.

In recognising the importance of the (often unconscious) act of adopting a point of view, we are not agreeing to dispense with truth. So perspective or point of view is important, but it still makes sense to talk of truth and falsehood – just perhaps more carefully.

Stories and the inner life

What I hope to have done in this chapter is to begin to show how we each live in a cocoon woven from our beliefs. Beliefs are stories and by making the shift to considering them as such we can become just slightly aware of what we are doing when we think about the world, or ourselves or others. It's hard, this; it's like glimpsing something from the corner of your eye, at the edge of your visual field, something which disappears when you look straight at it. Stories depend in turn on language, which is in turn based on some very complex habits and skills. We cannot deal with the world directly in what we think and believe, we have to go through language and language only works because of the way it makes distinctions, focuses on some features of the world and misses out others. So we can get the stories wrong just because we make a mistake or are misled, but even when we get them "right" we have never got the whole truth and we may even be looking at the world in such a way or from such a point that we simply cannot see some important aspect. Maybe we are just incapable, at times, of seeing what others see, like someone looking at one of those optical puzzles which could be a candlestick or two faces depending on which is the foreground and which the background.

All this matters for the peace of the inner life because language, thought and belief are such important components of the inner life. If we are not happy, some of our beliefs may well be at the root of the problem. It's not a question of make-believe, of bringing ourselves to believe what we know is not true. If I am short of money it doesn't usually help to pretend to myself that I am not. But even in this very concrete case it may help practically, let alone with my state of mind, to look closely at whatever conclusions I may have run to without much thought, to generate alternatives, to look at the issue from other perspectives, even to question why I think I am "short" – what do I need right now that I do not have, for it isn't usually money, it's something I need the money for. Again, it happens that people stay with violent or abusive partners because of a story or stories they accept about how staying is better than leaving. Story skill is not about persuading oneself that abuse is good or acceptable. It is about looking clear-eyed at the situation, examining one's own motives, beliefs and fears. Why is this acceptable, why are alternatives not acceptable? What benefits are there and why are they worth the price? How can the inner life be held together in these traumatic circumstances and how can the external situation be addressed? Not for a moment can we think that there are easy answers to these questions and often the key issues are purely external and practical, but sometimes it is story – belief – which imprisons someone.

So a basic skill is to confront and if necessary modify our beliefs rather than taking them as obvious and immutable features of the world. They are not features of the world, they are stories which pick out such features – but not necessarily the most helpful ones for our peace of mind. We often get stuck in a particular unhelpful story. The more we can step back, see the nuances and the alternatives, take different perspectives, see the hidden implications of the language we have used, the more chance we have to free ourselves. We can't go behind language, we can't go behind story as a whole. But we can move from story to story, perhaps from perspective to perspective. Being convinced that there is a way to un-stick ourselves is already a big step forwards. We can practice a few simple techniques which might take us further.

Chapter 12:
Story in practice

The uses of story skills

We can now look again at some occasions when beliefs cause difficulty for peace of mind and see how changing the story can help. In essence, this idea of using story is a very familiar process. We can all recall instances when small events upset us – a friend's chance remark, a decision going against us at work, an invitation which did not come. We usually have to reframe those events, find a different story to tell about them, and the upset will subside. The importance of finding the right story for our peace of mind is by no means an esoteric idea.

Stories are used explicitly in some traditions both to help develop mindfulness and to break the habit of reliance on finding a solution to every puzzle, which can be a problem for peace of mind when we stray into areas where no solutions are available. We have already met the Vietnamese Zen use of "gathas", which can be seen as stories to help focus attention on the details of everyday life. In the Japanese Zen tradition, "koans" are used both to develop concentration and to baffle the thinking mind into submission. A koan is a story-puzzle which has no intellectual solution but which the student must find a way of solving – "What is the sound of one hand clapping?" Worlds away, in that strange tradition called philosophy, the "language games" of Wittgenstein had a related purpose of ending philosophical problems not with a solution but by showing that (and how) a puzzle is illusory and arises from a mistake about the way in which language is used.

We can also see that much psychotherapy is a matter of developing and applying very specific story skills to the patient's situation. Depending on the school of therapy involved, the story might involve infantile sexuality, archetypes and dreams, layers of personality, hidden but mistaken beliefs or something else. One of the most successful therapies in use today, Cognitive Behaviour Therapy (CBT), focuses directly on the patient's own stories or beliefs and on challenging them, without trying to place them within a pre-existing theoretical framework at all. Indeed, it may be that the particular theoretical stories used in therapies scarcely matter. The important thing is that the patient can be brought to see and feel their problems in a different light, to reframe their genuine mental or emotional confusion within a different story, no matter which, offering a possible resolution. Psychotherapeutic theories are thus not like scientific theories for which the issue is literal truth or falsity, but more like toolkits for creating the kind of stories which will bring genuine relief to people who are too enmeshed to find relief for themselves. Such cases also show how powerful and deep-set problems with story can be.

Beliefs about ourselves

The stories we accept about ourselves can have a great impact on how we think and feel and of course on how we behave and act. Telling ourselves different stories about ourselves can therefore change us radically. If you see yourself as a victim or a damaged person, your outlook will be coloured by that story, and if you can accept a different story your life will change. This can happen in many ways, for example through therapy as we have just seen, but it also lies behind the idea of creating political change by changing the "consciousness" of people who for example see themselves as victims or are held in a subordinate role. "Consciousness" here means the stories people accept as setting the context of their own lives. The civil rights movement of the 1960's in the USA and the feminist movement in the 1970's are examples of stories used in this way. Just seeing that another story is possible is a huge step and is sometimes enough to create the momentum for change.

Stories are often used, however, to cover problems of the inner life and hide them from ourselves. We use stories like this to cover or rationalise fears ("I am frightened of dogs because..."), emotional pain ("My father abandoned me because..."), desires ("My wife doesn't understand me..."), negative emotions like anger or hatred ("I've got nothing against them but..."). The point in each case is not whether the story is true or false but that we accept it, in more or less good faith. The story may explain the problem, excuse it or hide it. Clearly, it is a great step forward each time we are able to become aware of such a story mechanism, because then we can look properly at whether the story is true or at what else might also be true. Awareness does not always in itself solve the underlying problem, but at least it gives us a chance to address it.

We often adopt unsubstantiated stories to fill gaps in our understanding, because we hate to think that we do not understand how the world works. Hence come myths and doctrines of many kinds which we accept as fact, as well as parables and poetic images which meet our need to grasp at something. We do the same about ourselves as we do about the world, adopting mini-myths which explain to ourselves why we do what we do, or like what we like, or why we are different from other people. We share these stories socially, even tribally: everyone likes to have a story or stories about where they belong and what their roles are. This results at its best in community and social cohesion, though the same habit in different circumstances results in hostility to outsiders, for example in gang culture. Social stories – social beliefs about ourselves – are often accepted and unchallenged by everyone in the group so we are unaware that our strong feelings and preferences are based on stories we have adopted from those around us. Recognising that other stories might also be true can free us from many consequent habits of thought and feeling.

Our habit bases contain so many stories about ourselves that they affect our inner lives in countless small ways as well as on major issues. I am this type of person or that, I like this and not that, blue suits me but not green, I am good at this but no good at that, I am too old, too tall, too fat, and on and on. These are all stories. They may be true, but they are never the whole truth. If they involve a judgement of value or taste, we should be especially suspicious. We allow our lives to be governed by these stories because we do not think they can be questioned, or we do not think to question them. We allow the peace of our inner lives to be eroded by the emotions and desires these beliefs cause us. Recognising them as stories at least shifts them from the category of unquestionable fact. Then we can begin to see whether they are really true or just, say, an expression of our fears. We can look at what else might be true as well, whether the condition they describe is permanent, whether we can reframe the situation, what we would do or feel if they were not true and whether we could do or feel that anyway, and so on.

We have already seen in the case of the skills of benevolence that imagining how another person might think or feel allows us to feel differently about their actions. If we only allow space for a different story to be a possibility, we have created the possibility of a different emotional response. There are some wonderful stories of Tibetan monks who have been imprisoned and mistreated but who have been able to draw on their training and beliefs to help them endure. They can, for example, see their ordeals as a great benefit, because by suffering they use up bad "karma", the result of evil actions they themselves have performed in previous incarnations, which stands in the way of their achieving their spiritual goal of enlightenment. Thus not only do they endure but they can also avoid hatred for their captors who are unwittingly helping them. This story only works because the monks have total faith in their underlying spiritual story, but it is a dramatic illustration of what story can do.

Telling a different story does not mean ignoring or avoiding facts or failing to do what would make external circumstances better. If the world offers problems, it is surely better to solve them if we can. But it is not always possible to change the world and sometimes we cannot see that change is possible because our story habits get in the way. So the story skills can operate on two different levels, first helping us to see more clearly and creatively what is possible for us to change, then helping us to deal with what we cannot change.

Story types / story techniques

If your inner life is clouded by negative emotion, it is likely that there is a negative story underlying it. This may not be the whole story – we now know it isn't! – but teasing out the elements of the story and why it makes you feel bad, angry, ashamed, hate-filled or whatever, is an important step. But which bit of the story you need to change may not at all be obvious. To take an extreme example, people who have been abused as children often have feelings of shame and guilt about it. To an outsider it seems obvious that the fault lay entirely with the perpetrator, but it can seem otherwise to the victim. Their inner story might thus go something like: I was abused, I was unable to stop it, therefore I was complicit, therefore I am guilty. This story can be tackled at many points and to do it skilfully clearly demands great experience and patience. But the first step is to be clear what the story actually is, what the hidden assumptions are and where there are false generalisations or inferences.

In this example a therapy like CBT might be needed because the story and the emotional scars run so deep. But in more everyday cases it is just as necessary to see clearly what we are assuming and what the weak links are in the chain of inference. Of course our emotions, especially our negative ones, are not decided upon by an explicit chain of reasoning. But they are usually triggered by a story and often sustained by a story. The habit or skill to cultivate is one of questioning negative emotions as if they were rational, in order to flush out the story. For example, your partner seems a little off-hand, you conclude he/she is cross with you and begin to feel defensive, or cross yourself, or guilty. Why have you assumed that your partner is angry with you? What other explanations could there be for their apparent mood? Is this an excuse for you to get cross in return? Does it help the situation? Are you feeling guilty anyway about something and expect anger, or are you cross about something yourself and don't want to admit it?! Why does his/her anger bother you? Do you perhaps think anger and love are incompatible? If you feel guilty, are you? Is it just that you always feel unworthy, or is there something you should be talking about? And so on. We think of ourselves as rational beings (other people are a different matter, of course!) but our reactions and emotions don't usually stand up to much rational scrutiny; the stories get very tangled. Teasing them out will not solve everything, but it often will change our perspective sufficiently to blunt the negative emotion. And if not, it will at least make it clear what it is we have to work on.

Alternatives

Sometimes we can tease out the story which underlies some part of our unhappiness and find that it seems quite coherent. We cannot attack it with logic or common sense because it seems reasonable. In such cases it helps to remember that no story is the whole truth: what we have is a partial story from one particular standpoint. From another perspective we may be able to see past this sorry tale. But to do this we need to be able to generate alternatives, find ways of shifting our point of view. If we succeed, we may see or perceive something completely different, or perhaps the same things form a different pattern and allow a different interpretation, like a puzzle picture. (You know the sort of thing. Doodle the outline of a cube on a piece of paper, all 12 edges. Which corner is nearest you? You can change your focus so that the cube seemingly "flips" in space.) The effect can be so dramatic that it is like seeing a different world. Change the story and you literally change your world. Change your world and you may change your life. Practice changing the story, therefore, and you gain the power to change your life.

This changing of perspective, as we have seen, is one of the functions therapy may perform but it is incidentally one of the great appeals of religions, because by accepting their doctrines we adopt a wholly different perspective on earthly problems and literally see things in a different light. It is, sadly, also one of the attractions of extremist views for the dispossessed and the angry. In both cases the new perspective may become our only perspective and we can move from being trapped in one story to being trapped in another. Whether this is a problem depends on the details of the story we have adopted.

We need some everyday techniques to help us generate alternative perspectives and help us change our "point of view". Here are four simple techniques for this purpose, but there are certainly many more. The first three of our quartet involve manipulating words, the fourth involves visualisation. We will call the verbal trio the "what if?", the "as if" and the "also" techniques.

What if?

The "what if?" story is perhaps the most familiar because it underlies so much fiction. It simply involves imagining that things are different from what we know or suppose them to be. We can imagine that one of our beliefs is wrong, or we can entertain a belief we do not hold to see where it might lead. We can do this even if we are convinced that our usual belief is right and that the temporary belief is definitely wrong, so this is a non-threatening technique even if we are deeply attached to our story. You don't have to believe in ghosts, vampires or aliens to enjoy a ghost, vampire or science fiction story.

"What if?" is the basis of much scientific method. Einstein's ideas about gravity implied that light should be bent as it passed a massive body like the sun. A solar eclipse offered a way to measure from two different points on the earth the light from a distant star as it passed the sun. "What if Einstein is right? Then we should observe...." The results were taken to indicate such bending and therefore as the first concrete support for the theory.

The "what if?" story is of course something we often practice (actively or passively) just for amusement or entertainment – in films and books and plays. This is one of the ways in which fiction can show us interesting aspects of the world, by changing some unchallenged assumption or received wisdom and showing us the consequences.

But "what if?" is most useful as an all-purpose imagination trigger, creative thinking 101. If a story has you in a box, "what if?" can be used to break out of the box. Any and every element of the situation you think you are in can be challenged, imagined differently, and perhaps you can find a story which helps you forward or helps you find peace. So you are a victim of this or that, but what if you were not, what would you do differently? How would you think and feel in those circumstances? Can't you go there now? Or what could you do now instead? It's not a matter of ignoring the facts but of freeing the imagination, allowing creativity something to work with. Maybe something needs to be changed in the external world and maybe you can do something about that. But keep focusing on your inner life.

How could you see or interpret this event, situation, predicament in such a way that it did not disturb your peace of mind? What if it were not an ending but a beginning (what would it be the beginning of?); what if what happened to you could help prevent its happening to others (how could that come about?); what if you refocused your life in a different way; and so on. Sometimes these stories are like inner sticking plasters to get you through a difficult patch, whereas the real answer is to change your habit basis in the longer term to cope with such situations. But sometimes they can be the source of genuine insight and a life-changing idea. What if this is one of those times?

As if

The "as if" story is the route of metaphor, allegory, model or myth. We also use it when we are trying to understand and absorb new concepts or knowledge. We relate the new to something we already know or understand so that we can get a grip on it, and then afterwards we can start to differentiate the new from the old.

Again, this type of story occurs frequently in science. For example, the structure of the atom might be (indeed was) represented as a little solar system with electrons circling a nucleus like planets around a sun. This is a model that helps enquiry to proceed because questions can be posed and tested: "If the atom is like this, shouldn't we expect such and such an effect?" and so on. In most cases (like this one) the model has strong and weak points so it may be modified many times before someone comes up with a better basic model, when the first model will be abandoned altogether.

"As ifs" occur frequently in religious thought and teaching. All religions make use of stories or parables to get across their meaning by likening the deeper message to something familiar to the audience. This creative use of metaphor greatly increases the ability to deliver the message to a variety of different types of audience and in particular to reach the uneducated and underprivileged. But "as ifs" play a part even at the more philosophical end of the religious spectrum. For example, in all the monotheistic religions there is a strong strand of opinion that God is unknowable or indescribable in principle because God is far beyond any human experience or power to understand, beyond the very concepts we have available. So everything that can be said about God has the quality of metaphor, approximation or even myth. In this way of thinking, God is not a myth, but everything we humans say or think on the subject is a myth or at best an approximation. These myths may nevertheless be very helpful because they satisfy our craving for understanding. No harm is done so long as we remember that they are metaphors and not the ultimate truth which remains ungraspable.

Like the "what if?" story, the "as if" allows us to stand outside a particular point of view or way of looking at the world. But instead of changing some basic fact or assumption, here we proceed by likening the aspects we are faced with to a familiar situation or interpretation. The "as if" world is the world of the poet. We do not (or need not) conflate the real and the model. The Assyrian may have come down like a wolf on the fold but, as Ogden Nash pointed out, we are not so confused as to suppose he was one. But because the metaphor or model maps some of the world as we know it, we look for other correspondences in the map and all of this may illuminate or add to what we know.

We are all familiar with myths from the past, stories which seem obviously false to us. But they may never have been taken literally: they may have been used to illuminate or just cope with aspects of existence which were important but otherwise impossible to understand at the time. They were "as ifs". Usefulness rather than truth is the appropriate criterion for choosing between alternative myths, if indeed it is necessary to choose. Sometimes we need to adopt or create our own myths: we can use the "as if" mode when it seems important to us to understand something but we know that we do not know the answer. We can piece together the bits that we do know with a model or a metaphor – like the "solar system" model of the atom. We know that it is not wholly true but it fits as many of the facts as we know and we can behave "as if" it were true and it may get us by. Although he would surely not have agreed, Freud's model of the mind can be seen as such a myth. Many models which correlate the activities of the inner life to the activities of supernatural beings (good and bad spirits, angels and demons) may also have started in this way. There is of course always a danger that we might forget that the "as if" was only a model and begin to take it literally – but every tool can be wrongly used.

"As if" can also be used in an active way to change ourselves, perhaps to help weaken a habit or build a skill. In this context it is sometimes called patterning or modelling. Perhaps you want to become better at public speaking, but you are nervous. One technique would be to study how confident and effective public speakers behave, how they stand, how they structure their material, how they use their hands, when they pause, and so on. If you could obtain this information, perhaps with help from a coach, you could start to behave "as if" you were a confident and effective speaker. As far as you were concerned, you would at first be acting, your nervousness might not allow you to believe that you were yet an effective speaker. But the audience would notice a change, you would be more effective and with this feedback and more practice your own confidence would grow. Thus the "as if" would allow you to build the physical aspects of the skill and use those to build the inner aspects. You would acquire confidence in this case from the outside in.

An "as if" story can thus be a matter of action, not just of words, and the "as if" technique can be used to build outer and inner skills. To do something "as if..." is to rehearse the feelings and attitudes required and thus strengthen them. This, in turn, can actually change the way we act and behave as well as the way we feel. We saw this in discussing the practice of kindness or compassion, and many of the "inner game" techniques now widely used in competitive sports also use this principle.

Also

The "also" story is not used counterfactually or metaphorically, but to draw attention to what is overlooked or missed out by a description. As we have seen, our language habits make the choice for us about what to notice and what to describe about the world, and we miss out more than we include. There is no such thing as "the whole truth" since the simplest description could be expanded to include more precise or varied information, without end. This incompleteness applies to simple things and events and even more to complex things like people. All of us are many things and fit many descriptions, including some good and some bad. We all fill many roles, have many dimensions, are part of many stories. And not all the stories need be consistent with each other, which is a driving force of much dramatic art but in life can just be confusing. "All descriptions are incomplete" – there is always something else. Whatever the situation, however clear cut it may seem, however stark and overwhelming the facts, it still makes sense to ask, "What is true as well?"

If you think this idea of incompleteness and even of inconsistent descriptions being true simultaneously is fanciful, think again about an everyday object and its scientific description. The example we used before is the table. It is solid, hard to the touch, does not move except when we move it, it is thoroughly familiar and holds no surprises. But switch to a very standard scientific story. Science says the table is made up of molecules, of atoms, of subatomic particles, of energy – pick your own level of abstraction/reduction. It is not static but buzzes with the movement of these invisible particles and most of it is made up of the space between the particles. We can't find out all the basic information about these particles, even if we wanted to. Which then is reality, the everyday sense that the table is solid or the science which tells us it is energy and space? Surely both are true, in their own ways, but neither can claim to be the whole truth. They are fit-for-purpose descriptions. Even when true they are never the whole truth. "Never the whole truth" doesn't mean that there is something mysterious and hidden, it just points to the way words work, picking out what we want or need to pick out, which is very useful but there is always a different way to do it.

It is easy to typecast other people with descriptions which harden into firm beliefs. Other possibilities are then shut out and we forget all the other categories which might more usefully be applied in one case or another. It is the way we create prejudices about others. It is common, for example, to hear arguments about what "America" should or shouldn't do, or what stance "the West" or "the Third World" should take on this or that question. It is easy to forget that these are just political slogans, whether the labels are self-applied or imposed. They may highlight certain common interests people have, but even if the group so designated is united on a particular issue, within each group there are generally as many differences as there are traits in common. These are people, not just members of a group, and each is likely anyway to be a member of many groups. There are many "also" stories about each sub-group and each member of such vast groups. All descriptions are temptations to simplify; that is their strength but also their weakness.

In the complexity of the inner life it is even more useful to remember the power of the "also" story and the incompleteness of all descriptions. Taking descriptions as complete is the way we create the ruts we occasionally find ourselves in. For example, a story which begins "I am only…" is a sure sign of self-inflicted prejudice. Of course we all have genuine limitations; not all descriptions apply to everyone. But a great many more descriptions could apply than we often think, and a great many do apply which we forget. "Also" stories help us to realise this and can create an enrichment of our inner lives. Many of the stories we suggested using to develop a sense of kindness or compassion towards others in the previous chapter were "also" stories. In the next chapter we will look at a particularly powerful set of "also" stories, the process stories, which reinforce the point that even a slight change in perspective can alter our inner environment beyond recognition.

Visualisation

Visualisation is a form of story and in most if not all cultures it is one of the most commonly used ways to create effects on the inner life. It is said that more of the cortex of the human brain is involved in vision than in all other functions combined, which is a possible explanation for the sheer power of visualisation, the inner use of deliberately constructed images. Mental "images" can involve sound and more rarely taste, touch and smell, so as we discuss visualisation these other forms should not be forgotten. But for most of us, vision dominates the inner landscape as it does the cortex and hence vision not only gives its name to the process of inner image-making but will be the focus of our discussion.

Images can simply be thoughts, whether memories or "imaginings". Beliefs, too, can take the form of images – don't we say things like, "I get the picture"? Often this is a source of difficulty because an image is nearly always capable of ambiguity and often it is simply ill-defined or incomplete. We have to take into account point of view, what the image shows and what it hides, why (say) people are doing things not just what they are doing – and many other things. But similar problems arise of course when we use words, so this is not an argument about the superiority of words to pictures or the other way round. It is perhaps a further way of showing that truth is always partial – we can just more easily understand that a picture, however clear on first glance, may need interpretation.

Images call up emotions and desires. We can, for example, have painful or embarrassing or happy memories in the form of mental images. Thus mental images change our emotions and we can even use such images to change our emotions at will, as some actors do. Even physical effects can be produced, since emotions and desires have such a significant physical component. Thus you can generate the physical "symptoms" of anger, sexual arousal or fear just by creating a mental image of an occasion when you were (memory) or might be (fantasy) in that state. Images can even be used to create desires, as when you make yourself hunger for a certain food because you have pictured it to yourself. Thus images and visualisation reach the whole of the inner life.

Clearly, visualisations and images can be part of a problem or they can be used skilfully to solve problems. On the negative side, you can imagine or remember images that arouse desire in you or frighten you or make you angry. People who have witnessed horrific incidents, for example, are often troubled by vivid visual memories, flashbacks, which are out of conscious control, and they may find it very difficult to dispel these images even with help. But on the positive side, because visualisation can also be consciously controlled it can be a skill with many uses. Imagining or remembering can be used to change difficult habits of emotion or desire. For example, putting yourself in the shoes of your adversary to arouse compassion and defuse your own anger involves imagining what that person must believe and how they must feel. To pull this off it might be useful to imagine them in situations in which they are vulnerable or suffering. Or again, a legendary technique to help nervous public speakers is for them to imagine the audience sitting naked or in their underwear. The idea is that you can't be frightened of the ridiculous or the vulnerable, so the image uses humour to overcome fear.

Visualisation has been a favourite technique in many traditions for many reasons. I have no special techniques to add to the list and it would be disproportionate even to attempt a survey, but here are some favourites. In some Tibetan traditions visualisations are used as concentration exercises. A precise, complex three-dimensional object such as a sacred building – think Natural History Museum or St. Pancras Station to give an idea of the complexity achieved – is mentally pictured and retained in the "mind's eye". At high levels of skill it is said that a practitioner may be able to change points of view with respect to the image, as if travelling round and through it, while the image remains as clear, sharp and detailed as if it were a physical model. Do not, however, be discouraged by this Olympian standard or jump to the conclusion that such a high level of achievement in this particular skill is essential for everyone. With all our skills the key issue for us is always whether we have enough skill to be happy and maintain our inner peace, not whether we are world champions.

Also in the Buddhist tradition are the gruesome charnel ground contemplations, in which one's own body is imagined in progressive states of post-mortem decay. These exercises are not for the faint-hearted, but they are excellent ways of weakening the habit – which we all have to some extent – of believing that our happiness is essentially tied to the state of our bodies. This is but one example of visualisation being used in order to weaken desires and attachments. Related exercises can be used to combat amorous obsessions, gluttony or pickiness in eating, excessive attachment to or desire for possessions (Imagine them in a hundred years' time, for example: are they really worth the trouble? Imagine yourself in a hundred years' time: what good will they have done you?) and many other problems.

In modern times many psychological methods, for example the techniques of Neuro-Linguistic Programming, use visualisation to very powerful effect. One common NLP method of helping with phobias is to visualise yourself sitting in a cinema watching a film about a phobia-inducing thing or event, let's say a large spider. You then visualise sitting at the back of the cinema watching yourself watching the film – the idea is that by stepping back and further back in this way you can progressively detach (dissociate) yourself from the fear which you would normally feel in the presence of the spider. Then you can learn to manipulate the "film" you are watching in the imaginary cinema so that it becomes less scary, and you can gradually re-associate yourself until you are acting in the film without feeling fear. Thus you have visualised yourself not being phobic, an important learning event which has the definite effect of weakening the phobia.

Other NLP techniques involve the use of visualisation to adjust emotional states. For example, if you had a negative emotional reaction like fear in certain specific circumstances, you could weaken this reaction by creating a positive emotional resource which you could call on when needed. A standard technique is to visualise in realistic detail, including sounds and if possible smells, an occasion when you felt supremely relaxed or happy or confident or whatever the needed resource might be. This visualisation "calls up" an echo of the appropriate emotional response – the stronger the visualisation the stronger the response. (One of the useful things about NLP is that the detail of the subject's problems and visualisations need not be disclosed to the practitioner. It is enough that the subject successfully visualises a positive occasion without having to describe it.) The positive emotion can then be attached to a physical cue or anchor, like a squeeze of the fingers for example, and this cue will in future set off the positive emotion, just like Pavlov's dogs salivating at the sound of the bell. This is surprising when you first hear it, but emotional responses really are that fickle! Thus the problem emotion can in future be countered by activating the physical cue and creating a countervailing positive emotional response. When this is skilfully done it has remarkable results and it is a good example of visualisation being used to alter emotional habits.

Finally, it is no longer unusual for top sports performers to be coached not only in physical ability and the specific skills of their discipline but also in psychological techniques to keep their confidence high in adversity and to prevent mental factors from interfering with their physical performance. We have already met the "as if" technique used in this context. Other elementary techniques might involve imagining (visualising) what it would be like to win the event, or mentally rehearsing the performance and success in it. This simple technique can have a significant effect on attitude, body language expressing confidence to opponents, and even physical condition.

There are those who claim that visualisation is the key to satisfying all our desires, that by visualising an outcome in sport or indeed in life we actually create it. This may be too optimistic, but it is certain that visualisation can have direct effects on our emotional and other mental states and therefore on our physical states to the very large extent that they are influenced by our inner lives. We may change our own bodies and behaviour, change the way other people perceive and react to us and thus change what happens to us and what we are capable of doing, all from the basis of visualisation. The stories we tell ourselves in words have a big effect on our inner lives and our external lives. The stories we tell ourselves in pictures are no less powerful.

Chapter 13:
Applications of the story skills –
Things and the self

In this chapter we will look at two stories which are deeply entrenched in language and (therefore) in the way most of us look at the world. First we have the story that the world is made up of things or objects. Second we look at the story of the self. The purpose is partly to show applications of the story skills and how they can be used to change our inner lives. But these two particular stories are sufficiently important to deserve examination anyway, because being able to step round them can be a source of insight in many situations.

Processes and things

Let us start with an important use of the "also" story type which is particularly helpful in counteracting entrenched habits of belief: the process story. When we look at or think about the world around us, inner or outer, animate or inanimate, we are used to dividing the world into "things" – chairs, people, plants, thoughts, buses, whatever. In European languages "things" are what nouns stand for and we tend to get locked into this grammar: we tend to think that the world is composed of things, which incidentally can be described by qualities (adjectives) and commit actions or have actions done to them (verbs).

It is a very convenient, practical and successful way of looking at the world to divide it up like this. But it is not the only way. (And incidentally, not every language does it.) Let us now try a different way, an "also" story. Everything could be described in terms of processes. We understand process from many familiar things. A fire or a flame, for example, is a thing with a noun to designate it but we understand that when we look at a flame we are looking not at a solid thing but at a process. The process is localised in space and time so a "thing" description works perfectly well but even while we look at a flame it is constantly changing. There is a process going on, a chemical reaction involving something being burned, using up oxygen to release light and heat. The same idea of a process can be applied, say, to "river" or "sea" or "wave": constant change. It still makes sense to say that this is one river, the same one we fished in yesterday perhaps, while that one over there is a different one. But it is also true that the river we fished in yesterday is gone, the process has moved on. If we could somehow tag the water we would see that yesterday's water is way downstream and this is a new lot. Hence Heraclitus' "You can't step in the same river twice" – it sounds a bit mysterious but we can see that it is true in a perfectly ordinary sense, the process sense, even while it is false in another sense.

Everything can be looked at in this process sense and it is not hard to develop the skill of "converting" things into processes. A wooden chair is of course a thing, but it is also part of a process. It was once part of a tree, and before that a seed, with the many nutrients which would contribute to the future tree scattered in air and soil, and before that something else. It will be a broken chair one day, and eventually the wood will be burned or will rot and the particles will go in different directions and become parts of different things. The chair is in fact only a chair for a small slice of time; what you sit on is a process, in fact a part of many processes. The process is rather longer and slower than a flame (and cooler, fortunately) but it is still a process. This is perfectly ordinary and not at all mysterious but when we start to think about things in this way we can sometimes experience a feeling of strangeness, a kind of dislocation. Everything can be analysed as a process, any "thing" is part of a process, usually part of many processes winding their way through time. We are aware, just now, of a little bit of them. You could alternatively look at this as thinking about things in four dimensions, restoring the time dimension we usually miss out.

Of course, "process" is a nice elastic term: it is a matter of convenience whether we see one process or many. We could see the wood of the chair as part of one process and the cushion covering it as part of another or we could see these processes as connected by their common "chair" episodes and therefore all the same process. There are thus many process perspectives. In at least one of them we could say that absolutely everything is part of one huge process which we can call the universe. So everything is connected, everything is One. This is quite reasonable although not very helpful when circumstances call for fine distinctions to be made. It is easy to understand, though, how someone might seize on this as a glimpse of a different kind of reality, maybe the True Nature of Things. It is more mundane than that; it is just a different way of describing, an "also" story which is true alongside the everyday way of describing. But it is not make-believe. This is a very important point about this kind of story. The process perspectives show us aspects which are just as real and true as the everyday one. They also show us that things have more than one side to them; dogmatism will always be mistaken.

The beginnings and the ends of processes may be well defined or they may not. A concert, for example, is a process which starts at the first note and ends at the last. A life is a process which starts at a birth and ends at a death. But concerts do not materialise from nowhere, they are parts of larger processes going on before and after and around them, parts of the life of a city or town, parts of the history of the performers and the audience, parts of the timelines of the music performed and the instruments played and so on. So it is with a life and so it is even with a person. Birth and death are noteworthy points in various processes but they can be seen as relatively arbitrary markers. Remember, this is not an attempt to persuade you that one view is true and another false; it is a matter of taking a different perspective. But you have to be willing to try to see things from this perspective.

Which processes actually begin at the birth of a baby? Possibly independent breathing, but not necessarily; that process often starts several seconds later. Not consciousness, that came earlier and/or will develop later, depending on your definition of consciousness. Certainly not physical development which has been going on for some months. Not even independent life, in fact, for few creatures are more utterly dependent than a newborn human. Actually, birth is more easily defined by the ending of a process, the process of gestation, than by the beginning of anything. Similarly, when is a tree born, when does it start? We could argue for one point in the process or another but we would be arguing about which linguistic convention is correct or most convenient, not much about the tree.

The boundaries of processes are thus conventional, conceptual devices which we impose to make language or our stories manageable. Examine any process and you will find that it is a slice of many longer processes and composed of many shorter processes. (The same may be true of things, of course, but is often much harder to see.) It is a slice both in time and in space because what you include geographically in the process and what you dismiss is just as much a matter of convention as the beginning and the end.

Living things are more complex processes. In a living thing, many thousands of processes are all co-ordinated, some starting in this instant, some finishing, some accelerating, some slowing down, some relatively static and so on. Your body is just such a bundle of processes, your mind is another related bundle of processes, your life is a bundle of processes. The processes which make up your life did not all start with your birth: some were going long before, some started only in the last second as you read this. But if we work this story thoroughly, the new processes all had predecessors and those that end are followed by something else. So there are many chains of events winding through time, winding through you and on to something else. (There may be jumps, too – processes do not have to be continuous.) You take in food, you take in air, you shed skin and hair, you breathe out and you excrete waste, you are constantly exchanging matter and energy with the world around you. The matter in your body is utterly different from what was there, say, ten years ago. Even if the chemical composition were similar (and it will have changed in many small ways) there would be different atoms in most places. It is difficult to draw real boundaries from a process perspective; the processes just flow on and through you, they start and stop and change and the term "you" is from this perspective a way to designate a segment where these particular processes meet and intertwine for a while. The process perspective is not a metaphor but an "also", an alternative description, true alongside everyday descriptions or scientific descriptions. It is another point of view, a change of perspective.

It is a good practice to try out this way of thinking, this generation of alternatives, on everyday objects from the most transient to the most long-lasting and solid. (Try "mountain". Try "planet", or "sun"!) This is a useful skill in itself, an antidote to complacency and rigidity of mind and incidentally a good technique for finding creative solutions to problems. Process stories can be used to shake us out of habit when we might otherwise get stuck in one pattern of negative belief or thought. Like all techniques, though, their efficacy and our ability to use them in serious situations depends on having practised them in less threatening circumstances.

What we gain above all from process stories is a deeper realisation that everything changes, in fact everything is constantly changing, even if the change is slow. Everything is a process or part of a process. Without this story we can unwittingly divide the world into things that change and things that don't. Then we can start to regret, for example, that things we like change and have endings while things we don't like are, we may feel, permanent. But this distinction is genuinely an illusion, created partly by the way we describe things. Everything changes, everything is part of a process. When we can not only acknowledge but actually accept and feel this view, a whole raft of illusions and mistakes falls away and our inner lives become easier.

The other helpful thing about process stories is that the boundaries of processes are much more obviously arbitrary than the boundaries of things. The grammar of "things" is useful in so many contexts precisely because it allows us to draw sharp boundaries in space and time, but we can get stuck in this habit and there are many instances when it just more useful to be able to see things as events or parts of processes. It is much easier in fact to join up processes, just because a complex of processes can be regarded as a single complex process. So a process story gives us great freedom to see the world in lots of different ways which ordinarily we ignore, ways which are genuinely alternative descriptions alongside the descriptions of more conventional speech, not contradictions of them but not fantasies either. Process stories help us to explore other perspectives and thus potentially free ourselves from unhelpful beliefs.

Self

The concept of self, essential though it may seem, can also cause confusion and problems for the inner life, a point recognised by many faith traditions. We can now use the idea of the process story to examine this important concept, which is full of hidden beliefs and habits.

The very fact that we have an inner life at all seems to confirm that there is an entity there, the one each of us calls "I" or "Me" or "Myself". We know, or think we know, more about this entity than does anyone else because we have what seems like privileged access to its inner ruminations, its thoughts and feelings and so on. We might speak or think, for example, of "the real me", meaning this entity as we know it from the inside (so to speak) as opposed to the "me" as known by the rest of the world.

This sense of self is much more than a belief – in fact, it seems to involve all the dimensions of the inner life. The self seems to be the actor in all that we do, externally and internally. It is the self that seemingly takes action, but it is also the self that seemingly thinks and plans, feels and desires, judges and perceives. At a social and physical level it is perfectly clear that you are one self and I am another, but I am also well aware in my inner life that I do not share your consciousness, your thoughts and feelings, which seems to confirm that we are organised as separate selves. We have layers (maybe tangles would be a better word) of beliefs, feelings and so on which depend on the assumption that each of us is a separate self.

A self sounds like a thing, but we can quickly observe that "it" is a unique kind of thing. There is a physical presence, sure enough, but the self is not to be equated with that. I am not just my body, if only because my inner life has to be added in. Perhaps it will one day be shown exactly how the inner life depends on the brain and the rest of the body, but the inner life will still be the experience of consciousness, not the explanation of it. Besides, as we have already noted, my body is not the same as it was 10, 20, 40 years ago, but I am still me, I still count as the same self. The self is not the body, or not just the body, although the body has something to do with it.

Perhaps then we can add in the mind or the inner life, or perhaps the self actually is the inner life. But the inner life changes with its contents as thoughts and emotions flit by, so if the self is the inner life we would have to say that the self changes from instant to instant and that isn't at all as it is meant to be. The concept of the self is meant to provide some stability and continuity, so it won't do to have the self changing every instant. What would happen, for example, to personal responsibility if the self of five seconds ago, let alone a year ago, were counted as a different self from the self now? "It wasn't me, officer, it was someone in this body but with different thoughts." I don't fancy your chances.

Maybe the self is somehow the inner observer of the inner life – you know, the one who watches when you pay attention to your inner life. But what about the inner observer's inner life? We can't go that way, it doesn't help to clarify or explain anything. The idea that there is an observer watching the events of the inner life unfold as if on a cinema screen can be a useful metaphor for certain moods and experiences but it does not in fact help to explain anything, let alone help to define the self. Every question we have about the self must now be asked about the "mini-self" which is the observer, and so on ad infinitum.

Well, what about these habits which underlie the inner life, this habit basis we have been talking about – perhaps that is the self? But the habit basis is not an entity; it is a term of convenience for all the dispositions and habits which give rise to responses and events in the inner life. The habit basis is not even part of our consciousness; we can be aware of some habits but not of all of them simultaneously. If we are to say that the habit basis is the self, we will be driven into some very difficult corners. Indeed, the self begins to seem like a strange and elusive kind of thing all round, some kind of combination of body and inner life and dispositions but we can't quite say what exactly the combination is.

Let us apply a process story to this strange thing and some of the strangeness will disappear. We have seen that any "thing" can always be described as a process and the description gives us a different perspective on it. In the case of the self, there are streams of events (processes) happening in the body, streams of events happening in the inner life and streams of events as this assembly interacts with the rest of the world. The self is the designation for a whole set of such processes, bringing them all together. Obviously "self" is a complex concept, which is perhaps why it is so difficult to define. But it is actually one of those concepts which fits better into the model of a process.

We know that rocks have a history, erode over large periods of time or get broken in other ways, so that even rocks can be regarded as processes. But they tend to be relatively slow so thinking of them as unchanging things is more useful for most purposes. The self is a fast-moving, fast-changing process, much more like, say, a river or a flame than a rock. The body changes over time, the character changes over time, the contents of consciousness change every instant, moods and emotions come and go, the memory undergoes additions and deletions, the skills this self possesses can be changed, and so on. So now the process story is not only a different perspective, it seems actually to fit our intuitions about the self more accurately than thinking of the self as a thing or an entity. One self can be distinguished from another just as one river or one flame can be distinguished from another, but none of these things is unchanged from one moment to the next. The concept of self is immensely useful not least because we are social creatures and it is important for us to be able to distinguish one from another. But we need not let grammar seduce us into thinking that by naming a self we have named an unchanging (even a relatively unchanging) "thing".

Regarding the self as a process may however lead us to think quite differently about it, compared with when we regarded it as an entity or a thing. When seen as a process the boundaries of the self become arbitrary, conventional. Even more radically, the idea that there is a core, an unchanging "essence" to myself or yourself makes much less sense. We are bundles of processes: every bit of us, physical and mental, changes or could change over time and what links the "me" of one moment to the "me" of another time are just these processes with different events happening in every linking period. If the self were thought of as an unchanging centre or even structure to this activity, we would have to say from this perspective that there is no self, any more than there is an unchanging centre to a flame.

Asking whether the self is real or not sounds like a fundamental question about the world. In fact, it is more like our previous questions about the birth of trees or babies. It is more a question of whether the "self" story is useful or not, and this varies from context to context. In the right context the self is real enough, individuality is real enough, the story is useful. In everyday life we can distinguish you from me and yours from mine. But the concept of the self can be an unhelpful story some of the time. It lies at the root of many habits which stand in the way of happiness. Any troublesome habit of will or desire (think greed, avarice, lust, excessive ambition, vanity, the desire for revenge, and also many less florid habits) is hard to imagine without a self to impose that will or desire. Likewise with any troublesome emotions – think of reactions like anger (you have wronged/annoyed/insulted *me*), hatred (you are *my* enemy), envy (you have what *I* want/should have). There are habits centred on the self which are just unhelpful to being happy. Dropping the unspoken idea that the inner life is organised around a central core, a self, can be a helpful way of approaching these difficult habits. It makes it easier to distance ourselves (!) from our own habits, which already lessens their power.

We could say that the concept of the self has its value in the external world, because it helps us to organise life in relation to others. Even in external contexts, though, we need to be careful because the concept encourages selfishness and separateness. But in the inner life the concept and indeed the sense of self have less value and cause more difficulties. For when we look inside for this central "self" we find nothing to hold on to. It is not any particular thought or feeling or habit, or even the sum of them. This can be a liberating idea, for often we "identify" with our feelings or our thoughts: we literally think that we are identical with them. So the feeling or the thought dominates our inner life. "I am angry", "I am sad", we say, and even the grammar encourages identification. If we said "There is anger at this moment", "There is sadness at this moment" – ignoring how artificial this sounds – we might be closer to seeing that these are just circumstances, temporary features of the inner life. If I am going to be peaceful and happy, these feelings are part of the context. Perhaps I have the skill to deal with them and perhaps not, but they are just feelings (or thoughts) of which I am aware; they are not me and they are not essential to me.

As far as the inner life is concerned, this ("they are not me") is true of every thought and feeling and everything else of which I am aware. In the inner life there is just thought and feeling and the rest, none of which could be said to be "me". In fact, in the inner life it doesn't really make sense to apply "me" and "mine" at all. There is only one inner life of which I can be aware, so I do not need to distinguish between yours and mine, which is the function the idea of the self usefully performs in the external world. Words have to have a function to have a meaning but if they apply to absolutely everything they have no function. If absolutely everything in the world were white, for example, what would "white" mean? Everything in the inner life (the one I experience) could be said to be mine, so the idea of "mine" is redundant here, it has no meaning in this context. There really is no "me" in the inner life. But language starts to fail us here and we begin to sound mysterious because language is difficult to bend in this way. We end up saying things like "I do not exist", which isn't quite right either! Some traditions indeed say that the self is an illusion, and these difficulties may be part of what they mean. But in any case, it is a very helpful practice to have an alternative to the story that the contents of consciousness are organised around a self, because it enables us to see the inner life and its habits from a different and more helpful perspective.

Chapter 14:
Letting go skills

Letting go

An old Zen master had retired to a cave in the mountains to practice. He was seated in meditation in the mouth of the cave when a vagabond spotted him from the nearby road and decided to see what he could steal. The robber crept up and slipped past the master, whose eyes were closed, into the cave. There wasn't much there, of course, because Zen masters tend to travel fairly light, but as stealthily as he could the thief started to gather up what he could see. Then he dropped a bowl which clattered to the ground. He froze, eyes on the master, but there was no sign of movement. After a few minutes the man continued but he again dropped something onto the hard rock floor, and this time he was almost sure he saw a slight movement from the figure in the cave mouth. He waited with bated breath but nothing happened, so he carried on. But as he turned back to the task he knocked over and broke a water pot. The Zen master leapt up and whirled round. "For heaven's sake try to be quiet!" he exclaimed, "Take what you want, but stop crashing around back there while I'm trying to concentrate!"

Without attachment to his few belongings, this master could let them go without a second thought, without any rancour or thought of recovering them. Perhaps he was left with a bare cave, but his peace of mind was not disturbed. He could see that the belongings were not essential to him. It's a nice story, I think, to introduce the idea of letting go, even if we suspect that reverent local people would soon provide replacements for the lost goods. But physical belongings are only one aspect of the attachments we worry about or which worry us. Even our Zen master was perhaps attached to his solitude and silence. Letting go involves a whole range of skills.

Change, again

One of the things we can learn from the practice of seeing the world through the lens of the process story, as in the preceding chapter, is that everything changes, everything is part of a process. You could call this an essential aspect of reality, but it is not some deep metaphysical insight, only a result of the way we constructed this particular story. It is true, nevertheless, and perhaps as near to an absolute truth as we are likely to find in the contingent world. The only permanent thing is the state of flux.

If you fight against or regret this aspect of reality, you will inevitably be unhappy because you cannot escape it. Things, events, states that you love or that give you pleasure will come to an end. Things, events, states that you dislike will come into being. Sometimes your actions may postpone change, or create a different change, but they will never eliminate it. Even people will change, day by day before your eyes. They will change their appearance, their minds, their habits and their relationship to you. It may happen slowly and subtly and the changes are not necessarily for the worse, but change will happen and nothing can prevent it. Sometimes this is how people get into trouble in their relationships: they assume that the person they know will always be the same and are surprised when years of slow change are finally noticed and it seems like a sudden big change. This is one reason that mindfulness is a key relationship skill: if you can pay attention to the constant changes in yourself and in the other person, you can evolve together. Or at least you have a better chance.

A possible way of trying to ensure that change does not distress would be to take pleasure in nothing, to banish feeling, or try to. Apart from the great difficulty of actually putting such a plan into action it is pretty obviously an arid and joyless path. Although it has had its adherents in philosophy and religion through the ages (some of the more extreme Stoics tried it, for example), it is certainly not attractive. But there is a better path anyway. Cultivating the skill of letting go offers a middle way between the two extremes of distress at change and extreme detachment. You can enjoy what is good about the world and other people but recognise that "all things must pass" when the right time comes, and allow them to do so, not indifferently or callously but in the full recognition that such was their nature and therefore without regret.

A small child given ice cream might enjoy it so much that she cries for more when it is finished. But gradually she learns that ice cream is only delicious in certain quantities and that it is in the nature of the experience that it has a beginning, a middle and an end. So the ice cream can be enjoyed and finished without distress and without negating the value and pleasure of ice cream. All we need to learn about letting go is contained in this example. Most of us learn the lesson quite early in the case of ice cream but we fail to generalise it, or else we think it does not apply to "more serious" things. But it does. It is just a question of learning to treat everything in life like ice cream!

Attachment (like its opposite, aversion) can be seen as a desire for the world to be other than it is. There are many things we can control and make choices about, and our desires and wishes in those respects can be satisfied by simply creating the change we want. If my front door is blue and I would prefer it to be green, this is a desire I can satisfy easily with a paintbrush and a pot of paint. But there are other things I cannot change, and wanting them to be different will disturb my peace of mind without helping to create the change I want. I cannot change the weather or the tides or stop the deterioration of the paint on my front door from the moment it is applied, however much I would like to. So if the world is in any respect not to our liking, it is good advice to change the things we can change and learn to live with the others. The problem, we might think, lies in knowing where the line comes between the two categories, as the famous prayer attributed to St Francis suggests. But this is a false problem, from the point of view of the inner life. Whether we succeed or fail in imposing our will on the world is an external circumstance and the product of many factors, some far beyond our control. Striving for change when change is needed, we can still be prepared to distinguish success from our inner peace. We need not allow ego to get mixed up with the goal. We can be useful in the world while maintaining our inner peace.

Thus it does not follow that we should just give up trying to do things. It is important that in letting go we need not become passive or inactive. Rather, we recognise a difference between arranging the world to our liking and having a happy mind. In an extreme case, you might decide it is worth risking your life to help create some vital change in the world, but is it ever worth sacrificing your peace of mind? I suggest not: what sense does it make to stake your peace of mind on imposing your will? So the key distinction is not after all between the things you can change and the things you can't – you won't know until you have finished trying anyway – but between creating change and being so attached to creating change that failure will take away your peace of mind. Letting go of such attachment can be seen as the key skill to counter the root cause of all problems of will and desire, this longing for the world to be other than it is.

Reconciliation or alignment with transience and change is, however, only a part of the power of letting go. To be happy we need to let go of many things which impede our inner lives. Letting go can mean freeing ourselves from illusions, compulsions, ideals, desires, beliefs – anything which prevents us from being happy. We could put it like this: happiness is about freedom from the inner tyranny of our own habits. Our habits have a grip on us, but then, our habits *are* us. So we are trying to free ourselves from ourselves. One of us has to let go! Freeing ourselves from our habits is the same as getting those habits to let go: getting the habits to let go is the same as letting go of the habits.

The first step is always just to realise that you *are* attached, that the habit has you in its grip so that your happiness will come second to the habit. Then at least you can be clear about where your unhappiness might come from. And then, if you choose, you can begin to look at how you might step away from that habit or let go of that attachment.

Non-attachment

Non-attachment is the willingness or preparedness to let go. It is both part of that skill and a way of developing it. "Non-attachment" is a clumsy word, but it names a very important skill and I can't think of a better word which doesn't already mean something distractingly different. ("Detachment" suggests something very different, such as indifference or lack of engagement, which is not the right flavour at all.) We might think of the model here being the love of a parent for a child. Implicit in such a deep relationship, if parental love is not to turn into something self-centred and damaging, is the willingness to let go, little by little, until the child becomes an emotionally healthy, independent adult. This is not indifference or detachment, as anyone who has tried it will readily agree. No caring parent likes to watch their child making painful mistakes and stumbling over hurdles the parent aches to remove or rearrange. It is excruciatingly difficult at times to know how quickly and how far to relax our protection, for we must maintain it fiercely at the beginning but equally be ready to abandon it almost completely in the child's best interest after a handful of years. This is non-attachment, the willingness to let go.

In the case of parental love, of course, we practice non-attachment for the sake of our child's happiness. But it is important to practice it for our own happiness, as well. This is not to say that it is helpful to let go of anything and everything lightly or at the first challenge, to be careless about belongings or cavalier about relationships. Part of the skill lies in knowing when it is time to let go. For those occasions when letting go is nevertheless painful, we can cultivate the recognition that this pain is ultimately less than the pain of not letting go.

The basic idea of non-attachment is, I think, relatively easy to understand and accept. What is much harder to understand and accept is that non-attachment is needed for absolutely everything and everyone in our lives, because change affects absolutely everything and everyone in our lives. The person you love most will change and perhaps even disappear, even the things you like most about yourself will change and disappear, and these changes are often very painful. Resisting or refusing to accept them will be even more painful and a sure recipe for destroying peace of mind. Only the ability, the skill, to let go when the time comes will be of any use, and that ability will be enhanced if non-attachment has primed you with the recognition and the willingness to let go.

Greed is the extreme form of attachment, in which we are attached not simply to what we have but to having more and more of whatever it is – it might be food or drink but might equally be wealth, power, sex, fame, possessions or any number of things. Some of these extreme attachments have their own names (avarice, ambition, lust, and so on) but they can be regarded generically as forms of greed. Most of them are regarded as "sins" by most religions but we could also say they are like diseases, hypertrophies, of the will and at their worst they are addictions. They are all severe obstacles to peace of mind partly because, as we saw earlier, they prevent any kind of equilibrium between desire and its satisfaction and also because they fix our attention on external circumstances as if such externals were essential to happiness. The attitude or habit of non-attachment is the antithesis of greed and thus its cultivation helps to weaken or eliminate a host of problems which can prevent peace of mind.

Past, Future and Fantasy

Letting go is particularly pertinent when we consider the past and the future. Spending time in the past or the future is exclusively an activity of the inner life: thus far at least you cannot do it in your external life. Such a use of "inner time" is not necessarily a problem in itself and indeed perhaps is no better or worse than any other form of inner activity. If I spend the next half hour inwardly reliving my past triumphs or the joys of youth, will I not have spent a happy thirty minutes? As far as it goes, the answer must be yes. It is escapist to reminisce, of course, but no more so than, say, watching TV. As for spending inner time in the future, it too might be positive as far as happiness is concerned. Looking forward in eager anticipation is a pleasant enough activity, provided I do not expect so much that the reality, when it comes, is a disappointment.

But there are some obvious problems. We might, for example, compare the present unfavourably with the past, in which case our thoughts about the past will be a direct source of unhappiness. And of course spending inner time in the past is not always pleasant or even voluntary. Spending inner time in the future includes instances of worry, fear, anxiety, even dread. As with the past, the future can be a standard by which we judge the present, in this case perhaps an excuse to rush through the present, at worst perhaps to rush through a whole series of presents, spending our whole lives longing for the next thing to happen. We can dream our lives away.

In the external world the real past and the real future are importantly different from imaginary ones, but still, neither of them actually exists now. In fact, particularly as far as the inner life is concerned, we could say that past and future are species of fantasy. Even true stories about the past and the future might as well be fiction except for their relevance to the present in the external world as causes and consequences. If the past or the future is in any way a problem for our happiness, it may be important to understand that what is making us unhappy is essentially a fantasy. The difference between a useful story and an unhelpful fantasy is often just this: you use the story, but the fantasy uses you. This is not a trivial distinction, for there are recorded cases where a person's fantasy has become so believable to them that their body responds and they develop physical symptoms or even die.

To escape from such fantasy we need to focus on the present, on the moment or *the now* as it is sometimes (rather portentously?) called. But what does this mean? Focusing on the present should clearly not preclude remembering where remembering is helpful, or planning for the future where planning is necessary, as it often is. We could see this focus on the present as a form of letting go, of letting go of the past and the future and in particular letting go of the twin habits which cause us so much trouble in regard to the past and future – namely, regret and fear. Apart from its external consequences in the present, the past is a problem when in any one of many ways we have regrets – about what we did or didn't do, about what was done or not done to us, about the fact that the past is no more or that something happened at all. The future can be a problem because we use it to fly from the present and thus live in our fantasies, but more often it becomes a problem if we fear it, usually if we fear what might happen to ourselves or our loved ones.

Regret and fear are thus major problems of past and future, respectively, for the inner life. Just imagine what your inner life would be like if you could free yourself from anger and hatred with the aid of the benevolence skills, on the one hand, and from regret and fear with the aid of the letting go skills on the other. No anger, no fear, no regret: how peaceful would your inner life be? How happily could you live? Understanding regret and fear and how letting go can help to deal with them is thus of vital importance.

Regret

Let us agree for simplicity that regret refers to our own actions and failures to act, including things we said or failed to say, rather than the actions or omissions of others. We know that regret is always futile, in a sense, for the past cannot be altered. However much we may regret what we have done or said, or what we failed to do or say, the only issue now is what to do next. We can resolve do better next time, or we can try to amend the present consequences of the past, but we cannot alter the past. This is quite obvious, of course, but it is remarkable how often we allow our inner lives to be disturbed by the unfulfillable wish or desire to change our past. "If only…", we say, or "If I could go back…" or "If I had my time again…". These are stories, but not skilful ones. They trap us into a fantasy about the past which can only make us unhappy, because the story cannot be true and does not illuminate or usefully change the present. The processes of the world and of our lives have moved on and we have to deal with today, with today's river, not yesterday's.

Our attitude to our own mistakes and misdeeds has a major impact on how much regret we have to deal with. Of course, if we make a mistake in our lives or our relationships, if we make a bad choice of action or words, it would be childish to excuse ourselves or ignore the harm we might have done to ourselves or others. Part of dealing with the past is to be clear-eyed about what we have done. But then it is a good practice to try to look at our mistakes as an essential part of the process of learning and living. We simply were not skilful enough at that point, whether the skill in question was inner or external. We may need to consider damage limitation, including putting right the consequences of the mistake, if that is possible. We might also use the recognition of error to bolster our motivation to increase our skills so that we do not repeat the mistake. But once we have faced the error and considered what to do about it, we also need to practice kindness towards ourselves in the matter of mistakes and even misdeeds. There comes a point at which we must decide: do we ruin our happiness in the present because we got something wrong in the past? Is this not another mistake in itself? There may also come a point at which to dwell on our past failings risks becoming an unhelpful habit in itself, an exaggeration of their importance and ours. To consider something as a mistake or a misdeed is already to have learned from it: the things we do and say which we do not even recognise as mistakes may be more harmful to others or to our own inner lives. And, as we learn to be kinder to ourselves, perhaps we also learn to be kinder to others who, we begin to see, are struggling with the same issues.

A sportsman who executes a bad stroke or gets an unfavourable decision from the referee faces a similar problem. He can put it aside and concentrate on the next play, or he can obsess about it and let himself be distracted. In the same way, we can forgive ourselves and move on or we can disrupt our inner lives and our happiness by clinging to our shame or our disappointment or our excuse.

Forgiving yourself

Letting go of regret is pretty much the same as forgiving yourself. When you forgive someone, the benefit to you comes from letting go of your anger against them, so that your mind can be at peace again. (We will look at this in the next section.) When you forgive yourself, there is that same benefit. You make peace with yourself and accept that you can be friends with yourself again. And you accept the forgiveness – which does not mean that the past is changed but that you agree to give yourself another chance. In extreme cases we sometimes hear people say: "I can't live with myself because of what I did." If another person had done it and you were on a desert island with them, you would surely find a way to live with them – murder being the only alternative. Well, you are effectively on that desert island with yourself. I don't mean to minimise how hard forgiving yourself might be in extreme cases, and it might require a lot of help. But in more everyday situations, once we decide that we are in the wrong we often hold things against ourselves for years which we would have forgiven in other people long ago.

We should above all not be misled into thinking that we do not deserve to be happy because of what we did in the past. We might still have to undergo some punishment or other hardship as a consequence of our past actions – for example, if we broke the law – but that is a matter of external circumstance. Happiness is a matter of the inner life. Nothing external can take away our right to be happy, but we have to choose the path of developing happiness to exercise that right. We can often feel that some difficulty in our external life is a punishment for actions we regret, when in reality it is no such thing but simply a random happening, or even something we have encouraged by our desire for punishment. In the external life we do not always get what we deserve or deserve what we get; the processes are complex and largely blind to merit and blame. Just look around you! In the inner life, though, we have the capacity to create happiness, moment by moment, building and using our skills. In the inner life we can look at the roots of our mistakes and misdeeds and change the habits which led to them. It can be a long process, looking closely at the present and knowing that whether we are happy now is a choice we have, or at least something we can move towards, whatever we did before. We ask ourselves, "What am I doing, what is going on in my inner life?" And we remind ourselves: "I have a choice here, I can develop my skills or not."

Sometimes forgiving ourselves involves realising that we have not lived up to an ideal we have adopted and trying again, but sometimes it involves letting go of the ideal itself. This is tricky, but there are undoubtedly times when it becomes essential to let go of an ideal if we are to be happy. We make mistakes in adopting ideals and causes just as we do in everything else. Why have you adopted this or that ideal, why do you follow it? Is it helping to develop habits which will make you happier, bring you greater peace of mind? Has it perhaps done all it can do to help you in that direction and is no longer helpful? If you asked for directions in a strange town you might be told, say, "Turn right, go down the high street until you see the large white building and ask again". This is an incomplete answer but it is still helpful up to a point and will not mislead you. Some ideals are like that: they take you part of the way and then they are done. So let them go, let go of them with gratitude for how far they have brought you. Be honest with yourself and do not abandon any ideal lightly – perhaps it is just that you are chafing at the discipline required – but be prepared to alter or abandon an ideal which no longer serves a purpose. Ideals are directions and there is a case to be made that all ideals are eventually to be let go. When you have arrived, you no longer need directions.

Letting go of regret may require that we seek help from others and at the least it may take time and effort and repeated attempts, but this is after all the nature of training ourselves in a skill. The ground rules are relatively simple. Let go of wishing the past had been different. This is a wish which cannot be satisfied and therefore you will always be unsatisfied while you wish it. Let go of anger or hatred about the past towards yourself or anyone else. These only disturb peace of mind and destroy or prevent your own happiness. Let go or work to change the habits which led you to do what you now regret. This is the best way to ensure no future regret and to put past regret behind you. Put things right or make amends when this is possible and appropriate. This is something useful to be done in the present and lessens the harm of what you did. Then accept that you did what you did and have compassion towards yourself for having been like that.

Forgiveness

Being unable to forgive chains us to the pain of the past, whether it be pain we caused to others, pain we caused to ourselves or pain which others caused to us. The past is gone, it is as we have seen just a fantasy, but if we cannot forgive it is a fantasy which binds us. The eminent Buddhist teacher and writer Jack Kornfield tells a story which is a perfect illustration. Two ex-POW's meet many years later and one asks the other whether he has yet forgiven their cruel captors. No, replies the other, he can never forgive what happened. Then, says the first man, they still have you captive, do they not?

We could say that forgiveness is a matter of letting go of emotion about the past. That emotion need not be anger – it could, for example, be guilt, embarrassment, shame, sorrow, exasperation, disgust, or despair – but anger is the typical and most common example. So there are two good reasons to embrace forgiveness as one of the skills of happiness. In the first place, without it we continually revisit the past pain in our minds, calling the event into our present memory and making the present share the unhappiness of the past. Secondly, we are angry in the present about what happened in the past and, as we have seen earlier, it is difficult if not impossible to be angry and happy at the same time. When we can forgive we can let go of the pain of the past and we can let go of our anger about it, both of which will increase our happiness and peace of mind.

This idea that forgiveness is letting go of anger and irritation about what has happened appears often in everyday speech. "Let it go", we say, when someone is obsessing about an insult or injury done to them which there is no prospect of putting right, or which could only be put right with effort disproportionate to the result or to the original harm. We all understand that letting go of such things is essential to our functioning in the world. If we did not do it we could become very bitter, angry people, troublesome to be with at best, maybe even unhinged and volatile. But the quicker we can let go of the emotions caused by petty insult and injury, the more able we will be to let go of emotions caused by more major hurts, and thus the sooner we can return to happiness.

Of course it can also be wonderful when we *receive* forgiveness. If a person we have harmed in some way can forgive us, it may help us to accept own sense of guilt or regret, deal with it and begin again trying to live a truly happy life. Religions recognise the importance of receiving forgiveness and most have institutions whereby a penitent can be forgiven or purified and can put down the burden of past actions. Maybe the person harmed is unable or still too angry to forgive, but if we believe, say, that God can forgive us or that we can in some other way be purified of guilt, we can at least begin to let go of our own regret. But being forgiven, like being loved, is an external circumstance, not a skill of the inner life. The *giving* of forgiveness on the other hand is a real skill. Forgiveness benefits the forgiver because the (for)giving frees the inner life from that needle of anger or hatred which spoils happiness. For this reason alone, forgiving makes sense even if the guilty person feels no remorse.

We have seen that against the habits of anger and hatred we can use the skills of compassion and kindness. The same techniques apply in forgiving, for even if their object lies in the past, the emotions we need to let go in order to forgive are in the present. Thus compassion is the way into forgiveness. With the weakening of anger and hatred we may be able to let go of the past incident and forgive. If we can, we will have freed ourselves from the past. This does not necessarily mean that we will be able, or even that it would be wise, to welcome the perpetrator(s) of past harm with open arms. They themselves might still be intent on more harm, for whatever reason. But just as you can recognise a shark and stay out of the water without being full of anger or hatred against sharks, so you can be cautious about new harm and still forgive someone, letting go of anger about the past. Whenever we can reach a point at which we can do this, it is a huge achievement and a great step forward for our own happiness.

If someone is intent on harming me, of course, it must be reasonable to do whatever I can to prevent the harm. Why would I accept that anyone should harm me if the harm is preventable? If the harm is in the past, however, prevention is not an issue, although restitution or recovery may be possible. But to abandon present peace of mind because of a past harm is simply not a good strategy. Anger and hatred are not compatible with peace of mind so they are not helpful habits. Developing forgiveness as a skill recognises this in respect of past hurts.

Forgiving and pardoning

It is worth noting that forgiving is not the same as deciding to take no action. Often we decide that there is no point in letting a past incident which hurt us stand in the way of being friends, or being pleasant to a family member – families are often where forgiveness is most needed. But this in itself is a decision about our external behaviour, not a letting go in our inner life. I will call this pardoning because it is a letting go of the insistence on punishment, revenge or even acknowledgement for the offence against us. It will often be a step along the road to forgiveness, but not necessarily. Forgiveness is about you and your inner life; pardoning is about your relationship with the person who has hurt you. Forgiveness is probably incomplete without pardoning, but pardoning can happen without forgiveness.

A friend whom I will call Tom told me about his father, who always seemed to undervalue him and let him down throughout his life. To take only one example, his father promised to help financially in Tom's business, but after Tom had taken risky decisions in reliance on this promise, his father refused to help. Tom in fact made himself successful after years of struggle, only for his father to decide that as Tom was now wealthy he could be excluded from the father's will. "But", said Tom through only slightly gritted teeth, "there's no point in falling out with the old man, I have forgiven him".

Now, I take my hat off to Tom, who made what must have been hard decisions to ignore so many let-downs and say nothing, to rise above them and neither expect his eighty-something father to change his ways nor to retaliate in any way. He pardoned his father. But did he, in truth, forgive? Did he let go of his own anger about all these past incidents and injuries? After listening to him tell the story, I think not. He was still angry, still disappointed and he had not yet managed to let go of these emotions. The memory of past incidents still troubled him although he bravely decided to do nothing about them. As a result, these negative emotions were still part of his inner life and still disturbed his peace of mind. Only when he could let go of his anger could he be said to have forgiven, and only then could he be free.

Fear

Fear is always fear of the future, of what is going to happen or might happen. No one fears the past; at worst they fear the consequences of the past. The present may have to be endured, but not feared.

We can understand, even if we are not yet skilful enough to pull it off, that if we absolutely knew we could meet anything and everything with peace in our inner lives, we would have no reason to fear anything. We would be able to cope with anything and, most importantly, we would **know** that we could cope, hence no need for fear. So the only reason for fear is that we are not ready for the future, in the sense of not being sufficiently prepared in our inner lives. The root of all fear is lack of confidence that we can deal inwardly with what will happen.

When people have prepared themselves according to their lights and beliefs, they can meet anything, even their own death, with peace and calm and without fear. I have seen it myself, and it is often reported by those who work with the dying: when people are ready, they can let go peacefully. At a more mundane level, we all know that if we have to exercise any skill or perform any task at work or at play, our anxiety is inversely proportional to our confidence that we can succeed. Think of taking an examination, going for interview, performing in public, even wiring a fuse. The more confident you are that a task is within your powers and capabilities, the less anxious you will be about the outcome. If you have full confidence in your skill, whatever the task and whatever the required skill, you will not be anxious. But happiness is also a matter of the exercise of skill, as we have seen, so the same principle will apply. The greater your confidence in your skills, in this case your inner life skills, the more confident you will be in facing any task and any eventuality without fear.

Thus, if your inner peace was firmly established and unshakeably supported by your skills, there would be nothing of which you would need to be afraid. Just as, for example, military training helps to reduce the natural fear experienced in combat, the ultimate antidote to fear generally is confidence in your inner training. This is an important and powerful story, for in this view the way to deal with fear is to train your inner life to be peaceful under all circumstances. All training of the inner life for inner peace and happiness is in itself training to eliminate fear. Knowing this, you know that there is a way to overcome fear and that if you practice to strengthen your inner skills you are on that way. You don't need to do something else. It doesn't of course follow that all fear will fall away immediately, but you can be confident at least that fear will diminish as you progress in your practice.

It is important to add that, even if you had perfect inner peace and confidence in your ability to maintain it, you might still feel fear on occasion. There is an aspect of fear which is instinctive, biological, something that happens to our bodies. So learning to deal with fear is not the same as never feeling fear, or as suppressing fear. It is about not being overwhelmed by fear, perhaps being able to say (or having the attitude), "Ah, yes, that's fear, I'm afraid", but still being able to remain calm and peaceful within, still retaining peace of mind.

Plans

If we were not so tied into outcomes, ambitions and plans we would have less anxiety and fear. We create a future in our minds and then get fearful and anxious if we think we might not bring it to pass, not to mention upset if we do not in fact bring it to pass. Or we imagine a future that we fear and get upset in case it comes to pass or when we fail to prevent it. If you are not concerned about, say, the outcome of a football match, you will not be anxious about the progress of the match or eager to know the result, but if you have some emotional investment it is very different. The same is true of many other events and particularly of our own schemes and plans. If we could be prepared to accept whatever outcome emerges and let the process unfold, we would have less anxiety, less fear, more peace.

But doesn't this turn us all into dropouts? Do we not bother to do anything, not even to prepare dinner, for example, because dinnertime lies in the future? No. It is not a question of not *having* plans or goals. It is rather a question of not being too *attached* to them so that if they do not turn out as we intend our peace of mind is not disturbed. Just as you don't have to do without possessions in order to practice non-attachment to possessions, you don't have to do without plans and ambitions in order to practice non-attachment to plans and ambitions. It is more a question of the attitude we adopt, a question of staying flexible, staying free. We have our preferences, of course, and one of them might be to have something for dinner, which requires action now. But as soon as we become attached to these preferences, start to invest emotion and desire in them, start to feel that our happiness depends on them, from that point they are in charge, they are running things. Our ambitions and plans are means to an end, and the assumption we make here is that the central underlying goal is to live a happy life. As soon as our other ambitions and plans conflict with that goal and begin to erode our peace of mind, they become hindrances, not helps.

For most of us this skill of non-attachment to plans is necessary because of the sheer complexity of the world and the impossibility of controlling everything. Because of complexity, even completely inevitable outcomes can seem random. Toss a coin. Heads or tails? It's random, is it not? In fact, tossing a coin is almost the archetype for what random means, at least in the macro, non-quantum world. If you had to explain the concept of randomness to someone who was completely unfamiliar with it, you might well start with a tossed coin by way of an explanation. But we know that the toss of a coin, like so many other seemingly random events, is at root a totally predictable event.

What makes the event seem random is of course that the precise data we would need to predict the outcome are not available and the calculations are too numerous to complete in the time the coin is spinning. There are too many variables and we can't work it out in time. Tossing a coin counts as a random event because we don't know the answer in advance, not because there is no answer. The same applies to much of our lives.

We spend a lot of time plotting and planning aspects of our lives, but we cannot in practice predict everything which happens; there are too many variables and we do not have the time or the skill to work everything out. So, many aspects of our external lives and even our inner lives might as well be random in something like the sense in which the fall of a tossed coin is random. There may indeed be order behind everything, just as simple mechanics governs the tossing of a coin. We might even believe there is a purpose or a plan. But if we don't know the details, it is just the same for us *as if* we lived in a world of complete uncertainty and chance. This doesn't mean that nothing is predictable or that there are never events which are more likely to happen than others, if only because we often do know some of the details, but it does mean that there is always a large element of uncertainty. If we want to live happily, we cannot ignore this very basic fact about the world in which we live.

Applying this to the question of plans and ambitions, we can see that it may make sense to plan but it does not make sense to stake our peace of mind on our plans. Uncertainty generates anxiety and fear in us because we are greatly attached to some outcomes and greatly averse to others. The more we can accept uncertainty and the less we are attached to our plans, the less vulnerable is our peace of mind.

Chapter 15:
The practice of letting go

Letting go in practice

Letting go is a key skill, but one of the most difficult skills to master, especially for those of us brought up in a self-assertive culture. It is hard enough to let go of external attachments – smoking, puddings, drinks, certain people, chocolate, favourite TV programmes, places we like to visit or just things we like to do – even when we know the habit is not good for us. The immediate satisfaction or release from need is stronger than the knowledge that we might be better off in the long run if we didn't do it or consume it or seek it.

With the inner life, letting go is certainly no easier than with our external habits. In fact, the very first step is often more difficult just because we are not aware of precisely what it is we need to let go, or even that we need to let something go. People with serious external addictions are often unable to see that it is the addiction which is the cause of other problems in their lives. We all suffer the same kind of blindness when it comes to our inner habits.

I find the following four "rules of thumb" helpful in the process and practice of letting go. They are intended just to give some structure to the process, a mechanism to use or a checklist to follow. You will not always need all four, but when a problem seems difficult or even intractable it helps to have a familiar pattern to apply.

Rule 1: Yes, you definitely need to let go

If your inner life is not peaceful and serene it is a very good rule of thumb that there is something of which you need to let go. Accepting that this is so is the first step towards helping you to identify the problem. Sometimes you will be able to see immediately what it is. But acceptance that there is something to let go will at least mean that you are on the lookout for what it might be.

This does not mean that you are always "in the wrong" – that if there is a problem it is your fault. You need to let go of something to restore your inner peace, but that does not mean that the problem is of your making. It might be, it might not be. Someone or something else may be a major or even *the* major cause of the difficulty, at least as far as the external circumstances are concerned. Thus, acknowledging that you need to let go is not about the rights and wrongs of the external situation. "Yes, but..." is not a helpful story. Instead, you could have a choice as to how to react to the external situation and in particular a choice as to how it might affect your happiness or inner peace. External problems are there to be solved if you can or endured if you can't, as the saint said. The first rule is a reminder that if your peace of mind is disturbed, the best and most potent remedy lies in your own inner life, your own habit basis. Focus your attention there and, however serious the external problem, do not be distracted into thinking that the problem is just an external one. Not every problem even has an external aspect, but every problem has an inner life aspect.

In many cases it goes very much against the grain to see a problem as an indication that there is something we need to let go. There are, for example, instances in all our lives when someone else wrongs us in some way. Worse still, for many people, is to witness injustice to others who are helpless. Why should the perpetrators get away with it, we ask ourselves, isn't justice important? Shouldn't we stand up for ourselves or the helpless, are we just going to take it lying down, be a doormat, let the perpetrators walk all over us? And so on. Thus we justify clinging to the very thing which is making us unhappy, very often our anger or outrage, in the name of an ideal like justice or self-assertion.

Justice and self-assertion, though, are about what happens in the external world. If we feel that an external situation is unjust, we might decide to fight and change it. But as we saw earlier, in real life as opposed to fiction strong emotions do not always aid clear thinking and good tactics, or lead to the best outcome. More importantly, if happiness is our primary aim, our first objective is surely to calm the inner turmoil and restore peace of mind. Then, if we still feel that genuine injustice exists and needs to be fought, we can do so from a calm centre and without negative emotions. Perhaps this means that we will find fewer opportunities to fight because some of the cases we might have regarded as injustice were actually about, say, injured pride. But putting inner peace first does not mean that injustice is to be tolerated, only that the unjust act is not to be allowed to dictate the conditions of your inner life. Would not such dictation be a double victory for the perpetrator?

The example of professional contestants shows us that fighting to right an injustice does not need strong negative emotions to succeed. A lawyer may fight injustices as a matter of professional choice, but she does not need to get caught up in hatred or anger against her opponents. In fact, to do so would make the profession impossible. It is an important practice to separate the external action and the inner reaction. It is also important not to use negative emotions to drive even positive actions, because to do so strengthens the negative habit and leads to further unhappiness.

Rule 2: Observe and respect

When you think you may have spotted the problem habit or attachment, just observe it for a while. Learn about this habit, see how it arises, what it feels like, what course it takes. One reason for doing this is that the habit you have identified may not be the real issue at all; it may be a side-show or even a scapegoat. But even if you are right you will have more chance of success the more you know about your "adversary". Look closely, take your time and get to know this habit or attachment which is disturbing your peace of mind. This is an important step but one many people miss out.

It is unlikely that you have any habits which are there simply to make your life difficult. Not many of us like to consume dangerous doses of poisons or jump from heights without parachutes, for example. We simply don't acquire habits which are that unhelpful, if only because we don't survive them! Although these are examples of external habits, the same point applies to habits of the inner life. If there is a habit of which you need to let go, it probably has some use to you, or had some use to you at some time. Perhaps it protects or did protect you in some way, perhaps it gives or gave you pleasure, perhaps it is even useful in some contexts but not in others. In the complexity of the inner life, even habits get confused sometimes! Something needs to be done about this habit or attachment, it seems, but it is not an enemy; it is operating for a reason. Observe the habit with respect and try to find out what benefit it is trying to give you and perhaps how it goes wrong. Then perhaps you can redesign it so that you can maintain that benefit yet also retain your peace of mind.

Do not be in too much of a hurry to force yourself in a different direction. You probably won't succeed anyway until you understand how the problem arises and how it works. Be patient and observe. You may well find that this activity helps to ease whatever problem you had anyway, because you know that you are on the road to sorting it out. But keep observing, because the problem may not have been solved completely and is likely to recur when external circumstances trigger it.

You cannot assume, incidentally, that the history of this habit and how you came to acquire it is the crucial issue or the key to understanding. Sometimes it may be, but often it will not be – why it operates in some instances but not others may, for example, be more relevant. You have a habit now which is unhelpful to your peace of mind and it is important to find out about it. But if you get lost in the archaeology of the problem habit you may miss other aspects which are more useful to you.

Rule 3: Objectify

Remember that it's not bad or a failing on your part to have unhelpful habits. It's just unhelpful, but in the hurly-burly of our lives it is very difficult not to acquire some unhelpful habits and you are by no means alone. An excellent way to make things worse is to blame yourself (or even someone else, parents being favourite) for the unhelpful habits you are saddled with. Having started on blame you then have that emotion to deal with as well as the original problem! Hence a good rule of thumb is to objectify the habit you have identified. Instead of saying "This is what I do", say "This is what happens", which is a more accurate story anyway as far as inner life habits are concerned.

By making this shift you remove or at least weaken the temptation to identify with the difficulty or see it as an aspect of your "nature". If you identify, you may be tempted to blame or excuse yourself, or see the only way forward as "changing yourself", a far more serious-sounding proposition than merely changing a habit. Your inner habits are very often not under your conscious control anyway; that's why they are called habits. You can become aware of them and then you can consider how to weaken or change them, but you cannot just stop them from operating by a simple act of will (whatever that is). You may have done things in the past which strengthened the habit in question – so may others whom you would like to blame – but the point now is to get rid of this disturbance to your inner life, not to dredge up the past. When you objectify the habit you make it much easier to let go without blame. It's not working so you fix it; there's nothing personal about it.

Rule 4: No one said it would be easy

Letting go is rarely an easy thing to do. It is usually easier to find excuses, easier to stay with the familiar. Letting go may take years to do, convincing yourself and re-convincing yourself that this particular habit or attachment really is an obstacle for your peace of mind. Everyone has relapses – ever been on a diet or tried to give up something you enjoyed, whether it was smoking for good or chocolate for Lent? And those were external attachments, much less subtle and even less tenacious than some inner attachments.

You may need to build up another skill before you can let go of a particular habit or attachment, so the process of letting go may be indirect at first. You know there is a problem and you keep an eye on it but you are not skilled enough to let go all at once. If the problem is one of belief, for example, story skills may help to show that there are alternatives to this belief, other perspectives. Ask yourself, "How do you know?" relentlessly. Could you be mistaken, are there other interpretations which fit the evidence, what is the evidence anyway? If the problem is one of fear, building up skill and with it confidence is generally the answer, but not a quick one. If the problem is regret or something else to do with the past, forgiveness is probably the key but it can take a lot of work. With anger, hate, dislike, resentment the benevolence skills are needed. And so on. Letting go may be a process of erosion rather than a dramatic gesture.

It often happens of course that an unhelpful habit has a pleasurable side, and this can be a real problem! If a peaceful inner life is your main goal and your central objective, however, anything which stands in the way, even pleasure, is an obstacle. Only you can decide in the end what is an obstacle and what is not, but if there is something you feel you cannot do without, there is already a potential problem. Letting go is not necessarily a question of austerity, however. A "portfolio" approach to pleasures, cultivating many pleasures so that no single pleasure dominates and any one pleasure could be given up without a great sense of loss, is one way of approaching non-attachment without austerity. It is a good practice to remind yourself that everything has to be let go sooner or later and that all attachment is therefore a potential source of anxiety and eventually of distress. But specific attachments have a way of creeping in under our guard. The political slogan "The price of freedom is eternal vigilance" was coined in a Cold War context but – a wonderful irony if you enjoy such things! – it perfectly sums up the situation we all face with our inner lives and specifically with our attachments.

Renunciation

Renunciation is an important way of practising non-attachment. Letting go of "worldly things" is indeed a theme of most of the world's faith traditions. In the name of faith people often renounce relationships, activities, homes, possessions and pleasures, adopting instead some degree of austerity. Sometimes what is given up is something unhelpful to health anyway, like alcohol or tobacco or certain foods. But sometimes the renunciation is more radical. So we have monks and nuns, anchorites and hermits, cave-dwelling yogis, wandering Sufis, Zen vagabonds, and so on. Part of the idea is simply dedication to the spiritual life. Getting and spending take up so much time and energy that they do indeed lay waste our days and the ambitious spiritual achiever has no time to spare. But part of the idea is also, to varying degrees, that the pleasures of the world may be an outright hindrance to spiritual progress.

In some cases, then, renunciation depends on beliefs about the relationship of the material world to a supernatural realm. But renunciation may also reflect that happiness is not solely or even mainly a matter of externals but of the inner life. No amount of external benefit will in itself guarantee happiness if the inner life is troubled, as we have agreed, and spiritual seekers have always recognised this. Having said this, inner lives being equal, a degree of external comfort may surely be more conducive to happiness than external distress so an emphasis on the inner life does not *by itself* recommend severe renunciation or austerity.

To understand the value of renunciation independently of any system of supernatural belief, we have to go back to the useful ideas of process and transience. Whatever external comforts we have today, whether in the form of our own good health and vigour, our relationships with others, material goods, status and recognition, or just warmth and a full stomach, we know that they will change as time goes by. If I know that the externals and even the current inner life states I experience are transitory and subject to change, I must be able to do without them, otherwise I am vulnerable to such change. "I am wealthy" – but I could become poor, it happens all the time, so let me not base my happiness solely on my wealth. "I am successful" – then let me enjoy it, by all means, but not depend on it for my peace of mind because things could change overnight. "I am beautiful" – ditto. "I am strong, or tough, or feared" – until I get older or someone stronger appears, as they will one day. "I am in love and nothing can ever change that!" – how wonderful, be mindful of such a sublime feeling, but there are circumstances in which such a feeling will turn to pain, even if you don't want to think about them. "I can achieve blissful states of meditation" – but what happens when you are disturbed or when your external circumstances make it difficult to reach that state? This is, of course, an exercise in non-attachment, the skill of not depending on circumstances being as you would wish them to be.

We can thus see renunciation as a way of furthering as well as testing our progress in non-attachment. If I can voluntarily do without something, then I could cope if I *had* to do without it. I can practice doing without to discover or show myself how much I depend on it and to train myself for its passing. So renunciation can be seen not as austerity for its own sake, nor as a form of negativity towards the blessings which life may bring, but simply as a way of practising and testing non-attachment.

This works perfectly well even if the renunciation is partial or temporary. Many faith traditions practice temporary renunciation in the form of fasting or abstinence from certain pleasures at certain times, such as during Ramadan or Lent. But even from a secular point of view such defined periods of renunciation are excellent practices which strengthen the skill of non-attachment. Permanently to deny ourselves something available and harmless which brings us pleasure and happiness might be considered perverse. But to remind ourselves by a temporary pause that enjoying it may not be a permanent blessing is simultaneously a guard against complacency, a reminder of our good fortune and a practice for letting go when the time comes.

Letting go of possessions

Attachment to possessions is one of the curses of this and perhaps of any age. As we have seen, to let go of all possessions and voluntarily embrace poverty or asceticism is a path with a strong and distinguished history, but it is unlikely to be practical or possible for most of us. There is much that we can do nevertheless to weaken the hold our possessions have over us. One of the simplest practices is to get rid of clutter, to throw – or better, give – away the things we no longer need. This simple practice has been advocated for many reasons but we can see it as a practice in the skill of letting go. Start gently: how many of your cupboards and wardrobes contain things and clothes you haven't used or worn for, say, two years? Is this because you only need them for special occasions which haven't arisen, or just because you haven't got round to disposing of them? If the latter, do it now! Get rid of them, let them go! Be as creative as you can in disposing of them, by all means, but don't let waiting for the perfect recipient stop you from letting them go. You will feel better, your house will be less cluttered and perhaps the things you do not use will find a use again with someone else.

If you wanted to take this practice a step further, perhaps there are things you do use, maybe even things you like, which would benefit someone else more than they benefit you. Perhaps you could part with one or two of them? Thus a practice in letting things go because their useful time with you has passed shades into a practice in generosity. But both are aspects of letting go. Take this to a reasonable conclusion and we arrive at the idea of "downsizing" – which amounts to the realisation that the most complicated and opulent lifestyle you can achieve is not necessarily the optimal one for you when you take into account the hours of work and the stresses of sustaining it. More is not necessarily better and less is not necessarily worse; it depends on which makes it easier for you to be happy, which means the effect each option produces on your inner life. And if your inner life demands more and more possessions, is this a good strategy for becoming happier and happier?

The same line of reasoning could be applied to a particular if ephemeral class of possessions, our food. We hear and read much these days about how western populations are suffering from obesity. Some of this has to do with the kinds of food we eat and some has to do with the lack of physical activity our lives require compared with the much harder lives of our ancestors. But one possible cause is that we just eat too much. There may be cases in which food, or particular types of food, become an addiction requiring special assistance to let go. But many of us eat more because we like it and we can. We might simply have become more attached to food and eating than is good for us. To adopt more discipline in this area could be a good practice in letting go or non-attachment at the same time as being good for our health. This is not to advocate ascetic eating habits, just a degree of moderation, or perhaps the adoption of occasional deliberate abstentions, like missing dinner now and again, using the additional motivation of knowing that this is a part of a general programme of training the habit basis. Such practices in relation to food are a common part of many religions, as we saw earlier. But look, this is only a suggestion. As with all practices and techniques, there is no need to feel (and no point in feeling) guilt if this practice in letting go does not suit you.

Perhaps the darkest aspect of consumerism is envy, attachment to or desire for things other people have, sometimes even because other people have them. One of the many advantages of learning non-attachment is that it frees us from this particular curse, which unchecked can cause great misery even to those who otherwise might be considered fortunate. If we can persuade ourselves of the truth that our happiness is not a matter of what we possess or what we consume, then there is no reason to be envious of anyone. If our happiness does not depend on our possessions, still less does it depend on having the same possessions as someone else. Anyway, we never see the whole picture of another person's life. They may have material plenty, but is there really nothing in their lives they struggle with? Everyone has difficulties, everyone has something which no one would envy. And whatever they do have will fade or be stolen or go out of fashion and in the end will be left behind for others to enjoy. Ownership is always a very temporary thing: it ends when you do, if not before. But perhaps the best story to tell yourself to combat envy when you recognise it in yourself is that envy changes nothing in the external world. Its sole effect is on your inner life, and that effect is to rob you of your happiness.

Letting go of image

Even the most insouciant among us spends much time and effort on the image presented to the outside world. Whether we want to impress, to shock or just to fit in, we are rarely indifferent to the image we project, although we often project an image different from the one we hope for. Probably this image desire we have is so deeply laid that we will struggle to get rid of it entirely, and indeed we could hardly function in society without our appearance and behaviour giving messages to others. But that is no reason to be unaware of what we are doing. We may also become aware that we are deeply attached to what other people think of us and how they receive our image. In extreme cases, but perhaps more often than we would like to admit, we can become trapped in creating or maintaining such perceptions, more and more attached to being thought of in a certain way and to the clothes, accessories and props, attitudes, opinions and behaviour which sustain our image. So firmly can this fantasy – for it is a story, however comfortable we feel in it – take hold of us that it becomes our world. Our happiness comes to depend on this image, on our being who we project ourselves to be, on our being taken for who we would like to be – rather like, say, a politician who creates and then becomes trapped by his own myth.

So much social interaction depends on the shorthand of dress and image that it would be foolish for any individual to dispense altogether with such things – indeed, to do so would involve deliberately projecting a particular image of unconventionality. But attachment to an image is a different matter. Not only does it tie our happiness to a set of external circumstances, particularly the reactions of other people, but it reduces the flexibility we have in dealing with life and its variety. We become stuck in one story and have difficulty in generating "also's" even when the story does not serve us. Circumstances may force us to abandon our central story or swallow painfully conflicting stories. We see this in parents whose children adopt lifestyles the parents cannot comprehend; in people who define themselves by their prejudice against certain groups only to find that a loved one has joined such a group; in disciples who are betrayed by their teacher. Attachment to image is an attachment no less dangerous and subject to disruption than attachment to material goods. Both are delusions when we come to believe that our happiness depends upon them.

Letting go of the menu

Have you ever looked at the menu in a particularly good restaurant and had trouble deciding what you want because it all looks so good? It can be hard to make a choice because choosing one dish means refusing all the others. In extreme cases, choosing feels more like depriving yourself of the things you haven't chosen than like giving yourself the pleasure of what you chose! It is one example of the difficulty of dealing with uncertainty, which I will call the menu problem after this illustration.

This example is by any standards a "high quality problem" – if all your problems were like this you might think your life would be pleasant indeed. But it is a trivial example of a type of problem which can cause great problems for peace of mind. We are so anxious to optimise, to squeeze the most out of every opportunity and experience, that we become permanently dissatisfied even in the midst of plenty. At the worst, we can become unable to make a decision and stick to it because "the grass always seems greener" somewhere else – whether it's food, holidays, pastimes, clothes or even work and partners. It can even happen with ideas and practice.

We often have to make choices in conditions of uncertainty or with a limited amount of information, so some of the time the choices we eventually make are bound to be less than the best. When we get things seriously wrong it makes sense to try again, of course, but to be obsessed with getting each such decision optimal is a poor strategy. We end up wanting to try all the options before making a decision, which is costly and fattening in restaurants and even more damaging when applied to major life choices like houses, jobs and partners. The menu problem is a form of what by now is a familiar mistake, namely that we equate happiness with external conditions instead of with the condition of the inner life. Choosing to be happy with the choice we make is a better strategy than insisting that the choice we make should make us happy. Once the moment for choice has passed, wondering about the menu simply distracts us from the present and from the enjoyment to be had from it. It makes more sense just to let go of the menu and concentrate on what happens next.

Thus the menu problem illuminates a general problem, even if few of us actually ruin a visit to a restaurant by acute indecision. Whether we worry about the decisions we have made or simply about how things will turn out for us, we find it difficult to live with uncertainty. The menu problem shows us that such worry is misplaced. If our inner lives are practised and primed to be happy under any circumstances, the outcome of external choices or happenings is not the main event. Certainly it will be easier, we will be less tested, if external things turn out to be wonderful. But whatever the externals are like, our happiness depends on our inner life. Once we really understand this, we can see that uncertainty does not matter because all outcomes are potentially happy ones. Thus our lives are like really good restaurants, if we could only see it. All the dishes taste wonderful!

Enjoyment

Finally we come to enjoyment skills, not only essential for living happily but also to help us sustain long-term practice to achieve and maintain happiness. Broadly, if you don't get enjoyment from practice, you are unlikely to keep going. But also, if you don't enjoy life as each moment passes, when are you going to enjoy it?

A very successful management consultant was on holiday in a tropical resort. As he lay on the beach, he watched the local fishermen bring in their small boats each morning and sell their catch to an always-eager crowd. Then the fishermen would do a little tidying of nets and craft and disappear around noon. After a few days the consultant grew curious and wandered over to one of the fishermen, bought a fish he didn't really need and started a conversation. First he asked how the man was planning to spend the rest of the day.

"Well, it's the same most days. I go home and have some fish for lunch. Then I have a siesta with my wife – you know how it is! Then in the evening we go for a walk along the beach, have dinner, and then I go to see my friends, maybe we have a few beers, tell stories, we sing, maybe there is a fiesta and our wives like to dance. It depends. And next morning I get up and go fishing."

The consultant quickly grasped that the fisherman fished for only four to five hours each day. He explained that in his own country he, the consultant, advised people how to get rich and offered to help the fisherman for nothing, if he wanted. The fisherman was happy to listen.

"First of all, after you have sold your catch, take the boat out again in the afternoon. That way, you can double your catch and make twice as much money."

"That's fine, but it won't make me rich", said the fisherman.

"It's only a beginning", said the consultant. "You save the extra money you make, and in a year or two you will have enough to buy a second boat. Then you will be taking four times as much fish as now, so a third boat will come even quicker. After fifteen, twenty years of working really hard you will have a whole fleet. Then you could sell out, if you want, and retire a rich man."

"That's wonderful, sir, but then what would I do?"

"Anything you want. For example, you might still want to do a little fishing in the morning, but for pleasure. Then you could have lunch, maybe spend a little time with your wife in the afternoon. Then in the evening you would be free to, well, perhaps have a few drinks with your friends, talk about the old days, go dancing...."

The four skill sets we have already discussed are good for more than combating negative habits, and the more they are developed the more pleasure and positive value can be found in them. But for most of us there will be a fair bit of work to be done in order to "eliminate the negative". The enjoyment skills focus directly on the happiness to be found in our lives already, even in the everyday and the mundane. To the extent that we may have unhelpful habits which blind us to the positive potential of the present moment, the enjoyment skills will help to weaken such unhelpful habits. So enjoyment skills do not differ in principle from the previous four sets, but they can be seen as much more focused on the injunction to "accentuate the positive".

Carpe diem

Sometimes we deliberately choose to forego immediate gratification, as when we save our money, diet to look good on holiday, go to the gym instead of relaxing (assuming you don't enjoy exercise for its own sake!), or donate time or effort to a good cause. Such calculated self-denial generally means that we postpone pleasure now for more pleasure later, or that we substitute a pleasure of one kind for a pleasure of another. However, this is a clear demonstration that pleasure and happiness are not the same thing, for the calculation which allows us to postpone or exchange pleasures does not work for happiness.

If we choose to forego our pleasure we must be happy to make the choice. If, for example, I give some money I intended to spend on myself to someone else, I must surely be happy to do so. My assessment of the benefit to the other person plus my pleasure in giving must somehow outweigh for me the pleasure of spending. So I have foregone pleasure or benefit but not happiness. Again, if I save rather than spend, I must presumably believe that this is in some way better for me in the long run and thus I must be happy with the decision. Saving postpones pleasure but makes me happy in the present. If not, then surely I am acting irrationally.

Thus pleasure postponed or discomfort undertaken (dieting or going to the gym) for a future benefit has a rationale, but happiness postponed is generally happiness lost. A happy life is made up of happy moments and each moment when its time comes is in this respect as precious as every other. So it is important to accustom ourselves to finding happiness in each moment and not to postpone happiness to some hoped-for future. As we have seen, this does not mean that everything in our external environment has to meet our most perfect fantasy at each instant. If this were the requirement, happiness would be impossible for most of the people most of the time. Happiness in each moment is rather a question of the state of the inner life and the inner skills we can deploy, which means the state of the habit basis. To live in joy is the end product of an art, based on skills we can practice.

Acceptance

At this moment – as indeed at every other moment – circumstances are just as they are, however much I might like them to be otherwise. If my external circumstances are not good (which could mean they are dreadful by any standards or it could simply mean they are not to my liking), I can perhaps take steps now so they get better soon. Or perhaps there is nothing that I can do and I must wait for things to change in their own time or through someone else's action. But if I am to be happy right now, these present unfavourable circumstances form the context in which I have to do it. Unless I am practised in the skill of accepting the circumstances of the present moment I must resign myself to being unhappy quite a lot of the time, even if I am good at changing things.

Equanimity or acceptance is thus the skill of inwardly acquiescing in the present moment and all it contains. It is not at all the same thing as indifference. The distinction here is very similar to the distinction we made between non-attachment and detachment. Perhaps, for example, you prefer your coffee with no sugar, but when visiting someone's home you are given a cup of sweetened coffee. Whether you explain your preference might of course depend on the circumstances – whether your host will be embarrassed, how easy it might be to rectify th\e situation, how much you want the coffee anyway. You might say something or you might not, but you are not indifferent, you know what you prefer. You would, however, be in a sorry state if the proffering of sweet coffee were able to upset you and disturb your mood. (We could imagine circumstances which would complicate matters, of course, but we won't!) Most of us take such things in our stride, they do not matter enough to ruffle us. We are not indifferent, but we can accept them. Acceptance is the skill with which we deal in our inner lives with adverse circumstances: how we allow them to affect our inner lives.

As we saw earlier, we constantly make ourselves unhappy by desiring that the world should be other than it is. And there is no denying that it would be pleasant if the world in general were other than it is – less cruelty, less war, less greed, less violence, less poverty, and so on. If we can change the world in some way, why not do it? But the world will still be imperfect. This is not to suggest that we should be passive in the face of evil or suffering, but one of the points about acceptance is to realise that these things exist and always will, so that our battles with them are part of a process. Furthermore, whatever exists today or at this moment is what we have to deal with. To want things to be different at this moment is understandable but in itself futile and unhelpful, like the tantrum of a little child who cannot wait for a promised treat. So we have to begin with acceptance of what there is today. From that point we can perhaps do something now to bring about change in the future. Things will change anyway but our action may be a needed part of the process of change, or may helpfully accelerate what might otherwise be a glacially slow process. Acceptance is no excuse for inaction, but neither is action an excuse for compromising our inner lives.

We also need to accept the circumstances of our own inner lives. Often we may be tempted to condemn our own inner reactions, becoming impatient, cross or even disgusted with ourselves for being as we are and reacting as we do. Indeed, the more we set our sights on training our inner lives, the more we might fall prey to this critical tendency. But your habits at any given time are as they are. Your habit basis is the product of processes stretching back in time even beyond your birth. If you can realise that some of these habits do not serve you and you can set about changing them, excellent. But the process of training can be prolonged and sometimes difficult. Training yourself often just consists of making mistakes, recognising them and trying again. Once you can accept this process and realise that you will improve your life steadily if you train yourself, the whole thing gets easier. But try not to become impatient about being at whatever point you have reached in this process of training or upset yourself because you are not already at the end of the process.

Obviously the skill of acceptance is of immense value in dealing with adverse circumstances, whether external or internal. Some of the great spiritual figures of history show this skill to an astonishing degree to which most of us will never come close. But again, more skill is always better than less skill. Practice, mindful application to the task, will inevitably improve anyone's ability to accept and not be disturbed by difficulties.

Less obviously, acceptance helps to us keep perspective when things are going well, for this is when many people come unstuck. If I achieve some success, be it in my career, relationships, even in my practice, my opinion of myself can easily become very high indeed. What a gifted, splendid person I must be to have achieved so much / acquired so much / be so famous / be so rich / have such insight! Perhaps such a gifted person has no need of further practice; perhaps I have already "cracked it"....

Well, perhaps. But just as likely, I am enjoying a streak of good fortune which is blessing my efforts with success at the moment, whereas the same level of effort and ability might have faced external problems which thwarted me, through no fault of mine. My happiness does not depend on this good fortune, any more than I should allow myself to be discouraged and depressed by difficulties. It is not that the success should not be enjoyed and savoured – of course it should: why not taste the sweetness of life when it shows itself? But I would do well to remember how contingent and how temporary this success might be and how, most importantly, my true happiness is still a function of how my inner life deals with whatever comes my way. Then I can stay focused. I can enjoy the present without losing sight of the need to be prepared for changes in circumstances. I can savour success, yet not get carried away with my own importance in the equation. I can suffer a setback, if that's what happens next, without being broken by the loss. Success is always, always temporary. Sometimes people say when they have achieved something, "No one can take that away from me". Perhaps no one can, but time already has. Even the richest and most powerful have to suffer loss, become ill or old or both and then die; their happiness, like yours and mine, lies not in what happens but in how they deal inwardly with it. So if you can win the glittering prizes and it pleases you to do so, then go ahead, but do not confuse winning with happiness. This is part of the skill of acceptance, the other side of the coin of dealing with difficulties, not indifference to your own fate nor to anyone else's, but genuine equanimity.

Moods

Happiness or inner peace is not the same as relentless cheerfulness. Just as the external life is full of ups and downs, so too the inner life has its tides and moods. Perhaps there is a quantity of practice which confers immunity from (say) waking up feeling just a bit out of sorts, but frankly I doubt we can become immune to our "inner weather" in this way. It is not even clear that we would want to. What we can seek to change by practice is the impact such changes and colours of mood have on us. If I am grumpy, for example, then I view the whole world through a grumpy filter. I am easily annoyed, my patience is short, I want to be left alone (but not of course to be left out!) and even those I love and whose company normally gives me delight seem determined to upset me. But if I can recognise that I am grumpy, I may be able to make allowances for the distortions in my emotional perception. I can at least avoid getting locked into a story about how everyone else is being irritating today. I can see, if I have made myself good at this, that "there is grumpiness going on". And I can either make allowances for the fact that I am receiving all data through this filter, or just retreat until the world looks normal again.

Inner skills do make a person generally more cheerful, both in their inner life and in their outward demeanour. Happiness, in our sense of inner peace, tends to make a person more cheerful because fewer external circumstances disturb and upset. But equanimity does not mean that we become immune to changes of mood. Whatever we do not control we have to learn to deal with, or it will control us and our happiness. Just as we can recognise that external circumstances are contingent and transient, that we cannot always arrange them to our liking and should not therefore depend on them for our happiness, so too there are moods and conditions of the inner life which are contingent and transient and we do not control them. We saw in discussing thought and mindfulness that there is much that flits into consciousness over which we have no obvious control. It is not possible to suppress such thought processes, so if they disturb our inner peace we have to find other ways of dealing with them. The same applies to moods. We have little choice but to accept our moods and deal with them; we cannot hope to control them because they are not voluntary or chosen in the first place. If we can become aware of our moods and the effect they have on our perceptions and interpretations of the world and other people, we can perhaps make allowances for them. Or we can just recognise them and avoid doing anything – taking important decisions, say, or reacting to the behaviour of others – which we know is likely to be affected by our temporarily distorted view of the world. Perhaps we can use one of the skills to change our outlook, tell ourselves a different story, let go of our disappointment or forgive a slight. If not, we can recognise that this is a mood or a feeling which will pass, like the rain, but which we may have to accept while it is with us. To change the metaphor, moods are like uninvited guests passing through our inner lives. If sadness is passing through, this is perfectly natural and there is no need to suppress it. But we can be careful not to feed it, either.

This accepting attitude to mood helps to explain one of the seeming paradoxes of developing the skills of the inner life as a route to happiness. We control the external world only to a limited degree, but we control our inner lives only to a limited degree, as well. In both spheres, we can sometimes directly change what we do not like and we can sometimes influence change, but we often have to wait for change to happen. Developing useful habits is one of the ways we can create change in and exercise influence over our inner lives, but that does not mean we can choose our thoughts and dreams and moods from moment to moment, any more than we can control the weather or the actions of governments. As we create change in our inner lives, we might expect more happiness, more of the time. And we will get it, make no mistake. We will become more skilful at dealing with external problems and we will become more skilful at dealing with inner problems as well, retaining our inner peace or recovering it more quickly in each case. But just as external conditions will continue to test us, our inner lives will throw up difficulties from time to time, as well. This is not a failure on our part and it is not a failure of training. It just happens, like inner weather.

At the risk of compounding (confounding?) metaphors about mood, they might be thought of as sea waves. The surface changes with the light and the wind and tide. Sometimes the waves seem angry, sometimes powerful, sometimes gentle or playful. Of course these are our projections; the sea is just the sea, just water reacting to the forces acting on it. The sea seems to change character, but we know that it remains the same massive body of water and that the change is a temporary and superficial effect. In your own inner life, moods come and go, you might be sad or cheerful, but these too are surface effects, reactions to whatever forces are operating. They will arise and they will pass, but if you are skilful you can remain calm underneath it all, remembering that these are just temporary effects. As you become more skilful, such swings will happen less, just because less disturbs you. People who have worked hard on their inner lives are usually of a calm and cheerful disposition. But if moods happen, they happen. They have to be accepted like external circumstances or distracting thoughts because you cannot do otherwise.

Another way to think about moods (another story which might help) is that they are fluctuations of your inner peace around the average – the average level which is usual for you, that is. If by your training and practice you gradually make yourself happier, the fluctuations occur against a rising trend, a gradually-increasing average level of inner peace over time. Such an effect will not be obvious on a day-to-day basis, but over longer periods you will observe that even your down days are "less down" than they used to be, and that your happiness generally is greater. Again, it's like learning any game of skill. If you practise and improve it does not follow that every day you will be better than the preceding day; you will still have good days and bad days. But you will nevertheless get better over time, so that after a year, say, you will be able to see clearly that even on your off days you are better than you used to be on your good days. Training in the skills of happiness may not make you immune to fluctuations in the exercise of your skills, but the upward trend in your skill levels and therefore your happiness will be obvious over time.

Patience

Patience, the ability to wait without irritation, is a most useful skill and a first cousin to acceptance or equanimity. Its essence is to enable us to enjoy what is happening even when nothing much is happening, or when what is happening now is keeping us from what we see as the main event. Patience seeks to treat each moment as a source of enjoyment even when the processes going on around and within us are unpleasant or dull.

The great thing about patience is the frequency and scale of the opportunities which modern life offers for its practice! Waiting for train or tube or bus, standing in a queue at the supermarket or anywhere else, waiting for loved ones to get ready, playing the same game yet again for a small child, repeating the mundane tasks of the day every day – the list is long. Patience is a matter of focusing on the joy available in what I am doing, not on the joy I think I am missing in what I could be doing instead or would prefer to be doing. A helpful prompt is thus the question: "What enjoyment can I find in this activity, in this place, now?" Of course the first, irritable response is likely to be, "Absolutely none!" My instinct, my habit may be to get irritated, to fume, to think about how much of my time is being wasted, to regret not being able to get on with whatever else I could be doing. You must have done it at some time. With a little creativity you can come to blame the other people in the queue or the management of the shop, the trains, the highways or the airline for all your unfinished work, for being late for an appointment, for missing the next showing of that film you wanted to see, in fact for all the troubles of your life. If you are really irritated, you might even flirt with the idea that these people are conspiring to slow things down, they're doing it on purpose!

But this too is a moment when I might have a choice about how to react inwardly, if habit had not got there first. Of course I can fume, but it doesn't make the wait any the less. And does it make me happy? Probably not. So why not use the time to concentrate on being happy, since that is what I would prefer to be doing? I do not control the external circumstances for now, so let me concentrate on what we know to be a better plan anyway – let me pay attention to my inner life. Well, what is there to enjoy, what can I find? Externally, probably quite a lot, once the focus of my attention is shifted. Is the surrounding environment really so unpleasant, are my companions or fellow sufferers really such monsters? I could focus on my own stressed body, note how shallow my breathing is in my irritation, perhaps I could breathe more deeply and slowly, perhaps I could become more aware of my breath entering and leaving my body, enjoy the usually unnoticed but pleasant sensations of breathing. I could play a game: find one beautiful, one funny, one touching thing in my surroundings. Or maybe just detach myself enough to notice, consciously to notice rather than be swept away by, my own irritation and maybe manage to smile at myself for my foolishness in getting upset about what I cannot change anyway.

Like all the inner skills we can develop, patience practised in small things and mundane circumstances will stand us in good stead when we are really challenged. It is after all one thing to endure when habit is petulantly crying out: "This is a waste of my time!" It is another matter if the events which challenge our patience are, say, delays which cause pain or even threaten our lives or our loved ones, like being on a hospital waiting list. Or perhaps the circumstances are even worse: imagine the patience required of famine victims, refugees, or the victims of natural disasters. But these cases are not different in kind, only in degree; the skill of patience is in essence the same. The people enduring these terrible circumstances offer us a master class in patience, but constant practice among the minutiae of life is the way to strengthen our patience and increase our skill.

Gratitude

One of the best ways to heighten enjoyment in everyday life is with the sense of gratitude. This, like so many of our skills, is no more than common sense – "count your blessings". In our sophistication, we usually manage to forget it or discount it because it seems too simple, but it is true and immensely powerful nonetheless. Gratitude is an art which can be practised in almost every situation and it will enhance every moment it touches. Most importantly, there does not need to be a "someone" to whom we are grateful. Sometimes there is, sometimes there isn't. But this skill is about being grateful *for* rather than *to.*

The power of gratitude comes in no small part from sheer awareness or mindfulness of what we have to be grateful for. Start from life itself, breath, good health if you have it and such health as you have if you don't. Everyday beauty, colours and sounds, art, music, friends, new things, old things, security however tenuous, shelter, food. However little you have, if you are alive there is something to be grateful for. If you have a lot of life's comforts and luxuries – and if you are reading this you already have a great deal, however little you think you have – you have a lot to be grateful for. Everyone has something.

Habit leads us to take most of what is familiar for granted. The fact that we have food every day (if we do) passes mostly unnoticed, for example. We forget to be grateful and forget that there are those who cannot take such a thing for granted. The excellent religious practice of saying grace or giving thanks before eating is a reminder of such good fortune. But taking things for granted is more usual. Several habits may be implicated in this. First there is the tendency to compare ourselves with others. No matter that I have ten times more than I really need, my neighbour has eleven times and so I count myself miserable. Second, there is the adaptation of expectations. I am used to having all that I have and so it becomes, so to speak, factored into the baseline of my needs. Every time I gain more, that increase quickly joins the realm of the essential and I cannot imagine how I could live without it. For example, as we get older and our material position (generally) improves, it is much more difficult to go back to what we had a few years ago, although we managed perfectly well at the time. Third, acquisition and the desire for novelty become addictions in themselves. I do not count what I have as valuable because, frankly, it's all so "yesterday".

Active gratitude, the deliberate looking for things for which to be grateful, focuses or refocuses our attention on our "blessings". Without such focus, our attention can easily be monopolised by what is missing or what is wrong. It is after all one of the key functions of the intellect to scan our environment for dangers and scarcities and initiate action to put them right – very useful perhaps in our evolutionary past when the external environment was so harsh and dangerous that we had to monitor it constantly. But we might speculate that this habit pre-sets our inner life to be dissatisfied, to focus on what we do not have. Even leaving aside the point that our wants are set relative to those around us, if we had 99% of what we could possibly need, the untutored inner life might tend to focus on the missing 1%. With the change of focus offered by gratitude we can keep a better sense of proportion. Focusing on each positive element of our lives, we remember to enjoy what we have instead of regretting what we do not have.

It is particularly easy to overlook gratitude for our own attributes and achievements. Perhaps you are clever, beautiful, talented or strong and you have used these attributes (even everyday language calls them "gifts" but we seldom stop to think why) to make yourself rich, famous or powerful. Perhaps you were born to wealth and authority or perhaps you struggled every step of the way but you made it. It is easy to think in each case that it is your birthright, your effort or your talent which has brought you success, so that you are beholden to no one. Gratitude is not in order, you might think. But this is a big mistake, a real howler. Did you create your parentage, beauty, talent or cleverness? Of course not. Could you have done without them? Of course not. So be grateful for them.

Remember, it is a question of what you should be grateful *for*, not whom you should be grateful *to*. Certainly you have worked hard, taken your chances, made your sacrifices, but were you not fortunate that you had the wherewithal to do so, the talent, the strength or whatever? So gratitude is definitely in order for all these gifts. Thank fate, thank your lucky stars, thank genetics, thank experience, thank whatever or whomever you believe in or thank no one, but do not make the mistake of not being thankful for your own gifts and your own achievements. If you fall into this error, you may miss out on much of the joy in your success. In fact, it is likely that with your focus only on external success you will neglect your inner life altogether and that happiness will elude you even while you are successful. But if and when adversity comes, you risk having to swallow a very bitter pill indeed. Since you have left no room for anything but you in your success, who can you blame for failure? You have a choice between bitterness at yourself and anger at others, neither of which is consistent with happiness.

Someone who honestly believes that all things are the gift of God will have no difficulty with the idea of cultivating gratitude for everything. The notions of blessings and grace will seem quite natural.

Everything is a grace, everything is a blessing, whether we understand the significance of it or not. This is a perspective which fills everyday life with wonders and can be an enriching, happiness-increasing attitude to life. The cultivated skill of gratitude offers the same benefits even to those who cannot accept the underlying theism. Practice gratitude *for* rather than *to*. This does not preclude directing gratitude at others, of course, and if you believe in a beneficent God it would be natural to direct your gratitude back. But even if you do not believe, the sense of gratitude, of blessings received and grace bestowed, will increase your awareness and appreciation of the good things in your life. If terms like grace and blessings make you uncomfortable, then stick to the sense of how lucky or fortunate you are or how good life has been to you. But do not miss out on being grateful.

Even without supernatural belief, of course, we are not always without a benefactor to thank. We live, most of us, in a social setting and our lives generally would be impossible without contributions from others, even if they are only "doing their job". Again, it is easy to forget this and to be aware of what others do for us only when they fail or we have cause to complain. Whether it is your partner, a family member, a work colleague or customer, a shop assistant or another service provider, we take for granted what others do for us a very high percentage of the time. Perhaps you are unusual in being invariably grateful for what is done for you by those with whom you have contact. But when did you last think gratefully about the unmet millions of other people – literally millions – on whom your daily life depends? Those who grew, picked, processed, transported your food, for example? Those who made machines and other inputs for the first set? Similarly for your clothes, cosmetics, papers and books, transport, entertainment? Those involved in any way with supplying you with energy, with water, or dealing with sewage and waste disposal? Emergency services, financial services? At one level these things come from faceless – and we may think unfeeling – corporations and organisations but we know there is another story and these things are also provided by people who are trying to be happy just as we are. What about those who taught you and all the others and those who taught the teachers, not just in school but anyone you or your helpers have ever learned from? What about everybody who did anything, ever, to enable any of this crowd to be alive and healthy and able to do their bit, however small, towards your welfare? There are plenty of targets for your gratitude.

In every case, being fully aware of what we have to be grateful *for* can help us to be grateful *to* the provider. It can be surprising how much more pleasant this can make our own external environment. But our inner life is helped as well, by feeling grateful for people's efforts and even by expressing it – in other words, by simply saying "Thank you". This is such an easy practice but often neglected, particularly the acknowledgement of people's genuine efforts when the outcome is not to our liking. "Thank you for trying" is always good for someone to hear and as the speaker your own inner life gains because you focus on what someone has *tried* to do for you. To see yourself as the recipient of someone's sincere effort is always more helpful to your happiness than focusing on your disappointment, let alone getting angry and taking out your frustration at the outcome on someone who was not responsible for it. It helps too to remind yourself of your interdependence with others

A further and more difficult practice of gratitude is to be thankful for setbacks. Perhaps only the saints get this right all the time, but anyone can have some success with it. It is easiest to start with a wrong or a setback which is now in the past – this practice can indeed help with the letting go of anger and the approach to forgiveness. "If X had not acted as he did, I would not have met Y/changed jobs/changed cities/done Z. And out of that change have come my current good circumstances. Thus even though helping me was the last thing on X's mind, that is in fact the outcome of his action. Therefore I can certainly afford to be grateful for what happened, maybe even grateful to X." In particular, adverse events sometimes make us focus on our inner lives in order to protect our happiness and out of such a shift comes a better understanding of how happiness works and hence a change in our inner habits. Then we really have occasion to thank the "wrongdoer", because they have given us an opportunity which might otherwise have eluded us for years.

The next step might be to see that the beneficial effects of change are, at the time of the wrong, still in the future and we cannot see what exactly they are although we know "something else" will happen. This is of course a sense of hope. Although this is difficult, if we can trust that the outcome will have at least some benign aspects, perhaps we can focus now on the fact that those benefits have been put in train. So even at the time of the setback or wrong we know that there are some consequences for which we will have cause to be grateful, even if we don't yet know what they are. It may not be much, and of course there are setbacks which seem completely devastating and overwhelming at the time, but this chink of hope is worth seeking because it reframes our predicament. Something good really will come after this, whatever this is. This is perhaps one way to take Nietzsche's idea that whatever does not kill me makes me stronger, as also the recommendation, deeply serious as the best comedy always is, to "Always look on the bright side of life!"

Humour

Which neatly brings us to the last of the skills of enjoyment, a sense of humour, the ability to see the funny or lighter side of things. We tend, rightly I think, to be suspicious of those who claim to be happy or to have achieved some spiritual progress but who lack humour. Laughter comes easily to those who are skilful. Perhaps some forms of everyday humour might appear less funny as the skills of the inner life are developed – deriding or making fun of the faults or weaknesses of others is not consistent with kindness, for example. But this doesn't banish humour, it just means the humour will be kinder and more understanding.

Humour is a way of looking at the world and the world is full of it. External circumstances will continue constantly to thwart and obstruct us. The universe, you may decide, has probably not been designed exclusively for your convenience and seeing the funny side of external circumstances, especially with the growing realisation that they are temporary and transient, can be endlessly if sometimes darkly amusing. Your own inner life and habit basis can also be pretty funny. Your habits will always try to lead you into negative or unhelpful reactions and you have to catch them at it and pull them back. This of course is the nature of training and it is a serious business, but it does not have to be a solemn one. You can afford to laugh at these habits and their continual urge to set off in the wrong direction. Negative habits are not your enemies, they are not doing it on purpose, they are just doing what they do. But of course your habits are you, so what this amounts to is that it is healthy to laugh at yourself and your own imperfections. This is hardly a revelation, but surprisingly often we get angry or upset with ourselves instead of amused. Don't take yourself so seriously! Laugh at yourself and your inner habits and then set about trying to change them. You can stop when you are perfect!

Playfulness

Which group of people in the world, would you say, is the happiest, enjoys the greatest, most robust and most easily restored peace of mind? Despite all the adult world's efforts to disturb and distract them, and despite the obvious counter-examples of children corrupted and childhood destroyed, children are surely the group which as a whole best fit the bill. Perhaps it is because they have had less time and experience on which to base bad habits, perhaps it is just because they have fewer cares and responsibilities. Perhaps they are in a state of natural happiness or innocence which all of us enjoy and abandon as we become older and more confused about what really matters to us. But the skill which children most obviously possess and which adults most obviously lose is playfulness – an activity directed towards nothing more serious than enjoying the moment, having fun. So playfulness is an aspect of humour we would do well to remember and cultivate. To condemn it as childish is to miss some crucially important points.

Playfulness keeps things in perspective, focuses on the moment and what joy there is to be had in it. It might make us feel better about being ourselves the plaything of circumstances, as we all are sometimes tempted to feel, for if the universe is playful what is there to be done but join in the game? Playfulness takes us away from obsession with ourselves and our plans, obsessions not infrequently at odds with happiness, as we have seen.

Playfulness has no agenda, it is not competitive – do not confuse playfulness with the serious playing of sports, for example, which is anything but playful. Re-learning to be playful, allowing ourselves to be playful, is one of the best practices to increase our enjoyment of life. So we have much to learn from little children, because we have lost the skill we naturally had when we were little but which we traded for other skills or allowed to fall into disrepair, or perhaps were discouraged from practising. A playful attitude does not mean that we cannot be responsible when need arises. It means that we practice enjoying the moment whenever we can.

It is so easy to fall into thinking of practice to develop peace of mind, particularly in its guise of spiritual training, as something rather solemn and serious. Practice is a serious matter, in the sense that the outcome is important and application is needed. But the skill of playfulness reminds us that the outcome, the central focus, is happiness. We know we can't control the external world, so why get uptight about it? Equally, we don't need to obsess about our inner progress and our difficulties. It will actually help our progress to lighten up, relax and let go a little. Playfulness is the difference, perhaps, between taking happiness seriously – which everyone would improve their lives by doing – and taking it solemnly, which is something of a contradiction. Children don't even think about this, they just get it right. We may not be so lucky, but we can win back the skill with practice.

Chapter 17:
Enjoying practice

Living happily doesn't have to make you miserable

Continuing the theme of playfulness, it is possible to make yourself quite miserable in the pursuit of happiness. Here's a little tutorial. First of all, you identify the habits which prevent you being happy. Right there is a first opportunity for gloom, as the certainty descends that you are without doubt the person most oppressed by unhelpful habits in the entire world. Also, what you thought were the annoying habits of others preventing your happiness actually have more to do with how you react to those others. Oh no, it's your fault! But you get over it and then you set about trying to reduce the hold such unhelpful habits have on you, conscious as you do so of every failure to live up to your new ideals, every mistake and every lost opportunity. When you think you are making progress and have one area sorted, you start work on something else and realise that you have to go back and work on the first area some more. It is surely a wretched business, trying to be happy! But that's all right, because when you have practised for ten or twenty years you will be happy, won't you, so it will all have been worthwhile.

Well, maybe. Caricature aside, people do fall into this way of thinking. We have all met good people, well-meaning people who become miserable in their pursuit of joy. I was once on a retreat where one day the teacher announced that he intended to play music in place of one meditation session and he wanted us to dance. He hoped we could take that natural joy from the dancing back into our meditation. Several people were quite thrown by this unexpected turn of events. I remember an earnest lady in the front row asking in shocked tones: "You mean…we're just supposed to *enjoy* ourselves?"

Happiness cannot be postponed even in the pursuit of happiness. Compound interest is not available in the inner life. We do need to work to change our habits, but we need to work with happiness and joy. If you are going to practice skills which help you to be happier, how do you know you are practising the right skills? You know because they bring you happiness as you practice them. You get happier as the work goes on, broadly speaking. Of course there will be dips and troughs and if you have a lot of work to do it may take some time to show strong effects, although improvements are often evident quite quickly just from your change in attitude. But at least you should not get progressively worse! If you practised a golf stroke or a recipe or a musical scale and found you were getting steadily worse – not just becoming more aware of how much work you had to do but actually getting worse – would you continue the practice? Probably not. You would quickly realise that there was something wrong with the method and look for another one. Likewise, if you adopt a practice designed to make you happier or increase your peace of mind and find that you are making yourself steadily less happy, something must be wrong. Possibly the practice just doesn't suit you or you need to work on something else first, possibly the external circumstances are too difficult, or possibly the practice you have adopted is flawed in some way. Or, of course, you are just not practising properly. There will be times when any practice is difficult or does not go well, or when real effort is needed to overcome some difficulty. There may even be times, especially at the beginning of your programme of practice, when unfamiliarity makes practice seem harder than the status quo. But it has to be possible to find joy in practice.

Finding your practice

With the five groups of skills we have a map – one among many – for developing the habit basis towards greater peace of mind. As part of the discussion we have looked at a few of the many ways each skill could be practised, but only a few. This focus on the skills themselves rather than on methods of practice is very deliberate. Each person's practice is like a training regime for the inner life, but a regime which takes into account their own needs, including not only their external circumstances but the particular set of skills and inner problems they face at any given time. One person might need to concentrate on mindfulness, and another on benevolence or letting go. Of two who decide they need to concentrate on mindfulness, one might be best suited to a sitting practice, and another might get more benefit from, say, martial arts, yoga or ecstatic dance. Your practice is your own, designed by you for your needs, using help and assistance where necessary. Practice in its totality becomes a way of life. You could of course adopt an entire regime wholesale, for example from one of the faith traditions, and it would no doubt be helpful, but it would not be specific to your temperament and the particular set of inner life habits you uniquely face. Our five sets of skills offer a rational framework on which you can build your own practice.

Just knowing about inner skills and why they are important is a big step forward on the path towards happiness and inner peace. Finding your own practice is the next step. It is not a single, once-in-a-lifetime activity but something to be repeated and developed constantly as you develop. The list of skills is a checklist for progress, a template for what any technique of practice should give you and a guide as to what to do and where to look if your life is not as happy as you would like it to be. It is good to remain open to new techniques, to try them and see if they suit you and where they take you. Trying something new can be helpful with motivation also, but beware of flitting from one technique to another, never mastering anything because you never give sufficient time for any practice to ripen. A balance is needed between innovation and determination, but generally we find our own balance, provided we bear in mind the objective, to develop the habit basis in the direction of happiness.

Difficulties with practice

Practice, we all know, is to repeat an activity purposefully in order to get used to it or better at it. Through practice what is at first difficult becomes gradually easier and eventually instinctive. What gets repeated is quite complex, though: practice of a musical instrument involves, as well as learning to play pieces, learning scales and exercises which develop dexterity, technique, intonation and musicality. Sport practice is aimed at developing fitness, strength and endurance as well as improving technique and understanding of whatever game is involved. In every case difficulties will be analysed, perhaps sub-skills will have to be learned, the performer may have to go back from time to time to correct a badly formed or no longer adequate technique. But when you practice assiduously, something happens which is difficult to explain. You change in ways you cannot necessarily foresee. You probably will bring about the change you want, but often your understanding of what you are trying to do changes, as well. The process of practice is among other things a lesson in not becoming too attached to outcomes envisioned at the start. At the highest levels, the results of practice can be almost transcendent, producing results which astonish even the performer.

There is always a danger that in our desire to make progress we do not sufficiently focus when we practice. We try to look at many problems at once and end up flitting between them. To concentrate on one issue at a time gives the practice a direction and makes it far more productive. Thus a musician, say, may play a problem passage over and over again, slow it down, dissect it, try to understand its difficulty and how to overcome the problem. Maybe the passage is then set aside for a fresh assault another day and the practice moves to something else, but at each moment there is a focus on one issue. So there might be half a dozen things you want to work on but they have to be addressed by turns, making as much progress as you can with one and then trying another. Trying to make progress on several fronts at once usually leads to you being frustrated and the problems remaining intact.

Repetition can itself be a problem, but the cultivation of the right attitude can transform it. The danger is that attentiveness becomes numbed by repetition and instead of remaining alert and concentrated we fall into an automatic state. There are religious practices, for example, where a prayer, mantra or sacred name is repeated over and over again, perhaps hundreds of times. If this is done mechanically, with just the thought that this task must be got through, then the exercise may be pointless. But if the task is undertaken in the right spirit, with attentiveness, then it will have a different effect – at the very least it will help to build the habit of attentiveness. You come to realise that each repetition is unique and repetitions welcomed in this spirit take on a different quality.

Sometimes when you practice an external skill you seem to be getting nowhere. You know the sort of thing. You repeat and repeat, knowing that something is wrong and having some idea of what you want to achieve. But it is as if your body will not obey: your fingers will not frame the notes, you cannot strike the ball as you wish or your body will not move as you have been shown. Dedication to solving the problem does not necessarily mean fruitless repetition *ad infinitum*, for you may not be able to solve the problem directly. Perhaps you need to go back a step, practice something else and take that skill into the solving of your problem. Perhaps you are just not ready to solve the problem yet. Not every problem can be solved at any stage you choose: you cannot play a concerto before you have enough skill at playing the instrument. This calls for a different kind of persistence, a patient, intelligent persistence which may take months or years to be satisfied.

It helps therefore to learn to savour the process of practice itself as much as achievement. Indeed sometimes the best practice becomes almost free of the goal. We find that we have met or surpassed our original goal almost incidentally; the path from A to B has just become a path worth travelling for its own sake. Training or practice is helped by dedication and effort but seldom by strain. I cannot just will myself or force myself to be better at whatever it is. The practice has to take its time. It is an organic process, like a tree which has to take root, grow to maturity and only then bear fruit. Habits or skills may be tended, helped, encouraged, but they still need time and process to grow. But with the skills of the inner life we are considering no less a field than the art of living well and happily. There is no completion of the process, unless it be the completion of your life. The process is all there is, so each moment has to be savoured, whether it feels like progress or a backward step.

Along the way of practice the problem you are working on sometimes yields, just a little, and it is a real epiphany. You suddenly realise how it could be. Realisation is something quite different from being told or having described to you how it could be. The swing of bat or club or foot is different and sweeter, the notes flow from your hands, the body moves without effort, the posture is easier. Or, in the inner life, anger gives way to compassion, joy and gratitude suddenly fill the moment, stillness suddenly expands. You can practice now with a lighter heart because you have a better idea where you are going and you know it is indeed sweet. This phenomenon is a common reward of persistence in training, as you will know if ever you have practised anything with dedication, however temporarily. It is true of external skills but equally if not more true of the practice of the skills and habits of the inner life.

You cannot hope to leap in one mighty bound from being a novice to being a master. It takes dedication and worthwhile progress is gradual. Of course you may find you have little trouble with some areas of the inner life so you need spend little time on them, but you will find plenty to occupy you elsewhere. Remember that getting it wrong is what practice is about so don't be discouraged when it happens. If you take on a challenge in any walk of life which is beyond your current powers, you will lose, of course. With the skills of the inner life we cannot always choose what challenges we face and when, which means that we often have to cope with challenges beyond our current level of skill. So we "lose". Our thoughts or emotions or desires get the better of us and our happiness is swept away, at least for the time being. But it is useful to remember (when we can recollect ourselves) that if we lose in this way it is just because the challenge was too great for us at this moment. There is no shame, no blame. It does not mean that practice is useless; it means that we need more practice. But unless we develop skills by practising on the easy challenges of life, we will have no hope of dealing with the major challenges.

Beware, finally, of the temptation to practice only what you are good at. It is very comforting but not a good way to make progress. You have to face the areas where you get it wrong, where you have unhelpful habits, where you make mistakes. You have to take some risks or you will not change the basis of your inner life. And taking risks always requires a balance between courage and prudence, even if the risk is just that of feeling or appearing foolish. It requires courage to change your habits, but you cannot run away from your own inner life. The only alternative to taking some risk is to remain stuck with whatever inner habits make you unhappy and allow them to go on doing so.

Four modes of practice

We have already touched on the distinction between practice in everyday life and practice at some remove from the complexities of everyday life, in more controlled conditions or "off-line", using techniques which can vary from watching the breath to martial arts to volunteering for a charity. There are in fact four different settings for practice of the inner skills, amounting to four different modes of practice:

1. Individual practice in time set apart for practice.
2. Practice in the context of everyday life.
3. Practice with a teacher or guide, receiving specific guidance or help with particular problems. This could be in the form of individual help, but it also might be in a group (as in forms of retreat), a class, or it could simply be a matter of reading something which helps us with what we need.
4. Group practice: practising together with others by agreement. Group practice might involve classes or exercises done together for motivational support, or discussion, or group activities – for example, a project to help others as a practice of benevolence or generosity.

A balanced regime of practice might contain as many as possible of these four modes at any time. Over a lifetime of practice it would be surprising if all four were not employed at various times. I will comment briefly on each of them.

1. Individual practice in time set apart for practice

If you are serious about developing the skills of the inner life, you will want to devote some time specifically to the task. At one extreme, there are those who are able to devote whole stretches of their lives, going on extended retreats or pilgrimages, for example, or even joining ashrams or monasteries. At the other extreme, most of us have intervals in our lives when there seems to be no time to spare for the merely vital, so pressing are the immediate claims of urgent tasks. But sooner or later we need to set aside time or we will simply not succeed. One of the most profitable uses of this time is to develop the skill of mindfulness, by practising mindfulness of breathing or some other technique. This is the area where most people are weakest. But we might also spend the time, for example, practising story skills and seeing how we can apply them to any issue which troubles us; contemplating the ideas of process and transience and testing whether we can let go of the past; reminding ourselves of our blessings; or considering how we might have dealt better with some incident which made us angry. How the time is used depends on need.

In an ideal world we would set aside some practice time for ourselves every day. Even if it was only twenty or thirty minutes, it would make a huge difference, for not only are the skills thus regularly reinforced but by building this time into our routine we help to keep the objective of happiness in the front of our minds. In this respect, 15 minutes three times a day can be better than a single block of 45 minutes. An analogy would be the laudable Islamic practice of regular daily prayers which helps to keep the religious objective in constant focus. But even if we can only find 20 minutes once a week, it is a great deal better than nothing. Progress will be much slower, naturally, like that of a weekend athlete. What generally happens in such circumstances is that people either find progress so slow that they cannot appreciate it and they give up, or they realise how important this time is and they find more, even if they have to get up earlier. If your life permits it, setting aside an occasional day or half-day is also very beneficial.

2. Practice in the context of everyday life

The inner life skills are of course intended to help with living our lives happily and for that they need to be applicable and effective in everyday life. It is of little use for everyday life to sit on a mountaintop becoming calm and full of joy, as in one Indian parable, if we become upset and irritated with the noise and the jostling crowd as soon as we descend to the town. We can practice and rehearse the skills privately, in peace and solitude, but unless we intend to be permanent hermits, sooner or later we have to use our skills in real life. The only way to do that is to make a point of applying them.

A distinction between applying the skills and practising them is probably not useful when we consider everyday living. If I try, for example, to overcome my rising anger with a dangerous driver in traffic or with a scheming rival at work by reminding myself that they are acting out of ignorance, I am both practising and applying the practice. Whether I am successful or not in dealing with the anger on this occasion I have, however marginally, reinforced the habit of thinking in this way and so I have practised well. I need to remember that my success depends on my level of skill and if I am not successful it just means that my skill level is not yet where I would like it to be. But that is no reason to be discouraged, still less to give up trying. I need more practice, not less.

Everyday life provides endless opportunities to practice every one of the skills. This is very important to remember if you are "pressed for time" and do not feel able to set aside time for private practice. If anything, the problem is likely to be that too many things happen at once and you do not know which skills to practice or when. Loss of focus results. It is much better if even a small amount of private practice is possible, because at least you can then review what happened in the day and reflect on how you might proceed on similar future occasions. Also, if you realise from experience that you are weak in a particular skill you can try to strengthen it "off-line" to help with the real life problem. One way round the difficulty of the complexity of real life situations is just to pick a skill and concentrate on practising that one skill for a day or a week. Then pick another and keep rotating around the skills.

You may find that a curious thing happens as you practice or apply practice in your everyday life: the more you practice the skills, the less you seem to need them. If you work on benevolence to deal with anger, for example, you may find that you are not merely better able to deal with anger, but fewer situations cause anger to arise in the first place. If you work on acceptance because you cannot avoid some unpleasant external circumstances, you may find that the circumstances come to seem less unpleasant. And so on. What is probably happening is that the skill is beginning to be internalised so that it operates as a habitual response to the first signs of the difficult situation arising, so that the difficulty, or at least your former inner response to it, doesn't have a chance to get started. This is obviously good news: the practice is working! At this point, however, the essential trick is to keep practising, not to be tempted to assume that the problem has gone away and that practice is no longer necessary. Progress is good, but real expertise takes a little longer and mastery takes a lifetime!

3. Practice with a teacher or guide.

Skills are often most easily learned from those who have them. Sometimes it is the only way, because the skill cannot be adequately described or explained except by observing it in action. Many craft skills are like this: there are so many nuances that it is not practicable to write them all down and certainly not possible to absorb them except by applying them under trial and error. The same applies to sport, martial arts, and often to the skills of spiritual traditions. There are spiritual traditions, particularly in Asia, where someone wanting to learn has to enter what is effectively a master-servant relationship with a teacher.

Does this apply to the skills of the inner life? There are without doubt many points at which a teacher or a guide can be invaluable. But although this is perhaps a cultural bias, the perspective we have developed in this book is that it is ultimately your inner life and your happiness at stake. The work can only be done by you and a huge leap of faith and trust would be required to hand responsibility for directing the work to another. Of course, the authentic Asian master-pupil relationship is predicated on the teacher's being whole-heartedly dedicated to the welfare and success of the pupil. In circumstances where this is genuinely the case, faith and trust may be amply justified. Perhaps it is more profitable, however, to understand the usefulness of teachers in the acquisition of inner life skills by examining the different roles which teachers can play. There seem to me to be six.

First, the teacher may set or help to set the direction or the goal of practice and progress. This is the inspirational role, the promise of fulfillment, what in the context of the faith traditions might be provided by the cosmological story, the provision of meaning and purpose to the enterprise. If you have at all agreed with the argument of this book then living a happy life in whatever circumstances is the goal. To the extent that you adopt happiness as your goal and direction, this often vital task of goal setting does not need a teacher.

Second, the teacher may so manifest the relevant skills that he or she provides a living lesson, an example for us to follow. The great spiritual innovators and teachers have all had this quality and performed this role. But people who have perfected all the skills of the inner life are not easy to find and are unlikely to advertise themselves. So this potential role which a teacher might perform may simply be unavailable. On the other hand, it may be incredibly helpful if we come across and are able to observe individuals who are better than we are at just one skill.

The third function of a teacher is to provide motivation, and with this we generally need all the help we can get, particularly in the early stages when we may still lack full conviction about the value of practice. It is important to note for this purpose that the teacher does not have to have mastered all the skills, nor even necessarily to advocate our five skills as such. For example, someone who advocates overcoming desire for religious reasons may be able to speak about it in such a way that we are inspired and motivated to examine how we can apply it in our own practice and to develop our skills. A teacher of meditation may have a religious affiliation inconsistent with our own but may be able to motivate us to practice mindfulness. A teacher of sport, or yoga, or a martial art may motivate us to practice their discipline and in doing so we may see how it relates to our own inner life skills. We may also find motivation – and teachers – in strange places. We may be motivated to practice because we can see that someone else lacks a certain skill and suffers because of it, so that a bad example can teach and motivate us. We may even be motivated by the need to overcome suffering inflicted on us by someone, thus taking our "enemies" as teachers.

The fourth role of a teacher is to help us assess our own needs and progress. We may be blind to our own weakness in one or more of the skills, particularly if mindfulness still needs work, as it usually does. We may even think we are particularly good at something when we are not. Or we may despair of our progress in one of the skills, not realising that what we lack is not the skill but the ability to appreciate it in ourselves. Thus a teacher can help us to keep a sense of proportion. A teacher in this sense need not literally be someone from whom we accept instruction. It can be a colleague or friend who understands what we are trying to do and whom we can trust to be honest in their advice. It could even be a support group. This is the role of the "spiritual friend" found in many of the faith traditions, but it is also one of the roles a coach may perform even for a champion in sporting contexts. The adviser or coach need not be more accomplished than the advisee, just objective and honest and skilled enough to identify difficulties and perhaps help develop solutions.

The fifth function involves teaching in a more conventional sense. We have our direction and we know which skills we want to work on, but the range of possible techniques we might use is vast. A teacher can help to introduce and instruct us in the use of techniques and may even devise new ones to help us deal with specific issues we encounter. For example, there are hundreds of different ways to practice mindfulness using meditation, hundreds more ways to practice the same skill using visualisations, exercises like repeated prostrations (a practice in some Tibetan traditions) or the recitation of prayers throughout the day. We might find any of these useful, depending on our temperament, beliefs and cultural background, but they must generally be accurately performed to be of any use. Thus we need a teacher to help us learn the technique, regardless of the skill we wish to strengthen by practising the technique.

Finally, a teacher may be able to help us solve particular problems in our practice, whether they be technical, practical or even emotional. This is the role of the expert or specialist. We may be unable to concentrate in a mindfulness practice, for example, and the teacher may be able to identify that we are adopting a mistaken or unsuitable technique, or simply suggest an alternative more suited to our stage of development. Perhaps we have a problem in our workplace and need help to decide the extent to which it is a manifestation of an inner life issue of our own and the extent to which someone else is being unreasonable. Or perhaps we find when we begin to quiet our thoughts and listen to ourselves that we have major unresolved issues of anger about the past, or grief, or anxiety which need to be dealt with. Sometimes such problems need the help of a counsellor because we ourselves cannot be objective about them: sometimes we may even need therapy of one kind or another. No shame in that, it is a major step to clear the ground on which we will one day build our happiness. Thus a therapist may in this sense be a teacher – they help us to solve a particular problem which we cannot solve on our own and which impedes our progress towards a skilful inner life.

4. Group practice

Only you can develop the skills which will enhance your inner life, but we are all first and foremost social beings. Practising with other people is not only helpful and pleasant, it is sometimes essential. In some spiritual traditions it is even said that progress on one's own is impossible or doomed to failure, if only because it sometimes takes extraordinary tenacity to keep going if there are no others with whom the path can be shared. If you can find just one other person who shares your goals sufficiently to help you and sometimes practice with you, the chances of success in developing the inner life skills are greatly increased.

Practices which develop mindfulness such as sitting and walking practice can clearly be performed in a group. It may not be clear whether the practice itself is enhanced but motivation most certainly is. And even with such essentially solitary practices there can be a helpful group energy. The story skills can benefit greatly from group participation because approaches can be shared and discussed, different issues and problems can be presented to the group for the collective imagination to work on different possible scenarios. Likewise, a group can work on specific emotional blocks and problems by discussion, role play and other techniques, making progress which it might be impossible for an individual to achieve on their own, although in such cases a skilled facilitator would be essential. The group activity of sharing positive thoughts from each member about their life or practice can be a strong incentive to develop and practice in developing the enjoyment skills.

Groups also provide an opportunity to undertake more outwardly-focused practices which might be more difficult for individuals to undertake alone. A group might undertake some charitable group activity as a practice in kindness or generosity, from fund-raising for a cause to transporting or visiting the elderly to feeding the needy. Even campaigning for a cause might be an act of kindness and generosity, particularly if the campaign is mindful of its impact on the inner life skills of the participants. Think, for example, of the many campaigns of Gandhi and particularly the spirit in which he conducted them.

Group practice has drawbacks as well as many advantages, of course. Good intentions do not protect against the usual hazards of group dynamics. There may be members who wish to impress with their superior achievements, insight, knowledge or eloquence, who wish to dominate the group or interfere with other people's practice, who believe themselves to be inspired, who ramble or have their own agendas, who may even be predatory. There may also be members who wish only to be spoon-fed, who are disinterested or disruptive. A once-focused group may slowly evolve into a social gathering, factions and feuds may arise, personalities may clash. A group would only be perfect if all its members were perfectly skilful, but in that case there would be little need for group practice! A group can never be a substitute for individual practice and practice in a group is not a soft or sure option.

Despite all these caveats, group practice is still immensely valuable. There are ways forward with all the problems which can arise. The regular presence of visiting teachers and speakers, for example, can help with focus and cohesion. The problems of group dynamics can be viewed as opportunities to practice the inner skills of forbearance, mindfulness and kindness in an environment which, for any faults it might have, is still likely to be greatly easier than the environment of the world at large. It is worth remembering also that group practice does not have to depend on continuous membership of a particular group. There are many opportunities to practice skills in groups on retreats, courses and even holidays. Religious practice may also provide many such opportunities. A supportive group is a great blessing and one of the most useful aids to practice it is possible to find.

Part Three

CONNECTIONS, SPECULATIONS, CONCLUSIONS

Truth and religion

In the course of the book I have often alluded to the faith traditions and the connections between parts of their practice and the development of the inner life in our sense. In this chapter I will consider some issues about practice and religion and also look at some issues with the other dominant mode of modern thought, science.

When people begin to think about their inner life and the way it relates to their happiness, their first instinct is often that they need to find "the Truth" – the capital "T" marks it as something special. Truth in this sense is one of the things which all religions and ideologies offer, in the form of a system of ideas which may include the following:

- a cosmology or outline story about how the universe, seen and unseen, is structured, what kinds of beings there are (including a supreme being if there is held to be one) and how everything works;
- a creation story about how things came to be as they are;
- a story about what will happen at the end of the world, if there is one;
- a story which explains what the role, purpose and meaning of human life is, and which accounts for such things as suffering and evil;
- a story which explains what happens after we die;
- an ethic, or story, which explains what we should do and how we should live if we wish to fulfill our purpose in this life, or in a future life or lives.

It is not at all my purpose to suggest that it is a mistake to subscribe to any system of belief, whether religious or ideological. If you are a believer, your faith will give you comfort in good times and bad, a sense of purpose and meaning in your life and a guide as to how to act when perplexed. It will, in short, help you to live a happier life – and how could anyone, particularly the author of a book about living a happier life, possibly object to that? Psychological studies have suggested that people who are devout believers or regular attendees at religious services are happier, less prone to stress and may even live longer, on average, than those who are not believers. Belief is very good for believers.

But what are you to do if you find it difficult to believe in any particular religion? How do you decide? We live in a sceptical age, when it is more than ever difficult to accept beliefs just because someone asks us or tells us to. We know that much of what we are ordinarily told is dubious. We are surrounded by advertising claims, people trying to sell us things, financial institutions assuring us that they are trustworthy, news media selecting and adjusting what they tell us for various reasons. Some people even think that our political leaders are not always frank with us! Scepticism in general is essential to survival, but it makes it harder than ever to accept religious doctrines. On top of this, science has explained away many of the mysteries which earlier ages found difficult to understand and therefore put down to supernatural causes. Also, people who claim to be religious, however dubiously, are among the worst perpetrators of violence in the world today, whether committing acts of terrorism or unleashing the military power of the state. Perhaps it was ever thus, but it does little to persuade the undecided that religious belief holds the answer to the question of how to live happily and well.

We may note also that most people, if they subscribe to a system of religious belief at all, subscribe to one which is false. This may sound provocative, but it is inevitable provided only that no such system commands the support of a majority of the world's believers – and none does. Even if one creed or sect did command a majority of believers, of course, it is not clear that democracy would be the right way to decide matters of transcendent Truth. But as it is, if all the many systems of religious belief are mutually exclusive, at most one can be true. Only the believers who adhere to that one true faith, whichever it is, are correct, but they are a minority since there is no majority faith. All the rest, the combined majority who believe in all the other faiths, are wrong, to a greater or lesser extent. This difficulty will not and should not deter believers since each one believes, obviously, that theirs is the true system and that it is the believers in rival faiths who are misguided. But the problem is devastating for anyone un-committed. The odds against finding the right faith among so many when all are convinced of their rightness make "seeking the Truth" a difficult and potentially very long-term undertaking.

However, it is worth questioning whether a concern with "the Truth" in this sense is well placed. There are two main issues. First, how are we going to decide what doctrine is "the Truth" when we find it? Second, does knowing "the Truth" take us any closer to living the happy life?

How do you know?

The first question is very difficult to answer, and perhaps that is an answer in itself. It is not clear how we decide between competing views on, say, how the cosmos is constructed – not in a scientific sense, which is hard enough in its own way, but in a sense which includes supernatural beings, spiritual realms and so on. A widely-held atheistic view is that there are no such things to be known beyond the purely physical, but that is itself a view which provokes the question, "How do you know?" The fact is that ordinary criteria for whether something is true or false break down when we think about such issues. If we disagree about whether Fred's car is blue, we know how to settle the matter. Of course we can get confused, be misled by colour blindness, misunderstand which car we are talking about, and so on. But there are ways round all these difficulties and in the end we can settle the matter. The most abstruse scientific dispute will in principle yield to the same kind of procedures, even though the evidence may be difficult, impractical or costly to obtain.

But if we disagree about, say, how many types of angel there are, what can we do to settle the question? We can't go and look, we can't do experiments. We might be able to agree that a certain person's word or a certain text is definitive on the subject, because we agree that the person or the writer of the text has special authority or has a way of knowing such things which the rest of us do not have. But if anyone disputes that knowledge or authority we are stuck again. We cannot go behind the authority's claim and the authority can offer nothing in support except, well, authority. The particular example I have chosen here is, deliberately, unlikely to be central to anyone's idea of the Truth. The point is, however, that all "supernatural" truths have the same difficulty – which is why they are supernatural. They cannot be tested by natural means such as we would apply to everyday questions.

Suppose a Martian were enquiring about a particular supernatural proposition. How would we convince the Martian of its truth or falsity? We will suppose she is polite, rational in the sense that she will not refuse to accept a conclusion if the argument is valid and the premises established, but also free of any relevant cultural bias. She will not accept that the oldest Earth culture or the most powerful or the most technologically advanced or indeed the most backward is correct just because of its status. She is also, obviously, immune to any kind of pressure, threat, or inducement. What arguments can any of us use to establish our view of the supernatural? The fact is that if she will not accept our assurance that the authority we rely on is unimpeachable, we will struggle. Authority is all there is, but the validity of the authority might just as well be the question as the answer.

People who are convinced of a Truth are convinced just because they are convinced. This is of course called faith, and to the extent that a system makes only consistent supernatural claims it is impossible to prove that it is false, just as it is impossible to prove that it is true by any means that we would apply to everyday or scientific issues. Many people are convinced because they have been brought up to be convinced, or because they have come across the doctrine at a time when they needed the help of such a belief, or because they have had experiences which they interpret as confirming the doctrine. In all these cases the Truth is accepted as the Truth because of the way it makes you feel. Many people are willing to say "It feels right", or more defensively "It feels right for me". Well and good: it is hardly appropriate to take away anything which brings people comfort. But we know that things are not made true just because they make us feel good. Otherwise we would all be rich, happy, important, much loved, and so on. And if we really want to base our happiness on Truth, we especially should not use the effect it has on our happiness as the criterion for whether something really is true. This is circular, it confuses "True" with "Makes me happy" as though they had the same meaning. Which, sadly, they don't.

This question of how to decide what is true in a supernatural sense is thus a difficult problem for those who believe that Truth is the key to a peaceful inner life or to happiness. But if you are going to search for Truth you have to know how you are going to decide when you have found it or the search can never end. So if you postpone being happy until you have found the truth – especially *the* cosmic Truth which underlies everything – you may have to wait a while to be happy.

Knowledge vs skill

The second problem may be even more serious for the idea that knowing the Truth, worthy aim though it may be in itself, will lead to happiness. It is simply that there is no essential connection between the two. It may give you comfort to feel, for example, that there is order and purpose behind events and that perhaps you understand how things work, or at least someone does. But you still have the rest of your emotions, thoughts, desires and beliefs to deal with and they may or may not leave you peaceful. Knowledge, in other words, will not necessarily deal with all the dimensions of the inner life.

Moreover, knowing that something is true is different from knowing what to do. Knowledge is not the same as skill. Knowing about dynamics doesn't mean you can ride a bike. Knowing about electricity does not by itself mean you can change a plug. Knowing everything there is to know about the physics of fluids would not help you to swim if you had not learned that skill. Likewise, knowing everything about the cosmos or about the underlying order of things, even if it were possible, would not necessarily make you happy. The kind of knowledge we are looking for if we want to know how to be happy is more like a way of doing things – in fact, a way of doing all things, a way of living. "The Truth", if it could be discovered, is about knowledge or theory; happiness is about doing or living.

But perhaps this general problem does not apply to some belief systems because they include or imply a specific set of instructions as to how to live as well as a set of beliefs. There may thus be no general connection between belief and happiness but there may be a particular connection based on the actual content of your candidate for Truth. For example, many religions promise happiness if we conduct ourselves in certain ways. We must observe certain practices and rituals, follow a certain moral code, cultivate certain qualities, and so on. Much of this emphasis on practice and the cultivation of qualities is truly helpful in bringing about the conditions for happiness, which is one reason why religions and their insights should be treated with respect even when we disagree with their doctrines. Many things can be learned from traditions whose practices are often hundreds or even thousands of years old and have been tested and refined over that time. But then it is the practices and their effectiveness which are of interest, not the doctrines. The helpfulness of the practices does not necessarily validate the beliefs.

It is moreover an essential element of many if not most faiths that belief in the relevant doctrines is a requirement, often the most important requirement without which the practices would be considered empty. In other words, the first and most important thing you must *do* is believe. Faith is a key quality or virtue; belief is itself a key practice. What are we to do then if we do not believe? If we do not at this point have faith in a particular doctrine, how is it to be found?

There is no sufficient answer to this question and we are back to the first problem.

The degree of emphasis placed on belief does vary between religions, it is only fair to say. It is of course particularly strong in some forms of Western Christianity and less obvious in other religions. Religions like Buddhism and to some extent Judaism and aspects of Islam could be seen as systems of practice, designed to bring believers to an awareness of the numinous or to perfect as far as possible their human nature or understanding. It would certainly be naïve to suggest that the essence of religion is the willingness to subscribe to a list of propositions, or that the essence of faith is to regard such a list as established in the same sense as, say, the multiplication tables or the map of the world. Many religious people would themselves accept that religious knowledge is knowledge of a different sort. But it would be equally wrong to suggest that belief in at least a core of important doctrine is not essential for most religions. Without such belief it is simply not correct to say that you are an adherent of that religion. If you are a member of one of the monotheistic religions, for example, it is not necessary that you are a theologian and have views on complex issues about the nature of God. You may have highly articulated ideas of what "God" means or you may not, you may even disagree with the orthodox account of divinity. It is difficult to be precise about what is a core belief and what is not and some religions are stricter than others on what amounts to heresy and what doesn't. But you must at least believe in such a case that there is one and only one deity, divine power or however you understand it – otherwise your adherence to the religion is cultural at most. Thus the issue of supernatural knowledge, of how you know what is true about the supernatural, cannot be sidestepped.

By way of an aside, there is a third sense of the word "know", which is the sense in which we know a person. ("Do you know Joe?") For many religious believers this is in fact the essential sense and what they seek is a personal acquaintance or relationship with the Transcendent. I acknowledge this but it is not relevant to this discussion, because to seek such knowledge only makes sense against the background of a system of belief already accepted, specifically including a belief in a personally knowable God. It does not help, therefore, with the general problem of how or what to believe.

A leap of faith

Thinkers of many faiths have offered as an answer to such problems that we should abandon the demand for rigorous proof in these matters, making thus an act or leap of faith. We just decide: "I will believe it regardless". It doesn't matter why we do this. It might be because we want the comfort which orthodoxy brings, or because we cannot bear not knowing, or because we are frightened, or because we want to experience whatever lies on the other side of faith. Or we might just be convinced without being able to say why. This is a replacement of reasoning with inner action, a form of letting go: we just let go of the demand for proof. And it has a great appeal. If we accept that we are dealing with transcendent truths which we cannot know by ordinary empirical means, and that anyway our minds are probably too limited to grasp such things fully, then just accepting that there are things we cannot understand but which may nevertheless be true is not a bad response. It could be seen as a letting go of our intellectual pride that we can understand everything, a form of humility but a realistic and even rational one in the circumstances. After all, most of us can't understand advanced physics but we know some of it is true, so although the two situations are not really the same because there are some people who can understand the physics, in a sense there is only one more step involved in faith. It helps anyway that most of us actually like mysteries. We are often disappointed when someone offers a rational explanation for some happening which seemed mysterious and which might have been evidence for spirits or aliens, magical or supernatural forces. There can be something quite satisfying about accepting that there is an impenetrable mystery at the heart of everything.

But there is still a problem. If I just let go and believe, which faith or which set of beliefs shall I believe? This is not usually a problem for religious thinkers, for they are generally concerned with belief in their own faith or in none: they see only two paths. But as we have seen, there are many systems of belief and most of them must be wrong. If you are going to take a leap of faith and are outside any system for the moment, how do you know which one to leap into? Exceptionally tolerant religious thinkers may hold that since transcendent Truth is beyond us, all religions are basically approximations or metaphors and one should accept the nearest one, so to speak. That is, one should accept and believe the faith which is culturally or personally most congenial, since all are only "fingers pointing at the moon", in the famous and beautiful phrase, and not to be confused with the moon itself. However, there is another solution for the undecided.

We can indeed learn to let go of the desire to understand everything. But instead of "leaping" into faith, we just stay still. The desire to know can be seen as an obstacle to happiness, another itch which cannot be scratched. Let it be. It will not of course be easy. If you are the sort of person who prizes knowledge or you have convinced yourself that there is a Truth to be known, then it will by no means be easy to let go this desire. But it may help to reflect as we have done that anything transcendent is intrinsically unknowable, not decidable.

The danger is that having let go we fall into a kind of nihilism, specifically a belief that nothing matters, and many people resist letting go of the desire or search for Truth because they fear such nihilism is the only alternative. But the search for Truth is after all just another activity of our inner life, driven by a habit, the desire to know. It might feel as if there were a mystery hidden from us which we must get at, as a detective might do in a story. But the mystery may have no solution; the story may not have been constructed in that way. The thinking and believing part of our mind thinks and believes that there is a puzzle to be solved, but in fact nothing will count as solving it. All there is, is the feeling of puzzlement, the unsatisfiable desire to know. Once we grasp this, the feeling may already begin to fade. To accept that we know nothing and perhaps never can is not the same as knowing that there is nothing. We just (just!) let go of a pointless activity which interferes with our peace of mind. To repeat, transcendent truth is unverifiable, as we have seen, otherwise it would not be transcendent. Therefore knowledge of it is unattainable. By insisting on searching for an unattainable Truth it is as if we have chosen this search instead of peace of mind. If this is the case, there are only two ways back. One is to make an arbitrary decision to believe something just to fill the void and allow ourselves to feel that the search has been completed. The other, more simply, is to give up the search.

In letting go of the search for Truth we can replace it with another activity, practice. We can practice the skills of happiness, whether we focus on the set of skills outlined in this book or on some other. Practice encompasses many things, as we have seen, enough to keep us busy for a lifetime. Our goal, if you like, ceases to be Truth and becomes happiness – Happiness, if you prefer. Happiness was arguably the true goal all along because surely the reason for seeking the Truth was that we believed it would make us happy. But the way to happiness, I have argued, is through practice and practical measures, working on the basis of the inner life, patiently weakening unhelpful habits and building up more useful ones. In this light, the search for Truth is, for the undecided, no more than an unhelpful habit.

Spirituality

Religion is not just about belief, of course, it also concerns spirituality. At its best it involves following a spiritual path, a concept which goes wider than religion, certainly wider than "organised" religion. Many people, religious believers and otherwise, would maintain that spirituality is the heart of religion. Indeed, if some forms of religion have lost their popular appeal it is perhaps because they no longer give people a sufficient sense of the spiritual. And a sense of the spiritual is something which people often still value and look for even when they are uncertain about or even hostile to religion.

What is spirituality then? A first attempt is that it must have something to do with spirits or Spirit – in other words, with the supernatural. Spirituality in this sense would concern the relationship of humans, individually or collectively, with the supernatural. All forms of spirituality would thus depend on belief in such spiritual beings. If activity or practice is involved, it is undertaken because of an under-lying belief about the supernatural and it only makes sense in the context of a particular supernatural cosmology. So what is a spiritual activity for you may not seem so to me if our beliefs are different. This means that spirituality and religion are broadly the same thing and there are many different spiritualities just as there are many religions.

But there is a potential problem with defining spirituality as concerning a relationship with one or more spiritual beings. It locates spirituality essentially as a matter of external circumstance, rather strangely since we tend to think of spirituality as quintessentially having to do with the inner life. If this were right, it would incidentally follow that spirituality had little to do with happiness as we now understand it, because happiness quite definitely is a matter of the inner life and spirituality would not be. There is of course no reason why religions or religious people should particularly cherish happiness or the inner life, even though it is the comfort given to the inner life which is the reason many people adopt or adhere to religion. But many people will find a disconnection between spirituality and happiness a curious and uncomfortable conclusion.

It will not by now come as a surprise if I suggest that spirituality as a concept can be rescued from being equated with religious belief or practice – in other words, that spirituality and religion are not the same thing. The development of the inner life is a spiritual activity, although quite separate from religion. It is a secular spirituality, a spirituality for sceptics. We can now bring together three reasons why it is genuinely a form of spirituality:

1. It meets the spiritual need to have meaning and direction in our lives;

2. It transcends concern with the physical and the material, but by focusing on the inner life and not by appealing to the supernatural;

3. It enshrines practice at the heart of our lives, so that although it does not coincide with what faith traditions say, it coincides significantly with what they do.

The quality of spirituality itself cannot be directly sought. It grows as a result of following a programme of training sincerely, aiming to weaken unhelpful habits and improve the practical skills of the inner life. Trying to be spiritual results only in religiosity, pomposity, hypocrisy at worst. The aim is to be whole and happy, not to be holy.

If you do not like this idea, note again that the rest of the argument in no way depends on it, for the argument is about how and why the cultivation of the inner life should be important to all of us. Secular spirituality is just another way to think about what is involved, placing it in a certain context and thereby relating it to other ideas and ways of thinking. This idea could be seen as an attempt to construct a place for spirituality, including very importantly those insights of religion which concern human happiness and the peaceful inner life, within the secular and rationalist tradition. I think this is much needed and that many people today feel this need and struggle with it. By defining and following a meaningful sense of the spiritual without supernatural belief, we can contribute directly to our own happiness, provide a basis for many of our ethical intuitions and incidentally rescue the secular life from materialism and consumerism.

Psychology

You might expect the scientific study of the inner life to fall under the aegis of psychology and that therefore psychology would have much to say about the inner life and happiness. But this comparatively young science has not been eager to tackle these subjects. In the first place, psychology grew out of and has been much influenced by medical concerns, which means that the pathology of the inner life, or the mind, has been its primary concern. It is hard to disagree if the first concern of research (and most importantly research funding) has been to alleviate suffering rather than to make healthy people happier, but it has inevitably meant that psychological science has traditionally had more to say about mental disease than about peace of mind. Also, there was a strong tendency for a long time, most pronounced in behaviourism but influential throughout the science, to view consciousness and the inner life as somehow suspect, not proper subjects of research. This suspicion is understandable because the inner life cannot be directly observed, or at least other peoples' can't, so the public visibility and repeatability of experiments which many feel to be the hallmark of science was compromised, to say the least. From a scientific point of view, it is no use using introspection as a tool and generalising from the observations I make about myself, when the features I observe may just be my own idiosyncrasies. This prejudice has been eroded over the years by the introduction of better survey and statistical techniques – basically, asking large numbers of people what they think and feel and extracting data mathematically from their answers – but there are still lingering doubts and difficulties. Whatever the reasons, psychological science doesn't say much about how to live happily.

There have been exceptions to this general if entirely under-standable neglect. Therapeutic techniques, some but by no means all of doubtful scientific provenance, have constantly leaked into popular culture and been taken up as insights into the human mind, applicable to healthy as well as stricken people. Indeed, such general applicability has been the claim of most originators of therapies, from Freud onwards, sometimes with the subtext that actually we are all more or less sick anyway. In another exception, humanistic psychology, pioneered by Abraham Maslow in the 1960's, tried to put the study of healthy people back at the centre of the subject, but made little headway against the orthodoxies of the day. But in recent years a whole new movement within the science has sprung up, created to a significant extent through the inspiration and efforts of Prof. Martin Seligman and attracting increasing numbers of researchers to its flag. This is positive psychology, intended to be the scientific study of what makes people happy and how we can all live happier lives.

Positive psychology will no doubt produce, over time, a new understanding of the mechanisms of happiness. The current problem is that it is a new sub-science, not yet a decade old although it draws on earlier work by lone pioneers, and it is very early to arrive at firm conclusions, particularly ones on which anyone might base their life. For example, people who score high on tests designed to measure happiness turn out to be more likely than average to have an active social life and to be romantically involved. But which way does the causality run? Are they happy because they are socially successful, or socially successful because they are happy, or do the same underlying personality traits incline them to happiness, help them to make friends and make them attractive? As yet, we don't know, which is not a criticism but a caution against basing behaviour on such findings.

Some of the emerging tenets of positive psychology are not in fact based on scientific evidence and may yet be revised radically. Again, this is not a criticism, because a research program has to start somewhere and have a sense of direction. For example, intensive effort has gone into compiling a list of virtues held to be ubiquitous throughout all human cultures. But the expressions used to name these virtues have had to be very vague in meaning so that the claim of ubiquity can be sustained. "Courage", for example, is one such virtue but it means different things in different cultures and contexts, which its proponents do admit, so actually courage as you or I might understand it is not a ubiquitous virtue.

But suppose we could fast-forward a decade or two and that positive psychology could tell us much more than it can today. Is it likely that the basic ideas we have been discussing – the importance of the inner life, the underlying basis of habit, the value of practice to build inner skills, the goal of inner peace, the recognition of this process as secular spirituality – would be thus superseded? No, it is not. The main reason is that these ideas offer a particular perspective on the world, a recommended way of looking at things which has certain practical consequences. They are largely normative, they are mainly about what to do, not about the way the world is. They clearly depend on some very basic assumptions about the mind, but nothing which cannot be observed by anyone for themselves – and if you find the argument does not resonate with your experience, you will not accept it anyway. It is highly likely that positive psychology will produce better techniques for developing the skills of the inner life. It is even possible that the list of skills will be altered, reduced or added to, but then I have been clear that the list presented here is by no means the only possible one, just a good one. It is just conceivable that science will demonstrate that kindness, say, or gratitude, or forgiveness is bad for us, in which case my suggestions would be at odds with science. But I think that the fact that these qualities have been prized for thousands of years makes such a revelation about human nature unlikely.

Neuroscience and the "reduction" of the inner life

In recent years great advances have been made in the study of how the brain affects the inner life. As always in the life sciences, some of this comes from studying pathology – in this case the pathology of the brain, as for example from clinical observation of what happens when different parts of the brain are damaged. Some also comes from experiments using technological advances which allow electrical, chemical, thermal and cardiovascular effects within the functioning brain to be observed. As this data accumulates, it becomes harder and harder for anyone to sustain a belief that the inner life is anything other than a high function of the body. It is of course still possible, as it always will be, to maintain that there is a supernatural element to human existence which neither body nor inner life captures, such as a soul. But to the extent that people believe in the soul as a way of explaining what today may seem mysterious about consciousness or the inner life, there will be less to explain as the boundaries of mystery are pushed back by research.

What does this mean for the inner life itself and particularly for the idea that training it might be a central focus for anyone wanting to live happily? Does neuroscience (to lump together under one term all the related disciplines which bear on the functioning of the brain and the mind) make all discussion of the inner life obsolete, even potentially? If the detail of the phenomena of consciousness will be explained by activity in the brain – few would claim that science is close to such an explanation yet, of course, but the bandwagon is moving – is there any point in observing and discussing the inner life?

The answer is definitely yes, there is. As an analogy, we know that the flat and smooth sheet of paper on which these words are written is made up of twisted, uneven fibres, which are made up of molecules, which contain atoms, which are made up of particles, until we get to a level of description where words fail and only mathematics will do. These levels are progressively more microscopic and we could say more fundamental. Knowing about each level may certainly change how we think of the one a scale above. But paper is still paper: we can still talk about it, use it, have opinions on different types, prefer one type to another. The everyday thing does not go away because we know more about its chemistry or its physics. Nor can you operate at the level of atoms or particles. If your printer runs out, you need to add paper.

The inner life is in a similar relationship with neuroscience. When we know all there is to know about the brain and how it works, there will still be thoughts and feelings. We may have more ways to deal with them: we may get technology to change feelings, even generate the thoughts we want. We may be able to change habits with the zap of a neurone. But we will still have an inner life and we will still, presumably, be interested in living happily. We will still need to operate on the level of inner-life phenomena, no matter how much science we have to help us. Science helps us to understand things and explain them, but it does not explain them away. We have known for a long time that a rainbow is an effect of reflected light in raindrops, but we can still observe and enjoy rainbows if we choose.

The technology of the inner life, that is to say the ways we have of developing the inner skills we need, might thus change beyond recognition as neuroscience advances. Most of us will rightly be reluctant to accept remedies like drugs and electronic devices for use so close to home without a very solid explanation of how and why they work, but one day such convincing explanations will be established. It is useful to distinguish again here between the skills of the inner life and the methods we use to acquire them. The ways of acquiring skills like our five groups of skills might change – for example, it might one day be possible to achieve the effects of practice from a pill, just as it is already possible, though banned, to enhance sporting prowess through drugs. Such a possibility would raise interesting questions about whether improving ourselves in that way would be appropriate or authentic. We might accept that we all take a happiness pill or have a happiness implant, but we should note that such a strategy would in fact be an external strategy for happiness. What do you do if the pills are in short supply, for example? In fact, it seems that most people when asked reject the idea of accepting a pill or a machine which would guarantee their happiness. (How would you feel about this?) The idea of a happiness machine was devised by the American philosopher Robert Nozick, who took our instinctive rejection of the offer to be made happy in this way as an indication that there was more to life than happiness. But it might just reflect an intuition that happiness depends on exercising skill in our lives. In any case, it is hard to see that the skills themselves would be redundant, if our aim remained the living of a full and happy life. Science may radically change our notions of what it is to be human and live a human life, but as long as we remain human we will need to pilot our inner lives skilfully.

Chapter 19:
Some thoughts about death and dying

The fear of death

In an earlier chapter I said that it was possible to imagine having no fear of anything, if only we were perfectly prepared for everything. If our inner lives were perfectly serene and – the difficult bit – we had the confidence that they would remain so come what may, there would be nothing which would induce fear in our minds. We might have a physical fear reaction but we would be capable of simply observing our bodies behaving in that way and our inner lives would remain tranquil. We noted further that since it is our own (inner) skill and our confidence in it which leads to the ending of fear, the path towards the ending of fear is the continued practice of the inner life skills. More skill means less fear, more practice means more skill, more practice thus means less fear.

Nothing is so frightening to us in general than our own death. If it is true that skill drives out fear, it ought to help in this extreme case and therefore sustained practice of the skills should help to make death less frightening. I believe this is true, but unfortunately the only genuine way to demonstrate it would be for you to practice until you perfected the skills and then see what happened when you died. Then it would be too late to complain if I had got it wrong! But we can look at some aspects of the issue as a "thought experiment" to strengthen the conviction that practice of the skills does indeed help with this most difficult and most human of problems.

Let us go back to the process story as it applies to the self. "I" turn out to be a bundle of processes which have come together, some for a few decades, some for longer like some of my DNA patterns, some for a few seconds like this breath I now take. The physical stuff in my body comes and goes throughout my life, forming and reforming patterns, but the atoms and their particles which currently constitute my body trace their origins back to the Big Bang. Many of the atoms and molecules which were part of my body ten years ago may now be part of someone else's. My consciousness will last as long as it lasts: it disappears at night for a while anyway and then returns. So what will happen when I die?

I do not know if I will be conscious at any time after my death. I suspect not, but how could I possibly find out for sure without dying? What I do know is that some of the processes (for example, molecules and atoms) currently part of me will continue after it is no longer appropriate to describe them as part of me. Other processes will cease – but then processes are starting and finishing within me all the time, so there is nothing unique or surprising about that. Each of the various processes which are in any way connected with me will at my death either stop, or start, or continue, just as such processes always have throughout my life.

Thus a different story about my "self", a story which looks at "me" as a bundle of processes of differing lengths, leads to a different story about the ending of that self. If I see myself as a unique entity or "thing" to be preserved at all costs, then death is indeed terrible, an abrupt ending amidst continuity. But if this "self" is a nothing more than a particular bundle of processes, then death becomes just another transition among these processes. If we regard a birth as the beginning and a death as the ending of an important process, we could say that each self experiences many deaths and many births every day. Or, switching to a different story, none at all: because the whole giant process that is the universe just continues and unfolds and flows on. If I were obsessed with the continuation of this self in this exact form, then every instant must be upsetting for me, because every instant something changes, and the processes move on whether I am aware of it or not. But if I can accept that it is the nature of being alive (or being at all) to change, then death is just another occasion when change takes place.

Perhaps, though, I feel that it is specifically the ending of my consciousness which is to be lamented. But again, whatever happens after my death, I will either be aware of it or I will not. If I am, then obviously some of the processes that constitute my consciousness are continuing and death has been greatly overrated. Whatever I am aware of, it seems safe to conclude that it no longer involves this body. Therefore if there is a continuation which can reasonably be said to be of "me", it must involve processes of the inner life, in some way. If this is even a possibility, the training of the inner life might be the only thing you can "take with you" – another reason to attach great importance to it.

On the other hand, if I am no longer aware of anything after my death, then there is no longer an "I", no longer any inner life. The situation for this self or consciousness will be as it was before I was born: the processes which continue will not involve or concern "me".

But even while I am alive there are many processes of which I am completely unaware, many of them part of me, let alone the billions of processes going on around me which are not part of me. Unawareness of process or change is no great event or anything unusual or different. And there will be processes and change after my death of which I am not aware. As usual. Thus death is itself not a fundamental change in this respect.

Because I am aware that I will die, I have to live with that knowledge, knowledge which can induce fear which stands in the way of happiness in my lifetime. But if I look at myself through the lens of a process story, this attitude makes little more sense than being upset throughout a sumptuous meal because I know that the meal will eventually come to an end. Processes go on, they start and finish. It is even a matter of convention which events we assign to which process and, as we saw, we could decide that everything is part of the same universal process. Death is an ending in some ways but just one ending among many others in my life. It is also the beginning of some processes, just like every other change. I have no reason to fear it, in itself, unless I desire the world to stop and for there to be no change, which paradoxically would be a more extreme death than the mere completion of a life. This train of thought won't make me instantly comfortable with the idea of my death, of course. But the more I entertain it, the more I get used to it, the more I practice it, in fact, the stronger will be its effects.

I am not suggesting of course that this is the one and only true story about death, just that it is an antidote to certain ways of thinking which make death seem uniquely terrible. If you have a specific set of beliefs about an afterlife, for example religious beliefs, your attitude to death will be shaped by those beliefs and you may not need this process story. It is just a way of looking at or thinking about death from a different but non-supernatural perspective.

Fear of the afterlife

There is another major reason why people come to fear death and that is the fear that something terrible may happen after death. This is not the fear that consciousness will end, but that it will continue and the experience will be unpleasant, even horrible. The stories of religious traditions often exacerbate this fear. How can it be dispelled? Well, if you are a believer, your religious tradition itself will usually explain how any dire consequences it predicts can be avoided, what has to be done and how you should live now in order to secure happiness after death. Unless your tradition prescribes a painful hereafter come what may, in which case to enjoy life while you can and develop courage against the future seems the only option, the reprieve comes with the sentence. Therefore you should live according to your beliefs and you need fear nothing.

If you do not subscribe to a belief tradition, there is no good reason why you should have such a specific fear of the afterlife. But you may nevertheless be infected with worry: "I don't really believe it but what if it is true? What if I'm wrong and am punished for it?" This is of course an instance of a "what if?" story but in this case a very unhelpful one, one which actually creates fear and disturbs peace of mind. What can be done about it?

You might think that it would be a spiteful, unmerciful and unreasonable Power which punished people for not believing things deliberately placed beyond their senses and understanding, but let that pass. We are dealing here with a worry and it is unfortunately true that worry is more insidious than fear based on firm belief. Since most of us have had some exposure, often as children, to some specific religious culture, we tend to have a very specific idea about what it is we *don't* believe. For example, assume that John Smith has no religious beliefs, or like many people, has only vague ones. But when he was at school he heard a story about Hell, a terrible place of eternal punishment. Although he may not now believe this story, it may still exist in his mind as a possibility, a "what if?" It is as if the story of Hell is first reserve: if it turns out that whatever John now believes about an afterlife is not true, then the story involving Hell might well be true instead and he might feel at risk in not believing it.

We can see that this happens partly because John's imagination does not present him with enough options – there are not enough "what if?'s". (He is in distinguished company: Pascal arguably made a similar mistake in his famous "wager" about the desirability of living a good Christian life.) If Hell is a possible alternative to what he now believes, so are many other stories, some to be feared and some to be welcomed. Clearly it would be easier and nicer for him to be convinced of a story about eternal happiness awaiting him or to have such a story as first reserve. But we cannot choose arbitrarily what we believe just because it sounds nice and still less can we choose what we do not believe but have worries about. John actually fears this Hell story (in our example) only because he is familiar with it. The selection of the Hell story was arbitrarily made by a chance of his cultural history. It might help to remind himself that there is an infinite variety of possible stories and also that, since they concern the supernatural, there is no way he can decide among them unless faith decides for him. But by assumption he does not have faith, so what can he do but give all the possible stories equal weight? Put all the stories into the frame and every imaginable outcome, good and bad, is there, with nothing to make one more likely than another. Crudely, they cancel each other out, leaving him with no idea what might happen. So the fear comes down to this: it is fear of the unknown and that the unknown just might turn out to be bad, although he has absolutely no basis to think that it will.

It is of no real help in these circumstances to seek the comforts of religion because he would still face the question, which religion? If he gets it wrong he is still in trouble, maybe worse trouble. If we assume it is specifically a Christian story he fears, perhaps the remedies suggested by that strain of Christianity would be the best antidote. This would be fine if his fear was, so to speak, full blown – that is to say, if he had a real belief in Hell. But it is a curious solution under our assumptions because he is led to try to believe doctrines that he finds difficulty with, because of a fear of something he does not really believe anyway. He might do better to bolster his central belief about what happens after death, although if he is honest he will understand that he cannot be certain about any story on such an issue.

It makes more sense – if, that is, we are troubled by such fears – to try to prepare the inner life to remain as steady and as peaceful as possible under any circumstances. But that is what we have been discussing anyway as the route to happiness in this life. We are likely at some stage to need such skill to deal with everyday pain and fear. Thus the pursuit of happiness in life, properly understood, turns out to be the best preparation we can make for death.

Letting go and dying

Another way to think about death is from the perspective of letting go. Indeed, a large part of the problem of thinking about our own death is the difficulty of letting go. If we have the habit of hanging on to our possessions, our relationships, our status, our physical fitness or whatever it is – and let's face it, we all have such habits – then to contemplate giving them all up will be difficult and will cause us distress. But to practice letting go is an alternative. If we were to practice and master the letting go of each moment as it passes, death would lose its importance for us.

As a thought experiment, just imagine that you have done this. You have cultivated the habit of being mindful of each moment as it comes and then willingly letting go of it and all it contains. Imagine you have practised until this has become second nature to you, it takes no effort, it is what you do, how you live. Each moment is unique and you take it for what it is, then you let it go and do not regret it but focus on the next, and so on. Consider now the moment immediately before your own death. You are mindful of it and then let it go. Now consider the next moment, the moment immediately after your own death. Whatever it contains, you will be mindful of it and let it go. Or alternatively, of course, you will not be conscious of it. Until we have died we cannot be sure which applies. But either way it is okay: either it is just another moment, or there is no such conscious moment. Nothing to fear, nothing to lose. Another moment, another letting go – or nothing to let go.

As before, merely following this thought experiment will not do the trick and banish all fear, of course. It is just an exercise to show what might be possible and how the skill of letting go could solve this problem. To gain the benefit of the exercise, though, it is worthwhile to take the time to "feel" it, meditate on it and try to imagine what it might be like. To reach such a state of equanimity as to be able to let go so completely is probably the pinnacle of achievement in training our inner lives, and at the least it might take years of effort. But it is there to be achieved.

Letting go and bereavement

As well as thinking about and perhaps preparing for our own deaths, it is useful to look at how the developed skills of the inner life can help us in coping with bereavement. When someone we love dies there is an obvious sense in which we have to let go of them. If we can bring ourselves to look at the prospect of such a loss when it is not an immediate issue, in the abstract so to speak, we can see several things about it. First, such losses are inevitable and it is a feature of our lives that they will occur. Loss is an aspect of the process of life, the continual flux of change, and it cannot be avoided. Every life has a beginning and an end and without the ending of each life that life could not have been. That is of course why many traditions celebrate and give thanks for a person's life when it ends, rather than mourning a loss. Thus gratitude, with its essential focus on good things received rather than on what has not been received – in this case more time with our loved one – is an essential coping skill. As the Christian tradition has it, "The Lord gives and the Lord takes away, blessed be the Name of the Lord." This prayer neatly expresses at once an attitude of acceptance for what cannot be changed, letting go of desire for things to be different and feeling gratitude for what has been enjoyed, even if it is enjoyed no more.

Second, our usual fixation with the future and with what happens next makes loss harder to bear. One of the things we have to let go is our own image or plan, no doubt a vague one but no less real for that, of the part the loved one might have played in our lives in the future. We have to accept that they will not be around to do new things with, they will not share with us as they did before. Hard though it is, if we could train ourselves to focus and be mindful of the present, such expectations and images of the future would be less troublesome in times of loss. Thus mindfulness and ability to let go of plans about the future (non-attachment to such plans) are essential coping skills.

Third, often what we miss most and find hardest to let go is the part the loved one played in our own habits of life, both inner and external. It is not, say, the happy memory of something we once did with them years ago that troubles us. Everything they did in the past, after all, which is to say the foundation of our love for them and the affectionate memories we have of them – all of that is still there as much as it ever was, as much as the past ever is. We know if we are honest about it that those times had gone anyway and could only be recalled in memory – which they still can. It is the everyday things we miss, the routines, the habits, because these now change abruptly. We are attached to all the ways in which our loved one was part of our daily life, which means that we have grown used to depending for our happiness on this fortunate external circumstance. But however much we resist the idea, it is the attachment which brings the pain. So although it is a difficult thing to practice, non-attachment is an essential coping skill.

It is important to remember again that non-attachment is not the same as detachment. We do not have to remain aloof from or indifferent to the living to guard ourselves against loss. On the contrary, being aware that our loved ones are finite and fragile makes them and the time we have with them even more precious. We might focus on each day, each moment, as the gift it is and enjoy and be grateful for it rather than focusing as we often do on how it might be better, until it is all too late and there are no more such moments. Just as seeing ourselves as processes helps to weaken the tendency to self-centred attitudes, so seeing our loved ones as processes helps to weaken the tendency to assume they are unchanging "things" to be taken for granted. People are longer-lived, on the whole, but no less fragile in the long run than flowers. If we are only going to love bits of them, the bits of them in terms of their time-lines that suit us and make our circumstances easier, can we say we love them at all? What we love when we love a person is inevitably a process and how that process intersects and interacts with the processes that are us. Non-attachment means remembering that all processes have ends, but that does not devalue them.

Lastly, we may need to be able to forgive both ourselves and our lost loved one. We may need to forgive them for our being left behind, for past wrongs, for things left undone or unsaid. We may need to forgive ourselves for anything we regret doing or not doing, saying or not saying. And perhaps we need to forgive ourselves for not dealing as skilfully as we would like with the processes of loss.

Here we are dealing of course with the past and our inability to be at peace with it. The past is gone, but we are unhappy because it is not now to our liking, whatever we thought at the time. If the lost one had been alive perhaps we could have said what we now want to say, perhaps we could have asked their forgiveness or whatever it was. But we have to recognise in most cases that it is only the trauma of their death which has made us rethink the past. Here in fact is a major clue about the way we might deal with others generally so as to be peaceful in our minds: if we speak and act so that we would have nothing to regret if they were to die tomorrow, we will save ourselves much grief on the rare occasions when that happens, but more importantly we will also have better relationships with the living.

But when anger or regret do arise, how do we deal with them? In the case of anger, the cultivation of understanding and compassion is just as effective whether the person is living or dead. In the case of regret, it is often helpful to follow as closely as possible what we might have done if the person were still alive. For example, if it is a matter of things unsaid or apologies unmade, perhaps we can still say what we wanted to say or wish we had said. We cannot expect a response, but we may not have received a response if we had done it earlier. If we do this, it is worth doing it a little formally to increase the impact for us, for we have to recognise that it is *our* inner life which needs healing, as would have been true even if we had acted earlier. Perhaps we can write down what we wanted to say, if we are good at that. (Many people put such a letter into the coffin.) Or perhaps we could go somewhere quiet, as if for an important and intimate talk, and say what we wanted to say, taking time to find the right words. If it helps to light a candle, or sit in a church or temple, or do anything which increases the impact of what we are doing, we should do it.

Mourning and grief

Grief can be a physical thing. It is as if the loss is a physical loss, as if the lost one had been an extra limb. This comes as a shock when it happens, but it is not so surprising that someone with whom we have shared some significant part of our lives should be quite literally part of who we are, part of our habits and part of our physical responses, as if hard-wired into our nervous systems. This may be easier to accept if you think of yourself and others from a process perspective, so that you and they are interacting processes. Whether the relationship was good or bad, the lost one really was part of the same process as you. We might think of it like this without going too far into scientific speculation: all those neural circuits and hormonal responses, all the physical patterns and habits of the body formed from the effort we have put into the relationship and from all the pleasure and pain we have received in it are all bruised and battered at once. This is only a metaphor of course but nevertheless it is a story which helps to explain why it hurts. Even if you are sure that the lost one is at peace, it hurts. Even if you didn't get on, it can still hurt. It is a physical thing.

It is reasonable to ask: "What is there to enjoy in such circumstances?" How could such a time be happy? Of course there is in truth still much to enjoy, the grass is still green, the sun still rises and there is still as much left of the infinite beauty of the world as before. There are plenty of "also's". The trouble is, we hurt too much to notice. Grief takes us over; it feels like we become our grief. We cannot see through to the other side of this time of loss. And there may of course be all kinds of subsidiary problems, particularly if were dependent on the lost one: on top of feeling the pain of loss we worry about what is to become of us, what our lives will be like when all we know is that they may be utterly different.

We would remember, if grief were not overwhelming us, that this bitter time will pass. We are full of pain but the pain, too, will fade. Perhaps it helps a bit to recall that the loss is itself an external circumstance: it is inevitable that there will be loss in our lives. Perhaps it is actually useful to think of this pain as a physical response to the loss, for we know that our bodies will give us pain from time to time and that this too is an external circumstance, part of the process of life. Just as we may experience fear as a physical reaction even if our minds are steady, so even the most accomplished practitioner may experience grief precisely as if it were a physical reaction. Mourning becomes something like an affliction of the body, a physical illness which we can do no more than allow to take its course. It's here, it cannot be wished away, but it will pass or at least fade in time. We feel the pain as we would feel the pain of an illness or a wound. If we are to retain some inner peace in these difficult conditions, we can only accept the pain and know that this is as much a part of the process of living as the good times we only dimly remember. If we have not developed the skill of acceptance then this will be hard indeed. There is a widely-known psychological model of the mourning process which emphasises that there are stages which must be passed through before the final stage of acceptance can be reached – denial, anger, bargaining, and so on. What we are saying now does not contradict this: grief is a natural process, even a physical reaction, which must be lived through and there are no short cuts. But if we recognise that acceptance is the destination and have prepared ourselves to accept, then the process may be very much easier and our inner equilibrium can be restored more swiftly.

Matters would often be much easier if we were allowed to prepare ourselves for the loss. Indeed, those who lose someone close after a long and clearly final illness often find it easier to cope than those suddenly deprived. There is an unfortunate taboo in our society which often prevents us from talking about and preparing ourselves for the death of loved ones. It is almost a superstition that we might bring about tragedy by being prepared for it, even though in other contexts preparation would be recognised as sensible risk management. The result of not preparing is that the loss hits all the harder. As we have seen, coping with such loss is a huge challenge which requires many inner skills. Because in general we have not prepared our inner lives, the skills to deal with the processes of loss are not there when we need them. We have to learn how to cope at the time when we are most vulnerable. Strange as it sounds, there is much to be said for training ourselves to cope with loss as a part of training ourselves to be happy. We know that all our loved ones will die sometime, just as we will, so such training should not wait until the danger is imminent.

A *way*

It is easy, I hope, to imagine from what we have discussed how practising the skills of the inner life could become a way of life, or at least the basis of one. This does not mean that practice becomes an obsession, or that it excludes the rest of life. The whole point of practising these skills is that they can be applied in whatever lives we lead and they will make our lives happier. Most of us will still be workers, parents, children, friends, lovers, campaigners, organisers, lobbyists, hobbyists, enthusiasts for this and that. We will live the lives we are drawn to, if we are lucky, and the lives we must if we are not. The skills entail a gradual change in attitude or point of view, living whatever life we lead as happily as possible, transcending difficult circumstances and being grateful for favourable ones. This requires constant attention to the habits of the inner life, herding them in the direction of greater skill. It will often seem like herding cats! The development of the inner life does require dedication, but it is a dedication to a particular way of living our ordinary lives, not a dedication to a different life.

There is a parallel between such a dedication to practice, founded though it is on a wholly pragmatic desire to live happily, and a Path or a Way as described in the spiritual literatures of many of the faith traditions, particularly those of Asia. The motivation may be very different, certainly if the spiritual goal of the faith tradition is a supernatural one. But the similarity lies in the idea that everything, our whole life and the world we live in, is changed by our commitment to this Way, even though little external may be changed. The change is an inner one, a change in point of view or perspective, a change in the background story among other things. But because of this change everything, every detail, takes on a new significance. As we observed earlier, meaning in life is largely a matter of having a purpose or a sense of direction and therefore practice of the skills gives meaning precisely because it gives purpose and direction. The most insignificant thought, feeling, action or event is meaningful because it contributes to developing the basis of the inner life. If we are practising diligently, everything contributes to a more helpful habit basis and therefore everything contributes to a happy life.

At first, practice is likely to be tentative and self-conscious. You may try sitting to watch the breath, for example, and succeed only in feeling foolish, or you may have to force yourself to reframe some everyday incident afterwards just to understand how you might have lessened the negative emotions it produced. "I have a choice here" is a helpful mantra as you react inwardly to other people's deliberate or accidental provocations. Another way into practice is to use a story: "What would it be like if I had these inner life skills, how would I react differently, how might I feel, think, believe, and so on?" The more we go through the motions of testing what it might be like to have the skills, the more we actually develop them. Gradually they start to be there occasionally when we need them, gradually they start to change our outlook. The more time we can devote to practising, whether it is time dedicated to practice exercises or time being conscious and mindful of the skills as we go about everyday life, the more rapidly the skills develop. But it is a matter of providing the right conditions for a process of maturation, not a matter of forcing the pace. We may all have to do a lot of faking it before we make it. Gradually we can weaken the unhelpful habits of the inner life and replace them with skills. Gradually also the process of doing this may infuse our whole lives.

Public policy and political choices

On the face of it, the development of the inner life might seem to have little or nothing to do with questions of society, public policy or political choices. It is not clear that this perspective has anything to say on all the many political and social issues which are in any case questions of expedience, effectiveness in meeting an agreed-upon goal or economic efficiency. No principles based on the inner life are likely to tell us whether, say, a hospital building should be publicly or privately funded, what the rate of vehicle excise tax should be, or how to structure and manage the police.

However, there are many political questions which do have an inner dimension. Not everything in the public domain is a matter of efficiency and effectiveness, let alone "spin" and expedience. We might approach issues of public policy by imagining what choices might be made in a society in which people generally understood happiness as a function of the inner life and accepted the importance of training the inner life. It is a "what if" test and of course it has to be in large part guesswork. But even though such a society is not even remotely like ours, or indeed like any existing today, this utopianism is still an interesting exercise. It entails making genuine happiness the centre of public decision-making, which is an idea many could subscribe to whether or not they accepted our arguments about the inner life. Many people advocate trying to maximise some measure of utility as the test of good policy. This book has argued that happiness is not a matter of external utility but of the inner life; on this view the cultivation of the inner life and the organising of public life to encourage and facilitate such a value would be most beneficial to society.

We live in a world divided by belief, most of us in societies made up of people with many different shades of religious and political opinion. Even disregarding extremists, consensus and even mere tolerance is difficult at times. One of the things we lack is any common basis of reference, particularly on matters of public ethics. We lack a shared set of values on which we can all agree and to which we can appeal to settle our differences. In some times and places the shared values of a religion filled or fill this role, but more commonly absolute power, even in the name of religion, less palatably settled or settles all disputes. If we were to have a common basis of values today, it would have to be defensible on secular grounds alone because imposing the dictates of one particular faith in a society, still less a world, which remained multicultural would involve horrific conflict. Not every religion could welcome a secular common denominator, but each religion would find it still less agreeable to accept the mandate of one of the others.

A commitment to the development of the inner life could provide a workable basis of common values. At least, it has many of the right qualities. It is a secular but non-materialist direction, which provides secular but non-materialist values. It incorporates and validates many of the ethical human qualities which the faith traditions have always upheld and which underlie much of the secular thinking on human rights. And it is based on individual freedom and the pursuit of happiness. Individual freedom and happiness have, it is true, to be understood in a more inward sense than the freedom to shop and vote and the satisfaction of being a consumer of material and political goods. But it is certainly possible to imagine people living har- moniously and prosperously with the development of the inner life as their highest shared goal. If it happened, it would produce an interesting change in the world. Before we dismiss the possibility, which we sadly must because it is ludicrously unlikely, we might reflect that there is one and only one way it could ever happen: if individuals, one by one, thought about it and made a choice in their own interests to live their lives in pursuit of happiness. For each of us, our part in that wider change is under our own control.

If we are willing though to indulge utopianism for a moment, we can ask what a society would be like if the members were focused on happiness as their central value and understood happiness to be a matter of the inner life. What political choices might such a society make? Our answers can only be tentative and painted with the broadest of brushes, but here are some thoughts.

First and foremost, such a society would be compassionate and tolerant. Since most people by assumption would be seeking to develop kindness and compassion in themselves, they would be prepared to help those in need. If the external circumstances of some were such as to make the possibility of their own practice difficult, those circumstances would be improved, even at the cost of some loss of comfort for the majority. Thus social support for the absolutely disadvantaged would be generous. On the other hand, society would not be consumption-oriented or consumption-driven, as ours is now. As a consequence, it would not necessarily be materially egalitarian. For example, it would not regard everyone as having a need for or a right to the consumer goods of their choice, nor would it be a problem if some had more material goods than others as long as all had sufficient to pursue life and practice with dignity.

At an international level, affluent countries would be keen to help economically struggling countries with much more generosity than today. This would be made easier because politicians would not need to offer electors maximum personal consumption as the price of their votes.

The education system would include a much stronger emphasis than now on the development of inner life skills, enabling people to grow up inwardly self-sufficient as well as externally able to take care of themselves. It would therefore naturally include significant discussion of the inner life and training in the skills which underpin happiness. Children would be given a clear sense of the importance of happiness and their choices in relation to it. In society at large dissent about aims and means of developing the inner life, as about beliefs, would be completely tolerated and even encouraged, provided only that such views did not intrude on or interfere with people's right to practice for themselves.

This utopian society would be ready to defend itself against internal disruption and external threat, just as today. The development of compassion and the lessening of anger and hatred do not, as we have discussed, imply passivity in the face of aggression. But defence would mean defence: aggression against another country, particularly invasion for purely political ends, would be unthinkable. The stirring up of hatred or anger as political weapons, even against the most unpleasant adversaries within the county or outside, would also be unacceptable.

Compassion would also drive us in the direction of a more environmentally-aware approach to living. If you imagine what it would be like to live in a future world blighted by pollution and depleted natural resources, or indeed what it would be like today to live in a local environment despoiled by economic rape or careless exploitation, compassion for and kindness towards the people who might have to live under such conditions suggests restraint. This is not some moral absolute, more a question of being aware of the real consequences for real people. There might be circumstances in which benefits accrued which counterbalanced an environmental dis-advantage, but ecological damage of any kind would never be something to be neglected or taken lightly.

On the economic front, consumption would cease to be the major goal and rising national income would cease to be the measure of success. Efficiency and full employment would be as important as ever, but the emphasis would be on everyone creating and having enough rather than maximising consumption. This is a profound change whose detailed consequences are difficult to predict. It might be expected to ease pressures on the environment and natural resources, for example, but perhaps the drive for innovation and change would also be lessened. Business conducted by business people steeped in inner practice might be expected to be more ethical, more mindful of externalities and less ruthless in the pursuit of profit than at present. A great deal of economic "froth" would disappear since people would not regard their external circumstances as critical once they had a satisfactory level of comfort. Frankly, the balance of many an economic nexus would be disrupted with consequences difficult to predict. As a minor example, advertising might be less useful and lucrative, but in turn that would make news dissemination more costly and difficult. It would be a very different world.

Economics tends to take people's demands for granted and asks how best and to what extent they can be satisfied. A society focused on the inner life would differ most radically from what we know now precisely in what people wanted. The drive to consume would be less, or to put it another way, people might be happy at lower levels of consumption, happier with simpler lives. But it is difficult to say to what extent this would happen. All we can be sure of is that the patterns of demand would be very different.

Much of our economic behaviour is not, in fact, very rational. For example, we all seem to want more than those around us have, regardless of absolute levels of affluence. Clearly such a demand can never be satisfied for everyone. Focusing on the inner life might be a way in which individuals could free themselves from these irrational wants, without any external compulsion or persuasion.

Many people will concede that the inner life is important to happiness to some degree, but rather as if inner peace were another consumer good to be added to the list for complete satisfaction. We need, such a list might run, somewhere to live, food and drink, clothing and warmth, health, entertainment, friends, satisfying work and finally inner peace – a bit like Maslow's hierarchy of needs. But the position we have now reached is more radical. Inner peace becomes the main event, happiness based on the inner life is the main objective, developing the habit basis is the main focus, with the arrangement or provision of suitable external circumstances a secondary consideration over and above an essential minimum level. Would such a society work? It would be very different from what we know today. It would most likely be a more caring and a happier place, but less affluent in total than we in "developed" nations are used to. The ramifications of all the changes involved are very complex and certainly beyond the scope of this book or its author. But if such ideas alarm you, do not worry. It isn't going to happen!

Self-sustaining practice

Coming back to individual practice, it is clear that if you are very skilful in your inner life you are likely to live very happily, in a state of peace and equanimity. The greater your skill, the more you will be able to preserve your inner peace in adverse circumstances. The sincere practice of these skills thus suggests itself as one of the best ways in which anyone can help themselves towards a better and happier life. But as we have seen the habit basis of the inner life does not ever stand still. It is a constantly changing and moving process whether we practice or not. Every thought, every judgement, every perception, every choice, every emotion potentially changes the habit basis and so it takes constant mindfulness and constant practice to keep the habit basis evolving in a favourable direction. On the face of it, therefore, the inner life could deteriorate back towards a less skilful and less happy state if practice were abandoned. Practice looks like a life sentence.

Is there perhaps a state we can reach where this is no longer true, where we can preserve inner peace in all circumstances without practice because the skills of the inner life have become so entrenched as to be unshakeable? Perhaps there is such a state to be reached, although it seems intrinsically unlikely that very many people would have the dedication and the application to reach it. What is more likely – and, crucially, would have very much the same practical effect – is that the habit of practice could itself become so entrenched that we are practising every moment without effort and so there is simply no opportunity for the habit basis to deteriorate. Practice itself could become second nature. If we practice enough, then, not only does the inner life become more peaceful and happy but the process may become self-sustaining. Practice of the inner life skills leads to a habit basis which is not only the foundation of a happy life but which itself supports continued practice, creating a beneficial spiral.

It is important to realise that all problems would not thereby fall away. External circumstances could still be difficult, we might still suffer injury, sickness or hardship, and one day the processes which make up our lives will inevitably move on to something else. There would still be injustice and war and famine in the world, unless by some miracle everyone else decided to adopt the same solution of seeking happiness by putting the development of their inner lives first. All we can say on that subject is that it hasn't happened in the last few millennia. Practice does not make external problems disappear; what changes with practice and greater skill is our relationship to our problems and the way they affect our inner lives. The external world presents problems to solve if we can and endure if we can't, but our happiness is something else, based on our inner life and on developing skill so that we can keep our peace of mind in any circumstances.

Nor is this a matter of being permanently "blissed out". If we crave happy, light states of mind and hate darker, more difficult ones, we are still at the mercy of circumstances, only this time the chance circumstances of the inner life. The goal of practising the skills is to retain equanimity through good and bad, dark and light. We realise that each event and episode will pass and move on to something else, but that whether we are happy right now, at this moment, depends on how we react in all the dimensions of the inner life not only to external circumstances but also to the circumstances of the inner life itself. If the inner life is troubled, we may be able to use our skill to interrupt the process and return to peace, or we may just have to wait patiently for peace to return. It can be a very complex business, of course, and we won't get it right all the time. Without sufficient skill any of it can so fix our attention that we lose sight of peace and happiness in the storm of activity. The skills take us to the eye of this inner storm where it is calm whatever else is happening.

The human spirit

The path we have been discussing is sensible, honest and free of superstition. A person adopting such a path might follow it with self-respect for the rest of their days. It is founded on a rational human objective, the desire to live happily in what is often an unhappy world. But we have shown how this desire leads to concern and compassion for others, to personal qualities which have been admired for millennia as basic human virtues and even as gateways to the numinous. The concern with the inner life requires inner attention, but it is not an introspective obsession because it is crucially about how we interact with the external world and it with us. Tolerance and understanding of others are implied, treating others as fellow human beings struggling, like us, towards happiness. But this understanding does not imply that we allow harmful actions or oppressive behaviour. I hope thus to have indicated a secular direction which offers meaning and purpose, which serves as a basis for behaviour and for ethical choices, and which transcends a fixation on the material and the external as sources of happiness.

You may choose to define spirituality as being about adherence to specific beliefs about the supernatural or about our relationships with particular spiritual beings whose existence those beliefs entail. But spirituality may also be about qualities of mind and heart – qualities of the inner life, in other words – and the development of those qualities. The qualities we have been discussing make us happier, wiser, kinder human beings. If we are sincere in the desire to develop such qualities and constant in our efforts to do so, I think we may rightly claim to be following a spiritual path, whatever our supernatural beliefs. This is a spirituality the sceptical mind need not reject, a rational, secular spirituality based on our humanity but transcending the material. For the truth is, we do not need the supernatural to be spiritual because we are already spiritual beings. In developing the inner life we develop the human spirit as we develop the qualities we need for a happy life. And thus, whatever we achieve or fail to achieve in the external world, we can reach the only kind of nobility and achievement which matters at all. We fulfill our potential as human beings.

Appendix:
Standing on the shoulders of giants

Personal debts

It is impossible to think about anything interesting without a leg up from the giants of past and present, often without knowing it. Newton, who coined the phrase "standing on the shoulders of giants" in modesty at his own colossal achievements, happened to be a giant himself which obviously helped even more, but for us ordinary mortals the view is definitely too restricted to see anything without standing on tall shoulders. The ideas in this book owe their origins to many people, most of whom I have never met, quite a few of whom I know only in translation. What I set out to do was to fit others' insights about the vital issues of spirituality and living happily into a single coherent structure, placing it in a contemporary context without making it dependent on appeals to the supernatural. If you think I have succeeded, I am happy to concede all the credit to the original thinkers. If not, well, there is only one person to blame.

This is not meant as a scholarly book, so I don't propose to adopt the scholarly conventions of citing sources and references. In general, the internet makes long lists of further reading redundant anyway: if you want to know more about a subject, Google it. In very many cases I have absorbed a story or an idea without retaining the least idea of whence it came and I apologise in advance if anyone feels aggrieved. But there are a few books I know I could not have done without. So in this short appendix I include a few acknowledgements, but by no means all, and some suggestions for further reading.

The subject of living happily, though of everyday concern, has historically tended to be thought about under either "philosophy" or "religion", although more recently it has begun to attract attention from psychology and of course psychology's love child, self-help. As for philosophy, the way I think owes whatever success it has to the way I was taught. My principal tutor in philosophy was an idiosyncratic former pupil of Wittgenstein and I would like to think (who wouldn't?!) that a speck of Wittgenstein's way of looking at complicated matters sank in. That pupil was Casimir Lewy, who probably wouldn't have approved of this book but it wouldn't have been written without him. In particular, he always insisted that we focus directly on the problem in hand, using historical attempts to solve it as sources of ideas rather than a subject matter in itself, however fascinating. That approach I have adopted here. Under the heading of religion I owe much to the Christianity of my childhood, including a lifelong conviction that the cruder forms of materialism were incomplete even if I couldn't say how until now. I also owe a huge debt to many teachers, writers and translators of and about Buddhism, about which more below.

The notions of habit, skill and practice are crucial to the idea of spirituality presented here and if I understand anything about them it is because of 16 years of practising aikido under Andy Hathaway at the London Aikido Club. There I have observed, in myself and others, the huge mental and physical changes which can be brought about, bit by tiny bit, with patient and regular practice.

It would be quite wrong not to thank publicly all the very kind people at Findhorn Press who have made the process of publication so smooth and pleasant. I thank in particular Thierry Bogliolo, Jean Semrau, Carol Shaw, Pam Bochel, Clarinda Cuppage and Damian Keenan for their help in all their different capacities.

Finally, external circumstances may not be the essence of being happy but the person who lives under fortunate circumstances has much to be thankful for. I am very fortunate in many ways, but particularly in my wife and my daughter who have taught me about loving and gratitude for being loved.

Further reading

The idea that the inner life is what matters if we are to live happily is very old. It arrived with me from two main sources, Buddhism and Stoicism, the latter being of course a creation of the Greeks but which I know best from Marcus Aurelius. It occurs in the scriptures of many religions but I have assumed it is not necessary to reference these, apart from the first reference below. These books I found particularly helpful:

> *The Middle Length Discourses of the Buddha* – Tr. Nanamoli and Bodhi (Wisdom)
>
> *The Meditations of Marcus Aurelius* – Tr. Hays (Weidenfield and Nicolson)

The Heart of the Buddha's Teaching – Thich Nhat Hanh (Rider)

The Art of Happiness – Dalai Lama & Cutler (Hodder and Stoughton)

Foundations of Buddhism – Gethin (Opus)

The idea that happiness or living happily is something fundamental comes again from the Greeks and in particular the notion that happiness is based on virtues or qualities, even if not yet skills, is the main theme of Aristotle's Ethics.

Ethics – Aristotle. Tr. Thomson (Penguin)

The notion of the habit basis is related to the Buddhist idea of store consciousness (see above sources), and also to the idea of the unconscious found in Freud and, more particularly, Jung. The idea that training or practice improves the inner life and refines our nature so that we can be both happier and more spiritual is found in many religions. That such training can be based around a small number of virtues, tasks or skills is also familiar, from the Old Testament's Ten Commandments and the Buddhist Eightfold Path to the New Testament's Two Commandments, the Pillars of Islam and the Sufi poets. Of course, the goal of training the inner life is not the same in each case, nor is it the same goal put forward here. As well as scriptures and other sources quoted in this appendix, I have found the following very helpful:

The Essential Rumi – Tr. Coleman Barks (Penguin)

Theresa of Avila – Rowan Williams (Continuum)

The notion that spirituality can be separated from belief is something which is often said about Buddhism, mainly because it is not theistic. But Buddhism in most forms retains a good measure of supernatural belief and there are obvious difficulties with any religion about selecting bits and pieces from the canon. An excellent attempt to deal with these difficulties is

Buddhism without Beliefs – Batchelor (Bloomsbury)

Turning to particular skills, mindfulness is the cornerstone of Thich Nhat Hanh's teaching and it was from listening to him one summer in Scotland that I grasped the vital importance and nature of this skill. He writes prolifically but I find the book cited above most helpful along with the early work cited next. I used to live near Amaravati monastery in Hertfordshire and found the place and the teaching there (in the Theravada tradition) a constant source of inspiration. Among other writers I have found the following particularly useful:

The Miracle of Mindfulness – Thich Nhat Hanh (Rider)

Full Catastrophe Living – Kabat-Zinn (Piatkus)

The Three Pillars of Zen – Kapleau (Rider)

Mindfulness: The Path to the Deathless – Sumedho (Amaravati)

On benevolence and compassion there is so much, from scripture to self-help. Personal favourites are these:

The Way of the Bodhisattva – Shantideva. Tr. Padmakara Translation Group (Shambhala)

Dzogchen – Dalai Lama (Snow Lion)

A Path with Heart – Kornfield (Rider)

Story has many influences. Ideas about the way language relates to "the world" were a speciality of Wittgenstein, but it is a tricky subject and has been a staple of philosophy for centuries. Frayn's recent book, appearing (unfortunately for me) after this one was completed, is an erudite and highly entertaining essay on this theme as it relates to the physical world. Campbell's famous series on the myths of the world shows another side of the story of story. The usefulness of story skills for altering the inner life is most clearly pioneered by cognitive behaviour therapy, which originates in the work of Aaron Beck and Albert Ellis. Persaud explains this, and much else, in clear and common sense terms.

Philosophical Investigations – Wittgenstein. Tr. Anscombe (Blackwell)

The Human Touch – Frayn (Faber and Faber)

Masks of God – Campbell (Penguin/Arkana)

Staying Sane – Persaud (Bantam)

Letting go is well dealt with in Thich Nhat Hanh (op cit) and Meister Eckhart (below), while Taoism is based on it. Jampolsky is good on the importance of forgiveness and much else.

Selected Writings – Eckhart. Tr. Davies (Penguin)

Love Is Letting Go of Fear – Jampolsky (Celestial Arts)

The Way of Chuang Tzu – Tr. Merton (New Directions)

As for enjoyment skills, it is difficult to single out particular sources because the usefulness of gratitude, humour and patience is well known to every culture on the planet and in different contexts they are recommended by most religions. Well, religions are perhaps a bit light on humour so I also include a representative work of one of the great sages of modern times, but any of his would do.

I Heard God Laughing – Hafiz . Tr. Ladinsky (Penguin)

The Thief of Time – Pratchett (Doubleday)

Other writings which provoked or continue themes in this book include:

Frogs into Princes – Bandler and Grinder (Eden Grove) A good introduction to NLP from the founders. Incidentally, if you ever have a chance to hear Bandler teach, take it. You will learn a lot about NLP and also witness a master class in how to handle an audience.

The Tibetan Book of Living and Dying – Sogyal Rinpoche (Rider) A classic, full of detail on Tibetan practices and beliefs.

A History of God – Armstrong (Vintage) And anything else of hers. If you want to find out about the beliefs of faith traditions there can be few better guides than Karen Armstrong.

The Feeling of What Happens – Damasio (Vintage) A virtuoso tour of neuroscience.

Authentic Happiness – Seligman (Nicholas Brealey) A superior self-help book written by the father of positive psychology.

Mystical Aspects of Islam – Schimmel (University of North Carolina) Classic work on Sufism.

A Thomas Merton Reader – McDonnell, ed. (Image/Doubleday) Introduction to a Christian spiritual master.

The Secrets of Happiness – Schoch (Profile) Good short history which I particularly like because it agrees with me in emphasising Buddhism and the Stoics!

Happiness: Lessons from a New Science – Layard (Penguin) A thoughtful attempt to reintroduce happiness into economics and politics.

The Pursuit of Happiness – McMahon (Penguin) Came out too late for me to have the benefit of it but it is lively and full of interesting detail on the history of Western thought about happiness.

Pensées – Pascal. Tr. Krailsheimer (Penguin)

Stumbling on Happiness – Daniel Gilbert (Harper Perennial) Not really about happiness as such, as the author admits, but brilliant about the errors we make in thinking about the future.

Happiness, A guide to developing life's most important skill – Mattieu Ricard (Atlantic) This book by French scientist turned Tibetan Buddhist monk Ricard appeared in translation after mine was finished, sadly for me because it would have been such a help. It shares the aim of developing an approach to happiness based on skill. It is understandably more rooted in Buddhism but I was greatly encouraged by it.

Destructive emotions – Daniel Goleman (Bloomsbury) One of a series of books with different authors reporting meetings between Western scientists and the Dalai Lama to discuss scientific topics, this one focuses on psychology. The meetings are held under the auspices of the Mind and Life Institute, an extraordinary and hope-inducing venture.

FINDHORN PRESS

*Books, Card Sets,
CDs & DVDs
that inspire and uplift*

For a complete catalogue,
please contact:

Findhorn Press Ltd
305a The Park, Findhorn
Forres IV36 3TE
Scotland, UK

Telephone +44-(0)1309-690582
Fax +44-(0)1309-690036
eMail info@findhornpress.com

or consult our catalogue online
(with secure order facility) on
www.findhornpress.com